Brian Freemantle is the former Foreign Editor of the *Daily Mail* but in 1975 he left journalism in order to write full time. Best known for his Charlie Muffin stories, one of which has been filmed, he has only recently turned to non-fiction. *KGB* was published in 1982 and *CIA* in 1983.

The Fix

Brian Freemantle

CORGI BOOKS

For Jonathan. And this time Ann, too.

THE FIX

A CORGI BOOK 0 552 12735 3

Originally published in Great Britain by Michael Joseph Ltd.

PRINTING HISTORY

Michael Joseph edition published 1985
Second impression 1985
Corgi edition published 1986

This book is set in 10/11 pt Baskerville

Corgi Books are published by Transworld Publishers Ltd., 61–63 Uxbridge Road, Ealing, London W5 5SA, in Australia by Transworld Publishers (Aust.) Pty. Ltd., 26 Harley Crescent, Condell Park, NSW 2200, and in New Zealand by Transworld Publishers (N.Z.) Ltd., Cnr. Moselle and Waipareira Avenues, Henderson, Auckland.

Made and printed in Great Britain by
Hunt Barnard Printing Ltd., Aylesbury, Bucks.

The chain of evil goes round the world

Kenneth Clarke, British Minister for
Health, at the Conservative Party Conference
at Brighton 10 October 1984.

Author's Note

As this book was prepared for publication in England, money is given in pounds sterling throughout. Where the original dollar figure is more relevant, the sterling equivalent is calculated on the average exchange rate for the year of expenditure as given by the Bank of England.

Contents

The Fix

Introduction

To illustrate the worldwide extent of drug-trafficking – and therefore, by obvious deduction, drug-taking – it has become clichéd to compare black-market profits against those of giant multinationals, like Exxon, General Motors and British Petroleum.

It is a faulty cliché.

While the financial results of multinationals are usually published, income from drug-trafficking can only be estimated. And those estimates are based upon a calculation using the assumed seizure rate of ten per cent against prevailing street prices, although British Customs insist they achieve a higher success ratio.

During the course of research I have become convinced – by cross-checking and checking again one set of supposed figures against another – that a truer figure of worldwide interception would be five per cent. Law enforcement officials from four different countries agree with me privately; some think that the figure is even lower.

In slave-trading, an interception rate of thirty-three per cent used to be considered an acceptable loss by human traffickers. But drugs are more easily concealed than a shipload of slaves, and drug-trading therefore more difficult to eradicate.

British Customs currently claim – particularly for heroin – an interception success far higher than ten per cent. I have agreed not to release the precise figure because it would betray to the smugglers and traffickers the very high quality of British intelligence, but in 1983 British Customs stopped drugs valued at almost £63,000,000. Taking this figure in conjunction with the overall average seizure rate for all drugs indicates that more than £1,500,000-worth of drugs illegally enters British airports and ports every week of the year. Another estimate suggests that a more accurate figure is £6,000,000 a week.

Which is a minuscule amount, compared with America.

In a canal-bordered office in Miami, a drug specialist official of the US Customs Service thought $100,000,000,000 (£66,666,000,000) a conservative assessment of the yearly smuggling figure. Conservative or not, this means that every week drugs valued at $1,923,000,000 are successfully imported into the United States for black-market street consumption.

In March, 1985, the House Select Committee on Narcotics Abuse and Control issued a report labelling drug abuse as America's number one health problem. The report stated, 'More than 20,000,000 Americans use marijuana regularly, approximately 8,000,000 to 20,000,000 are regular cocaine users, about 500,000 are heroin addicts, 1,000,000 are regular users of hallucinogens and 6,000,000 people abuse prescription drugs.'

President Reagan's adviser on drug policy, Dr Carlton Turner, declared himself 'cautiously optimistic' that by 1983 drug-trafficking in the USA was being contained and that abuse was diminishing. He produced statistics to support his contention.

After over fifteen thousand miles of travel and more than three hundred interviews with both East and West law enforcement officials, psychiatrists, doctors, drug experts, drug addicts and global analysts, I find Dr Turner one of only a handful of individuals prepared even to be cautiously optimistic.

The Vienna-based International Narcotics Control Board of the United Nations certainly don't share that optimism. In 1982 they said the world was suffering from a drug epidemic of 'staggering' social and economic proportions and in their most recent report (1983) they warned, 'The menace

of drug abuse has reached unprecedented dimensions.'
They still stand by that assessment.

Throughout the world, countries respond differently to
the narcotics problem – but rarely effectively. Certainly no
government will face the reality of the situation, because the
reality is politically unacceptable.

The United States, acting in accordance with the long-
established attitude of absolute prohibition to hard drugs
enshrined in the Harrison Narcotics Act of 1914, has
budgetted $130,000,000 (£74,285,000) a year on twelve
regional task forces – in addition to a pilot task force in
Florida – to curb trafficking. This is a country where eleven
states permit cannabis for personal use and the illegal marijuana crop from California in 1982 was worth $2,000,000,000
(£1,142,857,000) at street level, exceeding the profit from
grape cultivation, the supposed leading agricultural crop.

England has since 1926 been the envy of most countries
for its enlightened approach to drug addiction following the
dictum that abusers are ill and need medical treatment. In
1968 – following concern raised by unquestionable evidence
of doctors over-prescribing heroin and cocaine – that treatment was transferred from general practitioners to some
licensed doctors, predominantly psychiatrists and physicians at special treatment centres, usually attached to the
psychiatric sections of teaching hospitals. By 1984, it had
become obvious that the policy hadn't been given the opportunity to work, wasn't working and that a new approach was
necessary.

To advise on what that approach should be, a working
body was specially created by the Department of Health and
Social Security. It was chaired by Dr Philip Connell, who is
also chairman of the government's Advisory Council on the
Misuse of Drugs and has long and unrivalled experience of
the country's drug addiction problems, particularly those
related to amphetamines. The specific brief was to draw up
guidelines for good clinical practice in the treatment of drug
dependence and to consider whether licensing restrictions
should be extended to all opioid drugs. The effect of the

licensing extension would be that doctors prescribing any opioid to an addict – not just heroin, cocaine and, from April 1984, dipipanone – would need a Home Office licence.

The working group submitted its guidelines separately from its opinion of a licensing extention. Those guidelines were then sent by the DHSS to every general practitioner and hospital doctor in August 1984. The working party found it necessary to remind doctors of their professional duties and of the accepted British view that drug addicts are sick people. Part of their report said:

> Drug misusers, like other patients, are entitled to all the services provided by the National Health Service. We are concerned to learn that some doctors, both in general practice and in the hospital services, are unwilling or reluctant to see drug misusers or advise on drug-related problems, particularly in those areas where there are no specialist facilities or where referrals cannot easily be met by such services. It is the responsibility of all doctors to provide care for both general health needs and drug-related problems, as they would for patients with other relapsing conditions.

They further made the point that in many doctors' minds treatment had become synonymous with prescription of the drug of dependence or a substitute. 'By treatment we mean the care of the drug misusers, not just drug treatment,' insisted the experts. They added:

> Doctors should try to deal with the problems of the person who is misusing a drug or drugs, rather than concentrate on the drug-oriented approach. Treatment may or may not, depending on individual circumstances, include the prescription of a controlled drug, but, in our view, treatment is much more than this.
>
> The aim of treatment is to help the individual to deal with problems related to his drug use, and eventually to achieve a drug-free life. The role of support services, including family and friends, may be paramount in helping with problems of accommodation, employment and personal relationships.

In a previous report to the Department of Health and Social Security, the Advisory Council had criticised existing treatment facilities as hopelessly inadequate, unable to cope with the ever increasing numbers of multi-drug users. Among its forty-five recommendations the main suggestion was the establishment of regional facilities to help people with drug problems, permanent base treatment clinics and specialised treatment for all addictions, to include alcohol and tobacco.

Two years after that report, facilities remain inadequate. At the time of writing there are no specialised National Health arrangements in Cornwall, Devon, Wiltshire, Gloucestershire, Kent, Essex, Northamptonshire, Suffolk, Cumbria, Yorkshire, Hereford, Worcestershire, Leicestershire, Derbyshire, Durham or Bedfordshire. Throughout London there are only fifteen specialist hospital services. Norman Fowler, Secretary of State for Social Services, responded to the Advisory Council's criticism with the declaration, 'Our aim is to alert the country to the dangers of allowing the problem of drug misuse to grow and spread. Our overriding policy is first to contain and then to reduce it. We need to reduce the supply of damaging drugs.'

In 1984, Britain allocated £12,000,000 to combat drug abuse, which appeared to match the rhetoric. It was, however, spread over three years. And it was for the 1983 official addict population of 10,235. The real minimal addict population – based on official DHSS studies – was 50,000. Calculated against the official figure, it meant £7.51 was available to treat Britain's addicts each week: put against the unofficial but authoritative figure, it was £1.53 a week. By the end of 1984, the official figure had jumped to 13,274. Which meant unofficially 66,370. It also meant that for the registered addicts, over the three year allocation of that £12,000,000, the amount available was down to £5.79 a week. For the unofficial but nearer number of 66,370, the weekly allowance was down to £1.15 a week. During the first eight months of 1985, the addiction increase was 40 per cent up over 1984. On those first eight months' figures alone, that means £4.13 a week is allowed to treat the 18,583 officially recorded addicts. And just 82p for the nearer but still

13

low figure of 92,915. What that £12,000,000 is additional *to* is impossible to ascertain because a financial breakdown for drug addiction treatment is not made available by the government. Certainly it is paltry. Britain's annual contribution to the UN Fund for Drug Abuse Control is only £100,000 a year. And a £1,000,000 contribution to Pakistan – again spread over a period of years – to encourage farmers to abandon poppy cultivation is quite inadequate.

By April 1984, £5,000,000 of the £7,000,000 had already been allocated to eighty projects. Increasingly, in the following months, it seemed that the government was at last determined to face up to the size of the problem. In June 1984 – after a fact-finding visit to America – Mr Fowler demanded reports on the scale of addiction from the fourteen regional health authorities throughout Britain. Instructions from the DHSS to those regional authorities were to consult with the 192 district health authorities, voluntary organisations, police and probation services and report on the anti-drug plans by December 1984.

During 1985 the British government initiated its much promised programme against drug use among the young. Forefront was a £2,400,000 ($5,160,000) advertising campaign. More than 2,000,000 advisory leaflets were printed, for parents, teachers and health workers. A separate TV and press advertising series was created.

Announcing the programme, Social Services Secretary Norman Fowler said, 'Our approach will certainly not be soft but we do not aim to shock – all the evidence suggests that a shock/horror approach in this difficult area is at least likely to be ineffective and at worst counter-productive.'

The government, after a market research study, decided to mount the campaign against the advice of some doctors who feared that the publicity about drugs might actually tempt into experimentation people who might otherwise not have tried taking drugs.

Having toured British schools, leisure centres and treatment facilities, I consider this to have been a groundless fear: rarely did I find any group or gathering of young people to whom drugs were unknown.

I also consider the government's campaign to be ill-conceived, lacking any sort of proper thrust, and doubt it will have the slightest effect in cutting Britain's abuse problem.

Responsibility for the government's anti-drug crusade is that of David Mellor, Parliamentary Under-Secretary of State at the Home Office who, in June 1984, was appointed chairman of an interdepartmental group formed to develop an overall strategy. Mellor's appointment followed the publication of another report from the Advisory Council, entitled 'Prevention'.

The main recommendation of that report was that there should be better education at national, district and local levels of the country but that the education should embrace all aspects of healthy living and not concentrate exclusively upon drug danger. They further recommended an improvement in the training of those likely to come into contact with people misusing drugs – school teachers being the obvious body.

The figure of fifty thousand British addicts is estimated by another simple mathematical formula: by multiplying by five the number of addicts notified to the Home Office by doctors. Research commissioned by the DHSS has indicated that four-fifths of the addicts are either not notified by doctors or prefer to stay and buy on the streets.

But those Home Office notifications are predominantly for heroin, dipipanone, methadone and to a lesser extent cocaine. They give no indication whatsoever of marijuana abuse – because it is illegal and therefore not prescribed – and little guidance as to the number of people dependent upon psychotropic substances. Psychotropic is a generic description of drugs affecting psychic functions, behaviour or experience. The term embraces tranquillisers, sedatives, anti-depressants and psychostimulants and also includes lysergic acid diethylamide, more commonly known as LSD. This latter drug is also classified as an hallucinogen.

From my meetings with treatment specialists, police and monitoring bodies I consider a truer – although again conservative – figure of people abusing one or a mixture of drugs in Britain to be two hundred thousand. In a speech to

15

the House of Commons in April 1984, Conservative MP Sir Bernard Braine, a prominent anti-drug campaigner, said that in the five-year period since 1978, there had been a 57 per cent increase in addiction in London, 93 per cent in the south-east, 148 per cent in Wales, 437 per cent in Scotland and 480 per cent in the Midlands, a 'frightening' escalation.

By 1984, too, the number of British servicemen caught taking drugs – predominantly marijuana – had doubled over a four-year period. Although comparably the figure was extremely small – 259 convictions in the first nine months of 1984, compared to 153 in the whole of 1983 – service chiefs regarded it as a trend and were sufficiently alarmed to initiate anti-drug training programmes and to increase their surveillance and detection methods. The RAF appointed four specific training officers and at the time of writing are employing a dozen sniffer dogs at UK bases. In the Navy, the policy was adopted of giving offenders the shock of a period of close detention.

The belief that the ever-increasing growth of addiction is directly linked to the illegal supply of drugs – and that regulated control would undermine that market and reduce addiction – has resulted in suggestions of decriminalisation and legalisation being made to parliaments in Britain, Australia, Italy, Holland and Spain. Those suggestions have usually referred to marijuana, although in Italy and Holland there were some defeated efforts to include heroin.

This trend alarms the United Nations Narcotics Control Board, who said in their 1983 report, 'There are disquieting signs that in the face of the magnitude of the problem, determination may sometimes be giving way to permissiveness. To adopt such an attitude would be retrogressive.'

Retrogressive or not – and contrary to international treaty – such attitudes *are* being adopted, frequently unofficially.

Not so – federally at least – in America where, in June 1982, President Reagan declared that he was 'taking down the surrender flag that has flown over so many drug efforts'.

The flag may be furled, but there is still no indication that any worthwhile battle has been won.

And most certainly not the war.

1

He was a straightforward man, a scaffolder who lived an ordinary life in the north London suburb of Islington. Ordinary, that is, until his son became addicted to the drug Drinamyl, more commonly known as purple hearts, and changed 'from a lively, smart lad to someone listless and slovenly'.

He reacted immediately. He set out to find the prescribing doctor and learned that he was working from a surgery in Queensbridge Road, Hackney, described as the East London Addiction Centre. Then he broke in and attempted to do as much damage as he could.

He didn't try to run from the police. Instead he waited for them and explained the reason for his actions. 'I have no regrets,' he said. 'I feel it was my duty to save my son's life and possibly the lives of some other sons. I wish to stop this evil man. I smashed the place up so he can't use it to kill any other poor kids by giving them drugs.'

The doctor's name was Christopher Michael Swan. He was not destined to occupy his damaged office much longer. Two months after the break-in, he was arrested and charged with conspiracy to procure an abortion and with contraventions of the Misuse of Drugs Act. On remand in Brixton prison, he plotted to kill his co-defendants and was additionally charged with incitement and soliciting to murder.

The father, whose name was Michael Fagan, told police he had originally intended to murder Swan. 'But I changed my mind.'

The son's name was also Michael. Fifteen years after

17

becoming addicted to drugs, Michael Fagan twice entered Buckingham Palace. On the second occasion – 9 July 1983 – with blood dripping from a cut hand, he found access to the Queen's bedroom and spent ten minutes talking to her while she tried to summon help.

After the Buckingham Palace entry his father said, 'Once Michael started taking drugs his whole mind and character altered. He was never the same again. The damage they did is the price we have had to pay in seeing our son turn from a nice young fellow into a misfit.'

Swan was not the first nor the worst doctor guilty of over-prescribing. Another – regarded now by some drug experts as being one of the physicians most directly responsible for establishing heroin addiction in Britain – was even known at Buckingham Palace.

Lady Isabella Frankau accompanied her esteemed and respected husband – already a Commander of the Order of the British Empire and holder of the Distinguished Service Order – to the investiture at which he was awarded his knighthood. She was also in the congregation at Westminster Abbey on 6 May 1960, when Princess Margaret married Lord Snowdon. Which meant that the addicts to whom she regularly and grossly over-prescribed were kept waiting all day for their scripts at 32 Wimpole Street, the heartland of London's – and England's – expensive medical fraternity.

'Christ, we were angry,' recalled Mandy, her first-ever addict patient. Fifty-five years old now, dark-haired and fadingly attractive, Mandy has retired from prostitution. She lives with her heavily bearded addict husband Ray and a blind Pekinese called Sullivan – which bites – in a base-ment flat in West London. She added, 'We couldn't protest or anything, of course. She was a sergeant major, Lady Frankau. The worst you ever knew. If we upset her she'd make us suffer. Wait until last. Things like that.'

The monitoring – if not the control – of narcotic addic-tion in Britain has always been more efficiently maintained than anywhere else in the world. In 1934, in order to be able to supply addict statistics to the League of Nations, the

Home Office created an index, based on pharmacists' records of all narcotics transactions, and from 1968 – following recommendations from a government enquiry – doctors were officially required to notify the Home Office of any new addicts or suspected addicts. Until 1983, when they began to transfer the information onto a computer, that index was maintained by five clerks in seven stacks of file cards.

The Home Office, with the assistance of the police, also monitors the prescribing of controlled drugs. Which is how Lady Frankau was discovered.

'It was amazing,' said Mandy. 'She never decided for herself what the amount should be: she just asked what we wanted and gave it. The junkie community was close knit in those days – everybody knew everybody else – and once the word got around it was fantastic. You'd just go there, ask for whatever you wanted and get it! Marvellous!'

Mandy's eventual daily prescription from Lady Frankau was forty-eight grains a day. Today she gets five grains from her dependency unit.

'One girl was referred to her because she was hooked on purple hearts,' said Mandy. 'She sat in front of Lady Frankau who wrote out a script for heroin and for cocaine and gave it to her. The girl came out to us in the waiting-room and said, "What's this for? I don't know what it is." Can you imagine the rush to help her!'

Lady Frankau always wore a monocle and usually a severely tailored black suit. Fridays were bad days for her addicts because that was the day she always had her hair done and they had to wait until she got back from the hair-dresser's.

'She used me as a guinea pig,' remembered Mandy. 'Once, she made me "cold turkey" as a controlled experiment, under the supervision of herself and another. My withdrawal was awful. I was vomiting and had this terrible feeling in my back, like there was an electric fire inside me. And I couldn't stop my leg convulsions. Lady Frankau injected me with Pentothal [the drug thiopentone, an anaesthetic, also known as the truth drug] which stopped the convulsions. Then they began questioning me. I wasn't under the influence of the drug, not like they wanted me to be, to tell them secrets and stuff like that. So I tried to tell them what I thought they wanted to hear. Made the mistake of asking for a cigarette: the other doctor knew I wasn't knocked out and said so.'

Lady Frankau treated the addicts of the streets and adopted their language. 'Sometimes she got fed up with everyone hanging around in her surgery: it was posh, after all. Lots of titled people and things like that. So she'd say to me, "Go outside and tell them if they don't fuck off I'll stranglee them and I will never write another script for them." And that was the word she used, fuck!'

Aberdeen-born Lady Frankau didn't create the heroin outbreak in Britain. But she fuelled it, with the carelessness of a petrol-pump attendant smoking a cigarette. She did not do it through financial greed, like others. She was a rich woman whose non-National Health prescriptions – certainly often Mandy's – were frequently endorsed to be charged to her personal account, not to the addict; to one, Barry Ellis, she even – for a reason no one knows – gave a car. She innocently and naively believed that her abundant prescriptions kept her desperate addict patients from any illicit market, instead of realising she was supporting and feeding that market by providing more drugs than most of them – however fully addicted – could take. Heroin has a soporific effect. Having provided the sedative, Lady Frankau then prescribed cocaine as the stimulant to activate her patients into what she hoped would be some sort of useful daily existence. And all the time her prescribing was by the wheelbarrow rather than by the thimble; she therefore stands accused – rightly – in the history of British drug addiction as the person who re-introduced into England a cocaine culture that had flourished in London briefly before and then between the two World Wars but which was otherwise virtually unknown after 1945. And a heroin culture, as well.

Mark had started what Lady Frankau sustained.

That wasn't his real name, just the one he preferred to use in the jazz clubs and the coffee bars of London's Soho. His real name was Kevin Patrick Saunders and he was a porter at All Saints Hospital, in the London district of Chatham. Saunders wanted to be recognised and accepted. He decided drugs was the way. On the night of 24 April 1951 he broke in to the darkened pharmacy at the hospital, and from his knowledge of the drugs cupboards he found it easy to steal 3120 heroin tablets, which was 520 grains. He also took over five ounces of morphine and two ounces of cocaine.

'Bing' Spear, who possesses an encyclopaedic knowledge of the development of drug abuse in Britain, personally traced sixty-three people who became addicted directly as a result of Saunders' theft; in the records of British addiction, at the time it was the largest number from any one source.

Saunders got the recognition he sought peddling his drugs around the jazz clubs of Soho and the night clubs of Mayfair and Belgravia. One was Club Eleven. Another was the Contemporary Club, in White Horse Street. There was a brilliant jazz drummer at the Contemporary, a Nigerian named Geoffrey Aggrey. He bought from Saunders and by the time he met Mandy, he was an established, irredeemable addict. Aggrey came from a wealthy Nigerian family: he had had a university education. He taught Mandy to read and write: today, someone with a remarkable memory, she compares Somerset Maugham with other modern writers. Literature was not, however, the only thing that the hopelessly addicted Aggrey taught Mandy.

'He mainlined me, the first time,' she remembered. 'Everyone else was doing it and I wanted to do it too. It's like they say, in all the reports. You do what other people do whom you admire, either to conform – not wanting to appear scared – or to be part of it. Christ, it was wonderful, that first time! There's nothing like your first fix. Every one after that is trying to make it like it was the first time. But it never is, of course. Shouldn't say that to kids, not ever. Makes it sound attractive. Which it isn't later. Later it's

21

shit, awful shit. It's rubbish, about it being a sexual thing, too. Maybe initially, the first six months, say. But after that you're lucky if your husband comes near you. And I should know about sex. But the first time is wonderful. Really wonderful.'

Mandy was at one time a high-class call girl with a house in Mayfair – complete with maid – and numbered among her clients a still famous international musical comedy and film star whose fetish was having a phial of amyl nitrate, a vasodilator used as an aphrodisiac, broken beneath his nose during sexual intercourse.

Lady Frankau was interested in Mandy's sex life because she was one of Stephen Ward's girls.

Stephen Ward was an osteopath, who became linked with – and ultimately victim of – the biggest society scandal of the sixties in Britain, the disgrace and eventual resignation from Parliament of Secretary of State for War John Profumo because of his liaison with another Stephen Ward call girl, Christine Keeler. While sleeping with Profumo, Keeler was conducting a simultaneous affair with the Soviet naval attaché, Captain Eugene Ivanov.

A cottage, rented by Ward on Viscount Astor's estate at Cliveden, Buckinghamshire, was identified as the venue for sex parties, and in the rumour-laden atmosphere of the time there were recurring stories of The Man in the Mask. According to the gossip, the man who menially waited at table at dinner parties wearing – apart from the disguising mask – only a minuscule apron, was another minister in the Conservative government of the time who later retired and died in tax exile in the South of France.

'Lady Frankau was desperate to know who it was,' said Mandy. 'She wanted to be able to boast and appear to know things that other people didn't at her own dinner parties. She used to reward me with extra scripts for doing things for her – like baby-sitting for one of her most awkward alcoholics when no proper nurse would take the job – and she made it clear that I'd get extra stuff if I could confirm the name. I couldn't, so I didn't get anything extra.'

Stephen Ward committed suicide from a drug overdose. 'A lovely man,' insisted Mandy. 'These society men kept pestering him for women, that's all. He was a victim, really he was.'

Mandy fixed as we talked, properly, with sterilised needle and sterilised water to mix with her ampoule of medically-prescribed heroin. She had to do it subcutaneously because after thirty-eight years of addiction all her veins have collapsed so she can no longer mainline. She was proud of that, windmilling her arms and going through the charade of binding one of them to illustrate how she once made her veins protrude for the injection. Messy, she called it; blood spurting everywhere. She cleansed her skin with Diorissimo from an aerosol spray. Perfume was good because surgical spirit dried her skin and made it hard. She needs her skin soft, for the needle. No veins left, she repeated. Then corrected herself. The veins in the groin are always the last – she caricatured a friend, supporting himself against a television set, dressed only in his underpants with the hypodermic hanging from his crotch – and she knew she could still mainline there if she wanted to because the previous week at the clinic they had needed a blood sample and obtained it that way. Don't do it though, she said, proud of her self-control. Mandy has undergone fourteen detoxification cures. All have failed.

'I'm in love with the needle,' she said wistfully. 'I'll never stop. Don't want to.'

Mandy is a classic example of the addict envisioned in the first study of Britain's drug use in 1926. But the country's interest in opiates began much earlier than that.

Britain didn't start the opium trade – as early as 1729 the Portuguese began carrying the drug to an eager Chinese market – but it was the British who realised the commercial potential and soon took over, creating vast cultivations in India, which they controlled, and selling the opium on to China. Hong Kong's most famous trading firm, Jardine, Matheson, was established on the opium trade which its

23

founders, Dr William Jardine and James Matheson, originally conducted from Canton. The *Cambridge History of China* describes opium as 'the world's most valuable single commodity trade of the nineteenth century': by the early 1830s, 560,000 lb of the drug was entering China each year. Jardine's official history admits to 'a very considerable share' of the market. So lucrative did the business become that when the Chinese emperor, concerned about the effects upon his population, tried to stop it, Britain went to war to enforce its continuation. The first Opium War lasted from 1839 to 1842; the second from 1856 to 1858. China lost both and Britain established a world monopoly in the market. It is ironical that of all the addicted nations of the world China is virtually drug-free today.

Laudanum – the tincture of opium – was the product of the time and addicts averaged a pint or more a day of a potion in which one ounce of laudanum usually contained one grain of morphine. The poet Samuel Taylor Coleridge wrote 'Kubla Khan' under the influence of opium. Thomas de Quincey, English critic and essayist, was also a user. So were Edgar Allan Poe, Charles Dickens and Wilkie Collins. As in America, morphine, the alkaloid derivative of opium, became an ingredient in dozens of across-the-counter patent medicines, like Lancaster Black Drop, Battley's Syrup, Dr J. Collis Browne's Chlorodyne and Godfrey's Cordial.

Morphine was refined from opium in the 1820s but it did not become widely used until the 1860s, when Dr Alexander Wood, a Scottish doctor, perfected the hypodermic syringe and, with Dr Charles Hunter, publicised the benefits of injections to relieve neuralgia. Wood's wife is the first person known to have died from an injected overdose.

The medical profession, not improperly, embraced the new drug enthusiastically. In 1869 Dr Charles Wilson wrote, 'Few really important discoveries have glided so silently into everyday use as the subcutaneous injection of remedial agents. Slowly and surely this new method has won its way and established itself in the profession until

24

there are probably few medical men to be found who cannot bear testimony, from their own experience, to the marvellous power of narcotics beneath the skin.' The medical use of opium and its derivatives, attested Wilson, was the greatest boon since the discovery of chloroform.

In 1874 another derivative was discovered. A London chemist named C. R. Alder Wright experimented upon morphine by heating it in combination with acetic anhydride. And produced a drug that, for the time being, remained nameless.

By that same year there already existed a Quaker-based organisation called the Society for the Suppression of the Opium Trade. The official reaction to the idea of banning such a profitable business – and undeniably efficacious medicine – was strident. Sir George Birdwood wrote in *The Times*, 'As regards opium smoking, I can from experience testify that it is, of itself, absolutely harmless.' Surgeon General Sir William Moore insisted, 'Opium is not the destructive agent which anti-opiumists declare it to be. I assert that there is no organic disease traceable to the use of opium. Functional disorders more or less may be induced by excessive use of opium. But the same may be said of other causes of deranged health – gluttony, tea, tobacco, bad air, mental anxiety, etc.'

By 1878, however, there were warnings of the dangers of addiction. That year a German doctor, Edward Levinstein, wrote '*Die Morphiumsucht*', which was translated and circulated throughout the British medical profession as 'The Morbid Craving for Morphine.' Levinstein's recommended cure was complete abstinence for eight to fourteen days in a locked room, 'all opportunities for attempted suicide having been removed', with pain relieved by warm baths, bicarbonate of soda, chloral hydrate and unlimited amounts of champagne and brandy.

Levinstein was not the only German interested in opium and its derivatives. Heinrich Dreser, chief pharmacologist at the Elberfeld Farbenfabrik of Friedr. Bayer and Company, had been carrying out experiments – including tests on unknowing patients in the company's own hospital – with the drug Alder Wright had distilled in 1874. In 1898 he presented a paper about it to the seventieth Congress of German Naturalists and Physicians at Düsseldorf. He gave it a name, too: heroin. It was, he reported accurately, an excellent treatment for coughs, catarrh, bronchitis, asthma, tuberculosis and emphysema, without the disadvantages of morphine, which frequently caused nausea and constipation in patients. There was also a further advantage: heroin was not addictive.

Five years earlier, in Britain, William Gladstone's Liberal government responded to public disquiet about opium by establishing a royal commission to investigate its cultivation and use in India, with instructions to make any recommendations for change they felt necessary. The commission declared there was no danger.

That resistance to change persisted up to – and even after – opium conferences in Shanghai in 1909 and The Hague in 1911, which were convened largely because of American pressure. From the latter conference came an international agreement, signed by thirty-four nations, to impose domestic controls on the manufacture and distribution of cocaine, opiates and other drugs, so limiting their use to medical and scientific purposes. By the 1920s the need for monitoring was finally accepted in Britain. The Dangerous Drugs Act was passed in 1920 and the Dangerous Drugs Regulations established the following year. The Home Office was given responsibility for implementing the legislation.

In 1924 the Ministry of Health set up an enquiry whose function was to determine whether or not it was proper for doctors to prescribe to addicts; their conclusion – that addiction was a medical problem to be treated by doctors – was upheld for the next thirty-seven years. The composition of the Departmental Committee on Morphine and Heroin Addiction marked the difference which has always existed between British and American approaches. The committee's term of reference was to decide whether, under existing regulations, it was proper medical practice to supply addicts. The chairman was Sir Humphrey Rolleston, President of the Royal College of Surgeons, and the members of his committee were all doctors. From the beginning British legislators regarded addiction as a medical problem.

The Rolleston Committee, as it became known, held twenty-three sessions and heard evidence, in private, from psychiatrists, pharmacists, physicians, surgeons, civil servants, prison medical officers, the Director of Public Prosecutions and E. Farquhar Buzzard, Physician Extra-ordinary to the King. Their resulting report defined an addict as 'a person who, not requiring the continued use of a drug for the relief of the symptoms of organic disease, has acquired, as a result of repeated administration, an over-powering desire for its continuance and in whom withdrawal of the drug leads to definite symptoms of mental or physical distress or disorder'.

Showing a prescience about the possibility of cure to which modern treatment centres throughout the world can attest today, the Rolleston Committee declared, as long ago as 1926, 'Relapse, sooner or later, appears to be the rule.' If a cure failed, then they advised that the patient should be maintained upon the minimum dosage of the drug of his addiction guaranteed to enable him to function in daily life.

Realistically the Rolleston Committee recognised there would always be people, like Mandy, 'to whom the indefi-nitely prolonged administration of morphine or heroin may be necessary; those in whom a complete withdrawal of mor-phine or heroin produces serious symptoms which cannot be treated satisfactorily under the ordinary conditions of private practice and those who are capable of leading a fairly normal and useful life so long as they take a certain quantity, usually small, of their drug of addiction, but not otherwise'. The decision as to whether a patient should be weaned off or maintained should be that of the doctor, said the committee. And recognising, realistically again, that there would always be the risk of certain doctors over-prescribing, they recommended the establishment of tribunals before which

27

suspected doctors could appear and, if found culpable, have their prescribing authority withdrawn by the Home Secretary.

Provision for such tribunals was made in the new Dangerous Drugs Regulations of 1926 produced as a result of the Rolleston Committee's work, but in fact from 1926 until the end of the Second World War there were few examples of indiscriminate prescribing and those were usually dealt with by a warning visit from the drug inspectorate branch of the Home Office.

Through complacency and stupidity, the years of the mid to late fifties was a period of confusion and error as far as the British attitude to drugs was concerned. By 1955, the inspectorate branch of the Home Office became aware – from their check upon prescriptions – that a number of doctors, including Lady Isabella Frankau, were over-issuing scripts for heroin.

Amazingly, the tribunals recommended by the Rolleston Committee twenty-nine years earlier no longer existed to stop such practices: they had been omitted from the Dangerous Drugs Regulations of 1953, pending agreement with the medical profession about new rules of procedure.

In 1958 the Interdepartmental Committee on Drug Addiction was set up, chaired by Sir Russell – later Lord – Brain and therefore always known as the Brain Committee.

If the report produced by the Rolleston Committee was an example of clear thinking and intelligent conclusions, then the Brain Committee's first report was an illustration of bewildering and inexcusable ineptitude, even though their mandate from the Conservative government of Harold Macmillan went beyond the morphine and heroin of Rolleston's enquiry to include analgesics, barbiturates, amphetamines and tranquillisers.

Although officials from the Home Office and the then Ministry of Health provided background information, the Brain investigation did not officially call anyone from the Home Office Drugs Inspectorate – who could have told them verbally what they failed to appreciate from written reports about the rise in heroin abuse – and concluded, in spite of clear statistical evidence to the contrary, that there was 'no cause to fear any real increase' in addiction.

At a time when Lady Frankau was prescribing heroin pills by the hundred, the feeling among the blinkered Committee was that 'in spite of widespread enquiry, no doctor is known to be following this practice at present'.

The first Brain Committee conducted no such 'widespread enquiry'. Their most reprehensible recommendation, however, was that 'the Home Secretary should not establish medical tribunals to investigate the grounds for recommending him to withdraw a doctor's authority to possess and supply dangerous drugs'. Regrettably – during a period when the General Medical Council were equally reluctant to call a doctor before their disciplinary committee to question his prescribing – the government accepted that recommendation and did not change it when the first report was discredited and a second one found necessary. The result was that tribunals were not re-introduced as a control mechanism until the Misuse of Drugs Act, 1971.

The exposure of the first report of the Brain Committee as the facile document it was began even before its publication. Brain set out his Committee's findings in advance to a closed meeting of the Society for the Study of Addiction in London on 18 April 1961. He was immediately challenged by a pharmacist from one of London's all-night chemists – John Bell and Croydon, in Wigmore Street – to which addicts presented their prescriptions one minute after midnight, thus qualifying for a new day's supply. The man – Irving Benjamin – maintained his own register and told of one man who had presented a bona fide script for thirty grains of cocaine and fifty grains of heroin. In one day!

What Benjamin's figures proved – and Home Office experts already knew – was that the ridiculous over-prescribing of drugs, by a small but nevertheless dangerous group of doctors honestly believing they were preventing an illicit black market, was actually *creating* it. And it

29

is important to re-emphasise that few of these doctors, stupidly naïve in hindsight, were stocking the market for financial gain. Certainly Lady Frankau wasn't. Mandy insists that Lady Frankau – an aristocrats' doctor who considered herself an expert in drugs after treating a number of her patients for alcoholism – used her earnings from the rich to subsidise her treatment of the addicted poor, all of whom she considered mentally ill and all of whom she wanted to keep from the evils of the black market. That, too was the ambition of Dr A. J. Hawes, who never made a secret of his practices. After another doctor – Geoffrey Dymond, with a practice in the London suburb of Fulham – stopped giving treatment because of adverse publicity, Hawes wrote to *The Times*:'The most threatening portent is that addicts are telling me that there is plenty of the stuff to be had on the black market, even though the source from over-prescribing doctors is drying up. It looks as if big business, which has been waiting in the wings for so long, has now taken over the stage and is playing the lead. So we may look for an explosion in the teenage addict population as the months go by.'

So clearly out of touch with reality was the first Brain report that a second was commissioned in 1964. On this occasion its terms of reference were narrowed, rather than widened: the Committee was particularly charged with an investigation into over-prescribing doctors. This was a logical brief because police arrests were proving one fact conclusively: all the seizures well into the sixties were of pharmaceutical heroin or cocaine, meaning the drugs came from a doctor's prescription and were not smuggled in from abroad.

After hearing evidence about the titled doctor of Wimpole Street, Lord Brain turned to Home Office officials and said, 'Your problem, gentlemen, can be summed up in two words – Lady Frankau.'

For once in a discussion about drugs, it was not an understatement. In their eventual, second report, the Brain Committee recorded:

From the evidence before us we have been led to the conclusion that the major source of supply has been the activity of a very few doctors who have prescribed excessively for addicts. Thus we were informed that in 1962 one doctor alone prescribed almost 600,000 tablets of heroin [i.e. six kilograms] for addicts. The same doctor on one occasion prescribed 900 tablets of heroin [139 grains] to one addict and three days later prescribed the same patient another 600 tablets [i.e. 92.5 grains] 'to replace pills lost in an accident'. Further prescriptions of 720 [i.e. 111 grains] and 840 [130 grains] tablets followed later to the same patient

Lady Frankau's name was on every prescription.

The second report was altogether much better than the first. It blamed a small number of doctors – leading to a witch-hunt in the media – and recommended the creation of treatment centres, thereby making it possible to monitor and hopefully control the level of prescriptions to addicts. The report stated: 'If there is insufficient control, it may lead to the spread of addiction – as is happening at present. If, on the other hand, the restrictions are so severe as to prevent or seriously discourage the addict from obtaining supplies from legitimate sources it may lead to the development of an organised traffic. The absence hitherto of such an organised illicit traffic has been attributed largely to the fact that an addict has been able to obtain supplies of drugs legally.'

Things remained unchanged, even after publication of the second Brain report. And in view of the lack of co-operation from the British Medical Council, without the provision of tribunals there was little the Home Office could do about the doctors concerned.

Christopher Michael Swan was charging £2 for a consultation and while admitting he was probably one of the richest doctors of his age in the country, he declared, 'These young people are cracked kids from a cracked society. I see myself as rather like a worker-priest; someone with courage enough to carry out his beliefs in an unorthodox way.'

And leading the new order was Lady Frankau.

In 1935 she had become the second wife of Claude Frankau, already a legendary figure in British medicine. Knighted in 1945, Frankau was a consultant surgeon to St George's Hospital, the Royal Waterloo Hospital for Children, Woodford Hospital and consultant surgeon – non-obstetric – to Queen Charlotte's Hospital. He was the President of the Association of Surgeons for Great Britain in 1937 and 1938 and later examiner in surgery at the University of London, a member of the Court of Examiners of the Royal College of Surgeons and adviser in surgery to the Ministry of Health. In the First World War he was consulting surgeon to the 5th Army of the British Expeditionary Force, with the temporary rank of colonel, and was mentioned in despatches three times.

'Lady Frankau was overwhelmed by his achievements,' Mandy recalled. 'When he retired she determined to make a name for herself in medicine, like he had.'

She chose to do so in drug treatment. Convinced that she was an expert, she undertook a lecture tour of Canada, expounding her theory of liberal prescribing to keep addicts from the clutches of drug peddlers. Ninety-one Canadian addicts followed her to London and one of them told a Home Office official, 'London is a junkie's seventh heaven.'

Lady Frankau enjoyed her notoriety. She liked being known to the Home Office. And liked – strangely – the dependence of the addicts upon her every whim.

'Because I was her first I was special,' said Mandy. 'I used to try to advise her, tell her she was being cheated and tricked, but she wouldn't listen. Not often, anyway. She used to humiliate us, if we did anything wrong. I had to run messages for her. Do errands: anything she asked. Not a slave or anything like that: near it, sometimes, though. Still I liked her.'

John Petro, who took over the majority of Lady Frankau's patients when she died in May 1967, was a gambler – a contributory factor mentioned at his bankruptcy hearing – and apparently met some of the Canadian addicts she treated at the Golden Nugget casino in London's Shaftesbury Avenue. He had initially been introduced to Lady Frankau by his brother, Alexander, with whom he was in partnership for a time at 21 Wilton Place, London SW1. Alexander, who served for a period as Honorary Physician to the Queen, sometimes cared for Lady Frankau's patients at weekends when she and her husband visited their country estate at Ickleton Grange, near Saffron Walden in Essex.

The Petro family name was really Piotrkowski. John had come to England from Poland at the age of eleven, in 1916. And outstanding scholar, he gained a place at Cambridge and studied at Emmanuel College, from where he graduated with an honours degree in 1926. He then won the coveted Brackenbury Prize, while a student at St George's Hospital Medical School. In 1932 he became a Bachelor of Science. During the Second World War he was a surgeon lieutenant commander in the navy and was seconded, because of his ability as a doctor, to work with Sir Alexander Fleming. Petro, later to be vilified as one of the most evil doctors of his time, was the first to administer Fleming's wonder drug, penicillin, at a naval auxiliary hospital in Colombo, the capital of what was then Ceylon, now Sri Lanka.

A brillant doctor and surgeon, John Petro was privately an ineffectual man, unable to run his personal life. Two marriages collapsed. So did the partnership with his brother. An inveterate gambler, John was declared bankrupt. By the time of Lady Frankau's death, he had neither practice nor surgery. He prescribed first from the station buffet at Baker Street underground station. Evicted from there, he continued Lady Frankau's policy of indiscriminate issuing from a room at the Winton Hotel in Inverness Terrace, in London's Bayswater. His freedom with scripts spread addiction outwards from London to Hertfordshire and Welwyn Garden City. One of his patients was the heroin-addicted son of Sir John Rennie, head of Britain's external intelligence agency MI6. The boy frequently travelled with Petro on trips to Scotland. A £30,000 inheritance was squandered on drugs. And yet in spite of the fact that Petro was pilloried in the press, there remains within the medical profession a widespread belief that he was not a rogue doctor but a dedicated physician, someone who was genuinely trying to help the sort of people described in the document produced by the Rolleston Committee in 1926.

On 11 January 1968 Petro appeared on a television programme hosted by David Frost. As he left the studio he was arrested by drug squad officers and later fined £1700 for failing to keep a drugs register. Undeterred, he went on issuing from a former cinema at 17 Tramway Avenue, in the London borough of Stratford, and when he was evicted from those premises he wrote prescriptions from a Vauxhall Viva car parked in nearby Victoria Street. On 30 and 31 May, 1968, Petro appeared before the General Medical Council following his criminal court appearance; they ordered him to be struck from the register.

Petro appealed against that decision, which allowed him to continue prescribing. In April a new Dangerous Drugs Act had come into force, forbidding general practitioners to prescribe heroin. Petro switched to the injectable drug methamphetamine, sold as Methedrine and known in junkie jargon as 'speed', which he issued indiscriminately: in one month he prescribed a total of 24,906 ampoules to 110 patients – the average supply to one person being 46 ampoules a day. Petro lost his appeal and was finally struck off on 30 October 1968.

Petro was not the only doctor to prescribe methamphetamine. So, too, did Christopher Michael Swan, who later served his sentence for murder incitement at a prison hospital for the criminally insane, has been released and now works in London as a mini-cab driver. He is studying for an MA at a polytechnic on the outskirts of London. His chosen subject: deviancy.

Drug analysts say that before manufacturers, at the request of the Home Office, agreed in October 1968 to restrict the sale of methamphetamine exclusively to hospitals, the drug gained such a pervasive hold upon the black-market street culture that it provided the escalator to heroin in place of the marijuana at one time considered responsible.

And by now a very definite street culture had developed. It was centred around Piccadilly Circus underground station at the very heart of the capital, and particularly around the ladies' lavatory at subway 4. Piccadilly Circus was the centre because, like John Bell and Croydon in Wigmore Street, the Piccadilly branch of Boots the Chemist was open twenty-four hours a day and legal prescriptions could be claimed just after midnight. And the ladies' lavatory was a convenient bolt-hole for women carriers if a policeman suddenly appeared.

Petro remained on the drug scene. Barred from prescribing officially, he was frequently seen in Piccadilly, surgically lancing and treating the suppurating ulcers that developed on the addicts when they used unsterilised needles or mixed their injections with water from the lavatory bowl or with lemon juice or vinegar. And if they couldn't find a vein to use, Petro would help them to do that, too. On one visit he was accompanied by Margaret Tripp, a psychiatrist who ran the Addiction Unit at St Clement's Hospital in London for three and a half years and who wrote sympathetically of his efforts to help the addicts.

Few doctors knew what it was like to treat drug abusers. Initially there was a rush to obtain licences – there was almost a certain *cachet* involved – and six hundred were issued to doctors working from treatment centres attached to the psychiatric hospitals. Enthusiasm was quick to evaporate, however, and more stringent restrictions were introduced regarding their allocation; today there are only two hundred licence holders. In an article she contributed to the magazine *Drugs and Society* following her visit with Petro to Piccadilly, Margaret Tripp, empathising with him and doctors like him because she was aware of the unremitting pressure exerted by addicts, wrote: 'If I shut my eyes I fell into the light trance that follows extreme fatigue. It was a very pleasant feeling. It was easy to see how junkie doctors felt eaten alive by the unending demands of their patients. It was also easy to see why they took their own drugs.'

John Owens was a tragic example of a positive leader in drug treatment in Britain who became 'eaten alive'. A psychiatrist at All Saints Hospital in Birmingham, Owens established a clinic there before publication of the recommendations of the Brain Committee and successfully countered an outbreak of heroin addiction in the city. It set an example to other towns throughout the country and for more than ten years had a record of success, with an addict roster of 4500. So great was the pressure that in 1972 Owens introduced an emergency prescription service at certain Birmingham chemists and because of staff shortages at All Saints gave blank forms to his head nursing officer, Edward David Hill. The nursing officer was also under pressure. He began allowing addicts extra heroin and cocaine, in return for whisky and cigarettes, and some of the prescriptions were made out for Dexedrine, the stimulant drug dextro-amphetamine, which Owens used himself. In November 1976 Owens was prohibited by the Home Office from having anything to do with controlled drugs: at a hearing before the General Medical Council, the forerunner in the treatment of addicts in Britain was described as 'a fool, not a knave'.

There was a naïveté as well as some foolishness at other treatment centres, which developed uncertainly; because although the second Brain Committee had established them, it had not specified *how* they should operate, so individual hospitals and doctors created their own, differing models. And manipulative, inventive addicts were more used to dealing with doctors than doctors were to dealing with them. Initially, at least, there was over-prescribing, although not as recklessly as before.

There was, too, uncertainty among the addicts, for a variety of reasons. There was the fear that by going to a clinic they would have to be officially registered and thus achieve a 'record'. So a great many of them didn't go – and still don't, assessing official against unofficial figures. And those that did perpetrated the biggest misunderstanding of the British policy: that notification – it was never registration – gave them an *automatic* right to heroin. It never did and never has. The notification index is a statistical record and can sometimes provide a certain amount of intelligence: for instance, by isolating a sudden, concentrated increase in numbers it can locate a possible source of illicit supply. It also provides a central bank of information for doctors wanting to check whether an addict seeking help is already listed and receiving prescriptions or dosage from another clinic.

But the treatment and sort of drugs supplied – if any – is always the decision of the doctor.

While the clinics and the heroin and cocaine addicts tried to adjust to each other, the drug scene in Britain continued to expand. Methamphetamine had already been introduced, expanding the needle culture. Now barbiturates like Tuinal and Nembutal were being crushed and injected. They were the forerunners of Ritalin, Diconal and Doriden.

Considering the circumstances of the time, the official reaction to what many now view as an enlightened suggestion about marijuana was hardly surprising. A committee chaired by Baroness Wootton recommended in 1968 that the penalties for smoking cannabis – an illegal drug in Britain – be reduced. There was no evidence that it led to violent crime, said the Wootton Committee: it was, in fact, the equivalent of alcohol.

The Wootton Committee's findings marked the beginning of a change in Britain's attitude to marijuana, but their opinion was castigated by Home Secretary James Callaghan. He said: 'To reduce the penalties for possession, sale or supply of cannabis would be bound to lead people to think that the government takes a less serious view of the effect of drug-taking . . . Because we have a number of social evils in this country at present, it would be sheer masochism to add to our evils by legislation to make it more easy for people to introduce another one.'

But another evil had already appeared on the streets.

37

Not in any great quantity – although in succeeding years it was to increase vastly and rapidly – but sufficient to send the necessary warning to the more experienced officials at the Home Office. As early as September 1967, officers of the Metropolitan Police Drug Squad seized a light brown, granular powder. Not knowing what it was, they sent it for analysis and it was identified as a mixture of heroin and caffeine. Known as 'No. 3', it had been smuggled by the triads from Hong Kong for London's Chinese community, concentrated around Soho's Gerrard Street. Traditionally the Chinese do not inject their drugs. No. 3 is heroin for smoking, heated in such a way that the fumes can be sniffed through a straw or pipe. It's called 'Chasing the Dragon'.

Triads – known in Chinese as Huk Sai Wui, or Black Associations – are an established part of Chinese communities throughout the world, and their origins are not necessarily sinister. They were originally formed in the late seventeenth century as a political resistance movement to the Manchu dynasty. Today the most influential triad is K-14, formed in 1945 by the nationalist government of Chiang Kai-shek to oppose the Communist takeover and named after the house where it was formed, 14 Po Wah Road, Canton. It scattered after Mao Tse-tung's victory. Amsterdam has an active cell. So does London. It is regarded as a new society and therefore despised by another longer standing triad, Wo-Sin-Wo. The Wo-Sin-Wo were active in London, too, with an offshoot known as Tsui Fong.

The English clinics thought they knew how to treat heroin addicts . . .

As early as 1963 Vincent Dole, a metabolic research scientist, and his wife, Marie Nyswander, a psychiatrist with long experience of drug addiction problems, conducted a study at the Rockefeller University in New York. They claimed in their findings that methadone, invented because of the exigencies of war and first tested in the public hospital at Lexington, Kentucky, was the treatment panacea. Its particular benefit, they said, was that it blocked the euphoria from heroin, thus reducing the desire for the stronger drug. They called it the blockade principle.

Methadone became – and still is – the cornerstone of treatment in America. Britain adopted the same policy. In America, methadone was administered orally, usually mixed with orange juice. In England initially, after the establishment of treatment clinics, it was usually injected, but the British clinics that use it today have adopted the American practice and give it by mouth.

From the beginning addicts hated it, using it despisingly to wash out their syringes before turning to the black-market heroin being provided – in the 1960s – by the Chinese. They sold their unwanted methadone ampoules to finance their purchases in and around Gerrard Street of the Hong Kong-originated Three Crowns or Elephant brands – the packets carried their advertising motif and guarantee of purity – and Chinese Rice.

By 1970 treatment clinics were being approached for help by a number of people whose primary addiction was methadone. And two decades after the claims of Dole and Nyswander – claims that are still accepted by the majority of dependency clinics throughout the world – independent investigations have concluded that the harm done by methadone maintenance greatly outweighs the benefits.

In 1983 Dr David Ausubel, a New York psychiatrist, confirmed as a result of a controlled examination what British clinics had been finding since 1970, that the maintenance system 'has inadvertently created incomparably more primary methadone addicts than it has cured heroin addicts'.

Dr Patrick Mullin, the director of a dependency clinic covering the west of Scotland, and two of his colleagues – Roger Paxton and former drug squad head Jack Beattie – in 1978 published a report in the *British Journal of Psychiatry*, saying that the benefits of methadone maintenance had been exaggerated.

Methadone did not stop the craving for narcotics, they decided: 'It does not block receptors to the effect of opioids,

39

as do the true opioid antagonists. The so-called ''heroin blockade'' in methadone maintenance is merely an example of opioid cross-tolerance. Since opioid-takers develop tolerance, it is hardly surprising that those on prescription use extra drugs.'

From their experience they found few addicts maintained on methadone achieved eventual abstinence and said, 'Drug-taking is a complex social phenomenon, which varies greatly from one city to another. In some cities methadone may indeed be important in reducing crime. Unfortunately we have little firm evidence on this. In Glasgow it is not clear that it does so.'

Although by 1970 British clinics were already treating people addicted primarily to methadone, they still continued the maintenance programme with the synthetic drug. This wasn't the only new drug problem of the time. The emerging trend of barbiturate injectors, with their accompanying abscesses and ulcers, was sufficiently serious to be raised in March 1970, during the second reading in Parliament of the Misuse of Drugs Bill. The Advisory Committee on Drug Dependence, which was to become the Advisory Council as a result of the 1971 Act, was asked to report on whether or not barbiturates should be controlled under the legislation. The Committee couldn't decide whether the restrictions on narcotics had caused the outbreak of barbiturate abuse but concluded that barbiturates should also be covered under the forthcoming act. That judgement was made too late, however, for the necessary consultations with the professional bodies, and the Misuse of Drugs Act of 1971 – which re-introduced the never-before-used Home Office tribunal system to judge errant doctors – came on to the statute books without any control over barbiturates.

More and different drugs appeared on the illicit market, of which the worst has proved to be Diconal. Today in England – and in America, where it is marketed under the name Wellconal – it is frequently a drug *preferred* to heroin by established users. An analgesic, intended to be taken orally as a pill, it is crushed and mixed into a red injectable liquid with water and sometimes vinegar. The excellent monitoring system of the British Home Office – the index – indicated that supplies initially originated in 1970 from a treatment centre in Doncaster, and from an elderly Irish doctor called Brennan, who practised in Portsmouth. The treatment centre was quickly dealt with and, as the tribunals of the 1971 Act had not yet been established, Dr Brennan was personally exhorted not to prescribe any further supplies of the drug by Spear from the Home Office and Detective Sergeant Alan Russell from the Portsmouth drug squad. Diconal was also beginning to appear in the Republic of Ireland – first from pharmacy thefts, then medical prescriptions – spreading later to South Africa and finally the United States of America.

Although omitted from the 1971 legislation, barbiturates were not forgotten. The 1971 Act established the Advisory Council on the Misuse of Drugs, a group with no research funds that meets only twice a year and whose members include psychiatrists, medical doctors, nurses, educationalists, social scientists and – because they utilise drugs – a dentist and a veterinary surgeon. The inclusion of these last two has attracted criticism from some professionals more actively involved in drug addiction who argue that the Council is made less effective by its efforts to involve representatives from every profession who, although using drugs, are little involved in their abuse.

In their attack on the serious and growing problem of barbiturate abuse they certainly moved with the soporific slowness of the elephant motif on the Chinese heroin packet. It was not until September 1975 that the Council initiated the Campaign on the Use and Restriction of Barbiturates (CURB), and even that was a two-year project intended to persuade doctors voluntarily to restrict prescriptions and warn the public of barbiturate dangers. Not until 1978 did the Council recommend positive legal control.

At that time, however, public attention was focusing more upon another drug, the LSD that had earlier proved

41

so popular with California's flower children. England, according to evidence given at a trial in Bristol in February 1978, had become the world's manufacturing centre from just two laboratories, one at 23 Seymour Road, Hampton Wick, on the outskirts of London, and another at Plas Llsyn, near Carno in Wales.

According to the Bristol trial of a total of twenty-nine people, spread over several months, an estimated sixty million doses of LSD – at the street selling-price of £1 a dose – had been produced at those two laboratories over a four-year period. And that constituted half of the western world's supply and was sufficient for ninety-five per cent of the British demand. The brilliantly innovative chemist who led the ring, Richard Kemp, was given the doubtful accolade by police scientists of having produced the purest LSD up until that time ever discovered.

Public interest extended beyond the trial and the yet further proof of the staggering profits available from drugs. As it seemed, from the claims made at the trial, that the main supplier had been put out of business, there was an understandable expectation that the street price of LSD – if it were available at all – would rocket. It didn't happen that way. At most it was absent from the streets for a fortnight. But at the end of two weeks, another supplier stepped in to fill the gap.

An even more interesting revelation was the attitude – still, regrettably, to be found in some forces – towards drug squads. The task force that broke the British manufacturing ring was made up of policemen from ten provincial forces and worked under the code name Operation Julie. That Operation Julie came into existence at all was due to the determination of one of its leading officers, Detective Chief Inspector Dick Lee, who repeatedly fought against refusal at higher levels of authority to accept the existence of an organised LSD trade.

Soon after the conclusion of the case Lee resigned from the Thames Valley force. Diplomatically he refused to confirm a disagreement between himself and the Chief Constable,

David Holdsworth, saying only that his departure was 'on a matter of principle'.

In quick succession, there were other resignations among those who had formed the Julie squad. Sergeant Martyn Pritchard also left Thames Valley. Constable Paul Parnell quit the Dorset force and Constable Eric Wright left Avon and Dorset. Sergeant John McWalters and Constable Alan Buxton no longer felt able to stay in the West Midlands Constabulary. Buxton gave the reason. He said the official attitude was, 'Now that you've had your holiday and earned some money, you can get down to some real police work.'

A senior police officer who helped me on a non-attributable basis with the research for this book – the head of a major drug squad – said, 'There was then and there still is now a worrying lack of appreciation by some chief constables of how serious the drugs problem is throughout the country. Too often a few men are given the titular designation of "drug-squad" but they're the first to be hauled off onto something else during a panic or staff shortage. Even today I have chief constables tell me they don't need a drug squad because they don't have problem in their constabularies: how the hell do they know, unless they've men out on the streets, finding out!'

The English counties of Essex and Hertfordshire, for instance, still have a minimal commitment to drug squads.

By April 1984, however, the majority of police forces throughout Britain had recognised drug abuse as a problem that could no longer be ignored. Following a recommendation from the Association of Chief Police Officers, the government decided to strengthen Regional Crime Squads in England and Wales by adding to them 'drug wings' devoted entirely to drug-related crime.

Mr Colin Hewett was appointed as coordinator with these crime squads and the National Drugs Intelligence Unit. The Unit is based at Scotland Yard and is a computerised centre from which any of the crime squads or drugs squads from the forty-three police districts in England and eight in Scotland – plus Customs who have men attached to the Unit – can retrieve drug information. Drug intelligence is also constantly fed into this central bank.

It is the only centralised liaising facility in existence, although – through what one official described to me as an accident of history – a *de facto* national enforcement agency does and can operate in England: HM Customs and Excise. Providing drugs are unlawfully imported – which most are – by law customs investigators, unlike their counterparts in America and other European countries, are not restricted to border interceptions but can pursue cases anywhere in England. It is not even necessary for them to advise the local force of their enquiries, although they invariably do, both as a matter of courtesy and in case they need back-up – road blocking or armed enquiries, for instance.

There are indications, however, that some police forces resent the power of the customs authorities and that friction has developed between the two agencies. Some of the thinking behind the establishment of regional drug squads reflects the resentment of a number of forces at what they consider to be the encroachment of the customs authorities.

I understand Scotland Yard Drug Squad to be particularly concerned about growing evidence that there has been a complete change of attitude towards drugs among British criminals. One high-ranking officer told me, 'Twenty years ago none of the established villains of London or any other British city would dirty their hands with drugs. Because that's what they were regarded as, something filthy. Now that's all changing.'

Changing so dramatically, according to conversations I have had, that there is suspicion now of business links between British criminals and Mafia families in Sicily and New York. One Mafia group in both cities which I believe to have a British connection is the Gambino Family.

I further understand that there is a Scotland Yard file on a restaurant in London's Covent Garden, the Jersey-registered – and therefore concealed – ownership of which can be traced back to men with known FBI records for drug

44

trafficking and with connections to the Genovese Family.

Organised crime control is a new development in British drug-trafficking. The brief triad entry into the market was the nearest approach and that was not sustained precisely because it was not properly organised and because of swift police action. Then there were entrepreneurs, like Richard Kemp and Sydney Solly Frankel, a Rolls-Royce driving pharmacist who lived in London's exclusive St John's Wood and manufactured 16,000,000 diethylpropion tablets under cover of a company he established called Trynant Pharmaceutical Ltd. Muhammed Ashfaque Khan, who amassed a personal fortune of £250,000,000 smuggling cannabis, worked alone until a combined Interpol operation trapped him, resulting in a seven-year sentence at Reading, the Berkshire town in which London airport smugglers are frequently arraigned. Even the entry into the London black market of Iranian heroin was the work of individuals, although it is wrong to date its beginning from the time of the Shah's overthrow, when many Iranians used the drug as a convenient method of transferring their wealth. Before the accession to power of the Ayatollah Khomeini, there was a sizeable Iranian community in London, many of them students. Fearful always of the overthrow which eventually occurred, the Shah's secret police, 'Savak', maintained close scrutiny of that community and at one time had a network of almost a hundred informers. Payment for that information was frequently in heroin – the Shah allowed its use in a country in which there were a million addicts – and outlets were already established in Kensington High Street, Earl's Court and Notting Hill by the time of the revolution. Those outlets still exist.

A senior detective told me, 'The entry of organised crime – not just in London but in provincial capitals – is the most serious development in the past ten years, something we were always frightened would happen but always hoped wouldn't. We are very worried.'

So, too, are the experts involved in the treatment of existing addicts. The treatment centres created by the second Brain Committee cannot afford to operate. The 1982 report produced by the Advisory Council, which prompted the British Secretary of State for Social Services initially to advance an inadequate extra £2,000,000 a year, declared that the clinics had become nothing more than prescribing units – frequently taking new patients only after a two-month waiting period – and offering little other treatment. It said, 'During this study it became increasingly clear that problem drug-takers are being given low priority in many areas. There is no satisfactory comprehensive response capable of meeting current and increasing problems.'

According to Dr Ann Dally, a Devonshire Place psychiatrist and President of the Association of Independent Doctors in Addiction – a group that believes in returning the care of users to general practitioners – only five per cent of Britain's addicts attend clinics, which have failed to encourage their attendance or prevent an increase in the addict population.

David Turner, co-ordinator of the Standing Conference on Drug Abuse, a body that acts as the spokesman for thirty-one voluntary drug-treating organisations, says, 'We don't even have the facilities to help those who actually want to come off drugs, let alone the thousands of others who need treatment – we are not winning the battle.' And Jasper Woodcock, Director of the Institute for the Study of Drug Dependence situated in London's Hatton Garden, is similarly depressed by the grim outlook.

He is not the only one.

2

The idea that the British Home Secretary of the time, James Callaghan, refused to countenance in 1968 – that possession of cannabis for personal use should be decriminalised – was by 1984 a *de facto* if not a legal reality throughout much of Britain.

The constabularies of Merseyside, Northumbria, South Yorkshire and Suffolk adopted policies of caution rather than prosecute people found with small quantities of the drug for obvious personal use. And in January 1984, a spokesman for the Police Federation – reflecting the views of other forces in the country – said, 'The police do not have the resources to control possession of cannabis. The law on possession is fairly unenforceable and it points to a growing lack of conviction that it is a sensible law.'

West Midlands – the third largest force in England and Wales – is an exception: in 1982 there were 620 prosecutions for possession, compared to only 25 cautions. But the chairman of the police authority, social worker Edwin Shore, admitted smoking it himself and said he was unconvinced it could cause any physical harm.

Whether the police in general regard the law as sensible or not, there is little likelihood at the present time of any attempt being made in Parliament to amend existing legislation under the Misuse of Drugs Act – which does not anyway require prosecution – because the prevailing view of the government is that any change is politically premature and therefore unacceptable. This, too, is the prevailing view of some enforcement officials and agencies, but not that of an outspoken lobbying group within Westminster nor of the recommending body to the government, the Advisory Council on the Misuse of Drugs. In 1982 they suggested that possession of a small amount should not be considered an offence punishable by jail sentence. They also employed a panel of experts to report on the effects of cannabis use. Their findings were largely inconclusive but they did, in fact, say that there was insufficient evidence to indicate that it was harmful.

There have been studies, carried out both by the United Nations and in America, which claim there is harm, such as effect on short-term memory, male fertility, female ovulation and damage to both heart and lungs. But the overwhelming objection from those who oppose any relaxation is that marijuana leads inexorably to stronger, addictive drugs.

A number of surveys, conducted over several years by the Institute for the Study of Drug Dependence, have produced findings that can augment an argument either for or against that view. They have shown that alcohol usually precedes experimentation with marijuana. But not always. And that a heroin or cocaine user has usually previously smoked marijuana. But again, not always. And that a heroin user is normally, but not always, a heavy drinker.

The director, Jasper Woodcock, says, 'It is possible to support the argument of progression from one drug to another. But it is also possible to show that some users don't go on from one drug to another, but remain upon – or even stop using – the drug they originally began with.'

British Customs operate a summary – official designation is 'compound' – system when people are detected at Heathrow or Gatwick airport with 155 grains or less of marijuana. They are offered the choice of accepting either an automatic penalty of £50 or prosecution before a court. Introduced into the country's two main airports as an experiment in August 1982, the intention is now to expand the system throughout other ports and airports.

The multi-lingual Chief Investigation Officer for the

Customs, Peter Cutting, told me, 'This is in no way an addicts' charter, nor does it indicate a lessening of our efforts to stop and destroy the drug trade. The reverse, in fact. To prosecute people for minimal amounts of cannabis can tie several officers up in court for an entire day, often for a minimal fine. And seriously reduce the manpower available at checkpoints. Which means that while we are occupying ourselves with £20-worth of cannabis, someone can get through unchecked with £1,000,000-worth of heroin. We consider our compound system a tightening of our drug efforts, with the limited manpower we have.'

The summary system is only operated for people found with herbal or resinous cannabis, never the stronger cannabis oil. And never for anyone with a previous drug conviction. Which was why Linda McCartney, wife of Paul McCartney, was charged with cannabis possession in January 1984 when she landed at London airport from Barbados, where she and her husband – who after his Japanese conviction vowed 'never again' – had been fined for having the drug. Ms McCartney had 76 grains in a camera bag. It was worth £4.90 and was clearly intended for personal use. After she was fined £75 Paul McCartney said, 'I think the case for decriminalisation is stronger now and a lot of law enforcement officers agree with that.'

So do a number of treatment and rehabilitation specialists.

Cutting told me the British seizure rate is the envy of most other enforcement agencies throughout the world. The interception rate for herbal cannabis shows a fluctuating pattern. In 1984 – the last full year for which figures are available – the British Customs seized 15.49 tons, with a street value of £47,834,880. That compares with the seizure figure for 1983 of 9.84 tons, with a street value of £12,535,380. In 1982, 12.37 tons were stopped from entering the country. Certainly 1984 showed a marked decrease in the seizure of cannabis resin. That year Customs impounded just short of a ton – 19 cwt 70 lb – against the previous year's figure of 5.96 tons. The figure for 1982 was 3.72 tons. Cannabis liquid seizures also increased. In 1984 the amount was 60.78 lb – with a street value of £165,792 – against the previous year's total of 44.52 lb.

There were, however, street seizures of all types of cannabis which had passed the Customs first line of defence to be intercepted by the police. The additional street seizures of 1.89 tons of herbal cannabis brought the total amount impounded to a 29 per cent increase over the previous year. Street seizures of cannabis resin – 4.63 tons – represented an increase of 44 per cent over the total seizures of the previous year. It also represented the considerable success of smugglers to get it initially through Customs checks at ports and airports.

In 1983 Dr Gabriel Nahas, a United Nations consultant, concluded a fifteen-year research project into marijuana with the assessment that five million people used the drug in Britain. Rehabilitation experts attached to drug-dependency clinics within the country consider that figure gave an imbalanced view because it did not differentiate between the habitual and the occasional or experimental user.

The street price of marijuana in 1983 was eleven pence a grain. Cannabis resin averaged sixteen pence a grain.

The interception rate for cocaine also fluctuated. The year 1983 showed the biggest interception, 156.37 lb with a street value at 47 per cent purity of £12,491,639. In 1984 – the last full year for which figures are available – there were 76.45 lb stopped at entry ports into the country, with a street price of £7,297,700. In 1982, 26.65 lb were blocked.

Once again, however, police seizures on the streets brought the total interceptions for 1984 up to 30 per cent more than the previous year. In addition to the 76.45 lb detected by Customs, British police took from arrested dealers 68.2 lb.

Customs believe international drug traffickers treat Britain as part of Europe, not as an independent market, and long-term intelligence shows that Britain is frequently the entry point for drugs destined for onward passage to

Europe. But those same intelligence analysts believe that those 156.37 lb – a five-fold increase over the previous year – were all intended for the burgeoning UK market. The 1983 street price of cocaine fluctuated between £3.24 and £3.88 a grain in London, and was higher in Dublin, Edinburgh and Manchester.

The major concern remains heroin, however. In 1984 657.71 lb were stopped, with a street value of £47,834,880. That compared with 1983 with a seizure figure of 442.51 lb which had a street value of £25,343,083 and with 1982 with a seizure figure of 403.13 lb. Eighty per cent of that came from Pakistan and its Golden Crescent. At the beginning of 1984 Mr Michael Stephenson, a thirty-seven-year-old customs investigator, was sent on a two-year tour of duty to Karachi to work with Pakistani customs authorities in an effort to reduce the flow. The increased 1984 seizures were claimed by British Customs to show the effectiveness of Mr Stephenson's presence in Karachi. The Customs' union, the Society of Civil and Public Servants, still claimed that because of staff cuts the 1984 interceptions represented less than 10 per cent of what was being brought into the country. In the first eight months of 1984 – the last comparable figure available – 530 lb of heroin were seized entering West Germany, 528 lb at the Italian border and 587 lb in Turkey.

Once again the British figures represented what was stopped by Customs. In addition, during 1984, police took from dealers an additional 134.2 lb of heroin. The total heroin seizures for the year represented a 33 per cent increase over 1983.

In May 1984, Pakistan's Minister of the Interior, Mahmood Haroon, announced that the government was considering introducing the death penalty for trafficking. And in a further attempt at improving international liaison and control, Detective Chief Inspector Christopher Gibbons, from Scotland Yard's Central Drugs Intelligence Unit, was posted to The Hague which, with Amsterdam, is regarded as the main transshipment point from Europe into England.

Following the success of the overseas appointments –

particularly that of Michael Stephenson to Pakistan – David Mellor indicated in August 1985, that he was considering posting liaison officers to all the world's drug supply spots, which would include Bolivia, Peru and Colombia, as well as the Golden Triangle of Asia. He also announced his intention to visit Pakistan, where he hoped to meet personally with President Zia to explain, despite the increased interceptions, Britain's continued concern at the amount of heroin reaching the country from the Golden Crescent.

During 1984 the customs service appointed sixty intelligence agents specifically to concentrate upon drug interception, which did not placate critics of the government's slowness to react to drug problems. Those critics pointed out that Customs strength had been reduced by April 1984, to 25,309, compared to the April 1979 figure of 28,870. At the Conservative Party Conference in October 1984, it was announced that 100 more Customs officers were being employed, which still did not diminish the criticism.

It was expressed openly in July 1985, to the Commons Home Affairs Committee, where customs officers said staff cuts meant that drug smugglers virtually had 'free access' at British ports and airports. The MPs heard that only 509 of the third of a million containers entering Britain through the channel port of Dover were searched in 1984. And at London's Heathrow Airport only one passenger in 400 is questioned and fewer than that searched.

One customs officer witness, Tony Lewis, insisted that the service needed at least 500 new officers to tackle the drugs problem properly. And he cast doubt about the 100 new appointments declared at the Conservative conference. He believed that there were not 100 additional officers at all, merely men being redeployed.

In an address to the Pharmaceutical Society of Great Britain in September 1983, Metropolitan Police Commissioner Sir Kenneth Newman said so much heroin was entering Britain that the street price was dropping and the purity rising. Sources independent from the police put the 1984 price at between £3.24 and £4.53 a grain. In October 1980 it was £16.20 a grain. It is more expensive outside London.

In 1982, 8110 people were arrested in London for drug offences, an increase of twenty-two per cent over the previous year. Said Sir Kenneth, 'It would be wrong for me to suggest that the police service is making a significant impact in reducing drug abuse.' The relentless and apparently irreversible increase in that abuse can be gauged from the official figures. In 1960 there were 437 addicts for all drugs – heroin, morphine, cocaine, pethidine and methadone – listed on the Home Office index. By 1970 that number was 2657. By 1975 it had risen to 3425. The 1980 figure was 5107. By 1983, it was 10,235. Of that figure, 4371 were existing notifications, 4186 were new and 1678 were addicts who were re-notified. Using the recognised formula for statisticians attempting to obtain a true picture of the addiction problem in Britain, applying the multiple of five to the official figures, in 1960 there were 2185 addicts in Britain and twenty-three years later there were 51,175. Almost every treatment specialist and drug analyst to whom I talked during the preparation of this book thought that figure represented the minimum number of true heroin addicts in the country. Of the 4186 new notifications in 1983, 879 were under twenty-one and a further 1150 were aged between twenty-one and twenty-five. The increase in notifications was almost fifty per cent more than in the previous year and David Mellor, the Home Office minister heading the interdepartmental committee studying the country's drug problem, said, 'The figures underline the fact that drug misuse is a continuing and growing problem.'

It was a problem that continued to grow. The official figures for 1984 showed the total number of registrations to have risen to 13,274, of which 5,415 were new notifications during the course of the year and 1,995 were addicts who were re-notified. The rise continued to spiral. During the first eight months of 1985 the increase over 1984 was 40 per cent.

In London, heroin is sold from a Soho amusement arcade and public houses located around Soho's Frith Street. There is another heroin market in a bar in Berwick Street. Trading spots also exist in Kensington Market, Notting Hill and Earl's Court.

Piccadilly is traditionally regarded as the drug market-place of the British capital – although not for heroin – and it still flourishes, but less actively than it did when there was a branch of Boots open all night opposite the Eros statue. When it introduced shorter hours, drug prescriptions were made up at the chemist W. J. Hall, at 85 Shaftesbury Avenue, until that shop closed down in 1984. Piccadilly's main trading activity is in legitimate pharmaceutical drugs, obtained sometimes by theft but more often from over-prescribing dependency clinics or doctors.

The most popular – maintaining a hold established and built upon since 1970 – is dipipanone hydrochloride and cyclizine hydrochloride, made by the Calmic company under the brand name Diconal. Second in popularity is methadone, marketed under the name Physeptone and manufactured by Wellcome Foundation Ltd. Of lesser popularity – and less easily available – are dextromoramide, marketed by the MCP company as Palfium, dihydrocodeine, known as DF118 and produced by Duncan Flockart Company, and methylphenidate, sold as Ritalin by the Ciba company.

In 1983 a survey was conducted by two psychiatrists acknowledged in Britain as experts in drug addiction, Dr Thomas Bewley and Dr A. Hamid Ghodse, of St Thomas's and Tooting Bec Hospitals. The questionnaire sought to establish the attitudes to private prescribing of a hundred confirmed addicts attending the two dependency clinics. Sixty-nine of the hundred completed the survey. Of that number, not every one answered every question. Forty-four out of forty-eight said they went to private doctors because private doctors prescribed injectable drugs. Thirty-eight out of forty said private doctors allowed more than one drug. Thirty-six out of thirty-nine said the preference was because private doctors gave prescriptions which could be dispensed once a week, providing a bulk supply which could be sold through the black market for money to purchase illicit drugs on that same black market. Fifty-one out of fifty-six said private doctors gave what was asked for.

Thirty-six out of forty said private doctors gave larger doses. Thirty-seven out of forty-one said private doctors did not impose the sort of regulations that clinics did. Sixteen out of thirty-eight said private doctors treated addicts better than physicians and staff at clinics. Fifty of the sixty-nine openly admitted that private doctors were more easily manipulated than experienced clinic doctors and psychiatrists. Thirty-one out of thirty-nine said private doctors were prepared to sell scripts for money. And forty-two out of forty-five said they sold on some of the drugs they obtained to pay either chemists' or doctors' bills rather than to fund their own black-market purchases.

The purpose of the survey was not, according to those who prepared it, to argue a committed case for drug-dependency clinics against the supposed disadvantages of private doctors. They claimed it was to encourage legislation putting the abused pharmaceutical drugs under the same sort of control as heroin and cocaine. After its publication, however, there was criticism from doctors about both its impartiality and methodology.

From 1 April 1984 dipipanone hydrochloride and cyclizine hydrochloride – Diconal – were added with heroin and cocaine to the existing licensing restrictions. Dipipanone was already controlled under the Misuse of Drugs Act along with heroin, cocaine, morphine, methadone, opium and all opioid derivatives, LSD, mescalin, psilocybin, phencyclidine, cannabinol and certain derivatives. All these drugs are grouped under Schedule A of the Act. So are injectable amphetamines. Non-injectable amphetamines are controlled under Schedules B and C. Schedule B also includes methylphenidate, codeine, dihydrocodeine and cannabis.

Prescription of the following drugs requires notification to the Home Office index if the doctor suspects that the patient is addicted: cocaine, dextromoramide, heroin, dipipanone, oxycodone, hydromorphone, hydrocodone, levorphanol, methadone, morphine, opium, papaveretum, pethidine, phenazocine and piritramide.

After considering the results of their 1983 survey, Doctors

Bewley and Ghodse concluded that the extent to which private doctors were over-prescribing was as serious as it had been in the 1960s and said, 'There is an urgent need to control prescribing of this type. Also it is questionable whether it is ever desirable to prescribe controlled drugs to an addict when a fee is paid.'

They estimated that a doctor could earn more than £100,000 a year writing just twenty private prescriptions a day. In England addicts have to pay the full cost of drugs prescribed privately, as well as the doctor's and chemist's dispensing fee. Both psychiatrists believed a lot of addicts were making their drug-buying money by selling on the excess of their private scripts in Piccadilly, which they called England's 'Golden Triangle'.

This state of affairs was confirmed by an anthropologist with an intimate and detailed knowledge of London's drug scene, Dr Angela Burr, from the Addiction Research Unit of the Institute of Psychiatry. During a fifteen-month study of the Piccadilly area she also found evidence of addicts selling on part of the prescriptions they had obtained from drug-dependency units.

She published the results of that study in 1983 in the *British Journal of Addiction*. She wrote:

> It is difficult to estimate how many drug users were sell-
> ing part of their DDU (Drug Dependency Unit) scripts
> each day. There is a great deal of variation. Piccadilly
> drug-users themselves, when asked, usually say 'hun-
> dreds'. But never less than twenty persons a day would
> be a very conservative estimate and this is figure agreed
> with by the more observant drug-users themselves.
> Usually there is a great deal more on sale, especially on
> Saturdays. At least fifteen drug-users were encountered
> in Piccadilly who appeared to have injectable Physeptone
> ampoule scripts from private doctors, part of which they
> sold each week in Piccadilly to pay for their next week's
> script and they appeared to be increasing in number.

Dr Burr met drug-users who boasted of being able to obtain

prescriptions from several doctors at the same time. She found the Piccadilly drug scene apparently chaotic and disorganised on the surface but actually confined to definite trading hours, from 9 a.m. to 6 p.m. on weekdays with a weekend market on Saturdays.

She reported:

> Part of the market's general lack of 'cool' is clearly due to demand. Too many drug-users are fighting over too few drugs. But another cause is that the dealers themselves, fearing arrest, wish to unload their drugs as soon as possible. The openness of the drug market is a necessity for it to function properly, for the market is so large that not everyone knows everyone else. Although there is a hard core of regular dealers, most dealers and buyers vary from day to day. Someone may have drugs to sell one day and want to buy the next. If dealing was conducted in a secretive manner, drug transactions would be unable to take place on the scale that they do in Piccadilly.

Despite the open hustling and buying, it is not, however, the open marketplace of New York's Lower East Side. According to Dr Burr:

> The drug subculture that has developed in Piccadilly is well defined, inward-looking and strongly bounded. Although drug-users and the public pass each other by in the street all the time, the drug subculture is remarkably isolated from the outside world. Drug-users have little involvement with the general public, except for interactions with such as the police, local restauranteurs, shop assistants and ambulance drivers who pick up those who have overdosed and the occasional individual soliciting for sexual purposes.

The study established that the Piccadilly dealers – unlike a powdered heroin dealer – were usually addicts themselves. There are about ten 'scripters' – addicted dealers selling on part of their own prescriptions – trading every day of the week. Some act as middlemen for other addicts, buying the

57

excess from the addict's prescription and selling it on at a higher figure.

The cost of an illicit methadone or psychotropic habit is £25 a day. It is supported by shoplifting, prostitution – both male and female – and petty theft.

Throughout the latter part of 1983 and into 1984 another habit was increasingly concerning police, teachers, social workers and parents. It was solvent abuse – more often described generically as glue-sniffing – among schoolchildren and teenagers. Even – occasionally but increasingly – among adults.

There are three main chemicals which children get a high from inhaling. One is toluene, found in most impact adhesives, which has the effect of depressing the central nervous system, producing mood changes and symptoms of drunkenness or hallucinations. Another is halogenated hydrocarbons, which are found in most cleaning fluids and some fire extinguishers, the inhaling of which affects the heart muscles and can cause death. The third are gasses like propane or butane which, when sniffed, prevent oxygen reaching the lungs, causing death from asphyxiation. Police and hospitals have discovered gasses are sometimes sprayed directly into the mouth, freezing the larynx. If that happens a child drowns in its own body fluid.

The most common form of solvent abuse is glue-sniffing and, although medically this is considered the least dangerous of the three main abused substances, it can cause a child to suffocate in the plastic bag in which it puts its head to inhale the full effect of the glue's fumes. There have also been cases of children choking to death on their own vomit when they pass out, suffering irreparable strokes as young as twelve, or hallucinating, walking in front of traffic or throwing themselves off buildings.

From the outcry in Britain during 1983 it appeared that glue-sniffing was something new among children and teenagers. In fact the first publicly reported case occurred in the country in 1963. In Japan, in 1969, there were 161 teenage deaths because of the craze which then flowed – but subsequently ebbed – into America. Statistics maintained in Britain from 1971 until mid-1983 recorded 236 deaths. The British government came under increasing pressure from the medical profession to introduce some controlling legislation, particularly when specific kits began to appear in some do-it-yourself or ironmongery shops; but constitutional lawyers argued the difficulty of enforcement. The Magistrates' Association suggested that the law covering drunkenness in a public place could be extended, partly to enable the police to take some action.

In March 1984 two High Court Judges returned a ruling with important implications for the opinion of the Magistrates' Association: that a person found intoxicated from glue-sniffing could not be charged with being drunk and disorderly. In a finding that lawyers saw as strengthening the case for reform of the existing legislation, Lord Justice Goff, sitting with Mr Justice Mann, decided that under the present law an offence was not being committed where intoxication was caused by a substance other than alcohol.

While the government agreed to 'consider urgently' a ban on the ready-made kits, it refused to introduce or even consider preventative legislation because of the enforcement difficulty. John Patten, the then junior Secretary of State for Social Services, instead issued new guidelines to retailers, but they lacked the force of any law and left unscrupulous shopkeepers free to continue selling. Part of Mr Patten's voluntary code included display signs saying the retailer reserved the right not to sell certain products – similar to signs governing the selling of alcohol in off-licences and bars to children under eighteen – and removing solvents and glues from open display.

The government's slowness in reacting to the problem of solvent abuse was criticised in July 1984 by both the Magistrates' Association and the Justices' Clerks Society, composed of the legal advisers to those magistrates. Both organisations said the guidelines – which included advice to police to adopt an informal approach to glue sniffers – actually hampered police in attempting to confront the problem. Their opinion was that the police should have some statutory power to detain a solvent-abusing child in a place of safety to enable its parents, a doctor or social worker to be contacted.

The government's attitude to solvent abuse appears, from some examination, to be ambivalent if not confused. While there is a reluctance to attempt any sort of legislation from the Home Office, the Department of Education and Science seemed sufficiently aware of the problem in June 1984 to issue a circular to every school in the country specifically warning authorities to ensure that any solvent or chemical capable of abuse is locked away and that during lessons teachers keep a strict check on what is given out and returned. The warning was not confined to science laboratories. Domestic science buildings and classrooms used for secretarial instruction – typewriter correction fluid is a substance of abuse – were included in the warning. The Department of Education and Science estimated in their warning that up to ten per cent of British children between the ages of twelve and seventeen have experimented with glue-sniffing.

The Department of Health and Social Security co-sponsored with other government departments a film called *Illusions: a Film about Solvent Abuse* to be shown to teachers, social workers and police. But not to children.

The decision not to show it to children was derided by some treatment agencies. Release, a voluntary agency, said, for instance, 'It is like refusing to show a sex education film on the grounds that children should not be encouraged to know about sex. Young people are inevitably going to know about glue-sniffing and it is in their interests that they get the best unbiased information they can to avoid making mistakes.'

The rebuttal from the Department of Health and Social Security stated that the film was not intended as a warning, but as a training film for professionals and parents who might have occasion to identify and attempt to stop such abuse.

Although there is no clear evidence, doctors believe solvent abuse can damage the liver, kidneys and brain. Memory loss is also common among frequent users. Often boils or ulcers develop around the mouth and nose, and sickness and loss of appetite are common symptoms, with a consequent loss of weight. Children on glue or solvents also lose their co-ordination, appear confused and are unable to talk coherently, have blurred or double vision, permanent running eyes or nose and often hallucinate.

Legislation was finally put onto the Statute Book by a Private Member's bill. Introduced by Mr Neville Trotter, Conservative Member from Tyneside, the Intoxicating Substances (Supply) Bill imposes a maximum sentence of six months jail or a £2,000 fine for the unlawful supply of solvents to children.

Britain lagged behind Scotland in the establishment of a law governing glue-sniffing and in its use for a successful prosecution. The legislation is the Solvent Abuse (Scotland) Act of 1983. In November of that year three judges in the Court of Criminal Appeal ruled there was a case to answer against Khaliq Raja, 23, and his brother Ahmed Raja, 28, who sold and provided glue together with crisp packets or plastic bags from which to inhale its fumes from their shop in Saltmarket, Glasgow.

The two men paid children, some as young as eight, in glue for odd jobs carried out in their shop. They also accepted stolen goods in payment for glue. Each of them was jailed for three years.

Scotland also led in introducing legislation to seize traffickers' profits. In February 1985, Michael Ancram, Minister for Home Affairs and the Environment in Scotland announced that changes were being introduced into the Law Reform (Miscellaneous Provisions) (Scotland) Bill empowering courts to impose fines commensurate with the possible profit from trafficking, as well as jailing the pushers. Any imprisonment imposed for non-payment of the fine would be additional to the separate period of jailing. No limit was set on the amount of the fines.

Drugs is a £50,000,000 a year business in Scotland, where in August 1984 the Chief Constable of Strathclyde, Sir Patrick Hammill, increased the strength of his drug squad by eleven because of the ever growing size of this problem. Drug cases in 1983 showed a forty-four per cent increase over the previous year and in the first six months of 1984 there was a sixty-three per cent increase over the matching period in 1983. The largest marijuana shipment ever seized by British Customs – eleven tons – entered through Scotland. And when, acting on information supplied by the Home Office, police arrested three Dutchmen – Jan Stuurman, Dick Ruiter and Albertus Merks – in 1979, they found at their factories in West Linton, Peeblesshire and Monikie, Angus, amphetamines valued at £72,000,000. Evidence given at their trial established that there were sufficient materials to make a further 60,000,000 tablets. A police scientist said experimental material he found at the factories indicated that Stuurman, a chemistry graduate, was attempting to create a synthetic heroin.

The Possil, Gorbals, Hutchesontown, Balornock and Castlemilk areas of Glasgow and Kilmarnock are bad drug areas. There is also widespread abuse and trafficking in Edinburgh. Detective Chief Inspector John Veitch, ex-head of Edinburgh's drug squad, told me, 'We do our best but we're not beating the traffickers. The profit is just too big.'

The Edinburgh street price for heroin is about £9 a grain with purity often as high as forty per cent. The traffickers frequently get new addicts by offering a 'loss leader', like supermarkets, giving away as much as thirty-one grains for nothing until their new customer is hooked. Common in Edinburgh – and throughout Scotland – is the bartering of stolen goods for drugs. The Scottish expression is 'resetting'. Chief Inspector Veitch's men have found that a common way of procuring money for drugs is to steal frozen meat which can be sold, no questions asked, around council estates. Dealers wrap their heroin in cling-film and both they and the addicts customarily carry it in the palms of their hands so that it can be quickly swallowed – for later recovery – if they see police approaching. Another drug common in the Edinburgh area is dihydrocodeine.

In Glasgow Superintendent Charles Rogers, head of the drug squad, said that although heroin remained their primary problem, cocaine abuse was increasing. Speedballing – injecting a mixture of cocaine and heroin – was not uncommon.

'We're after the dealers, not the users,' says Superintendent Rogers, who sees as an important part of his job the extensive lecturing tours, warning of the dangers of addiction, he undertakes around the city's schools and youth centres.

Geoffrey Isles, the principal addiction officer for Strathclyde Regional Council, called the rise in drug use in Glasgow 'massive'. He blamed the squalor of many of the inner-city areas for tempting children to experiment. 'I can easily understand a child sniffing glue to try to blot out the surroundings in the Gorbals,' he said. There had been cases of children as young as fourteen becoming addicted to heroin. And graduating to the drug from glue-sniffing.

Mr Isles thought a drug task force should be formed, but conceded, 'Try as the law enforcement authorities will, I don't think we'll ever be able to kill the black market. Increasingly organised crime will always find a way to deal in heroin.'

In March 1985, Scottish Labour Party member Gordon Craig estimated at a conference in Perth that Scotland's addict population was 6,000, of which 3,000 were centred in Glasgow. He estimated that addiction in Scotland was growing at 40 per cent a year.

The main centre for the treatment of addicts in western Scotland is the dependency unit at the Southern General Hospital, Glasgow, run by Dr Patrick Mullin. He and his staff say one of the biggest barriers to addicts seeking treatment has been films like *The Man with the Golden Arm* and *French Connection II*, both of which showed supposed junkies writhing with the agony of withdrawal.

'The discomfort of getting off heroin unaided is no worse

63

than a case of bad 'flu,' said Mullin, a diagnosis supported by the twenty-eight-year-old Marquis of Blandford, heroin-addicted heir to a £40,000,000 estate that includes Blenheim Palace, who isolated himself on the Scottish island of Luing and went 'cold turkey' to kick his habit.

Dr Mullin admitted that attendance at his clinic dropped dramatically when his patients realised he was not going to prescribe methadone. But if he believes an addict cannot stop without some sort of chemical assistance, he prescribes Librium, a tranquilliser. The average time for withdrawal is five days the longest he has known, two weeks. Depressingly Dr Mullin, who supported the *de facto* decriminalisation of marijuana, estimated the relapse rate of addicts who come to the clinic for help to be as high as ninety per cent.

At Dr Mullin's clinic random urine samples are taken to ensure that an addict is not shooting up while attempting to achieve a cure. Anyone arriving under the influence of either drink or drugs is told to leave but they are invited to return the following day. One of the unit's rules states: 'If you have a hit after being stopped for a while come back and sort out what happened. Don't feel you have cut yourself off from the programme.'

Methadone is still prescribed at Manchester's drug dependence clinic at Prestwich Hospital, which covers the north-west region with a catchment area of 4,500,000 people. But it is prescribed on a dosage decreasing over a period agreed in consultation with the psychiatrist until it is stopped altogether. An official of the Manchester clinic who helped me on a non-attributable basis said, 'Agreeing the cut-down time in discussion with the patient is important because it involves him in his own cure, gives him a responsibility for himself.' The Manchester doctors do not, however, permit maintenance to go on for years, as sometimes happens in clinics in southern England. They usually attempt to achieve a cure over a three-week period, with ten weeks being the maximum. The methadone is always administered orally, never by injection. Medical staff have treated addicts who inject into the penis or vagina, or even through the nose tip. They have also had cases of addicts unable to get drugs who have injected beef extract, melted cheese and salad cream.

William Skelton is chairman of the Merseyside Drug Council, a dedicated probation officer who began counselling after personal experience with a heroin addict. The man – who was on probation under Skelton's care – was in hospital when his wife and a male friend were trapped in a house fire and burned so badly that both died. Skelton accompanied the bereaved addict from hospital for the funeral.

'He bought a suit especially for the funeral but it was too small,' remembered Skelton. 'His disinterest didn't register, not then. After the funeral I took him to his parents' home and asked them to care for him. We got there at about seven-thirty. At ten o'clock they found he'd killed himself, to fulfil a suicide pact with the woman. They orphaned two children.'

Skelton also spoke of a mother who has already bought a dress for the funeral of an addicted son whom she knows will soon die, and of a husband and wife who have both become alcoholics from the strain of having a boy – now serving a jail sentence – whose addiction they did not know how to handle and dealt with by giving him £245 a week to buy drugs.

Skelton calls the drug problem on Merseyside 'acute' and research carried out by the Council of which he is chairman indicates that fifty per cent of youngsters aged between fourteen and twenty-five are regular users of heroin. Heroin on the street costs £3.56 to £3.88 a grain but is pushed for as little as £2 a sachet.

'Dealers hang around the roads leading to schools in Liverpool and let the kids have it for nothing, until they're hooked,' Skelton told me. 'They don't call it heroin, to avoid frightening the kids. They call it Happy Powder or some other fanciful name. And they say it's not necessary to

65

inject, in case the needle frightens them, too. They teach them how to "Chase the Dragon". After the introduction, of course, the paying starts. And the price goes up, from £5 to £10 a shot.'

Between January and June 1983, forty-eight children sought help from the Council at its premises in the appropriately named Hope Street, Liverpool. From July to September of the same year, the number was one hundred. The youngest – a boy and a girl – were twelve. Jason Fitzsimmons, from Norris Green, Liverpool, never had a chance to get to Hope Street. He became addicted to heroin in just six weeks, starting in June 1985, and getting his supplies easily in the city's Croxteth area, a place of large housing estates. Hooked, he tried for a better sensation and made himself a cocktail of heroin and methadone. Almost at once he lapsed into a coma. He was connected to a life-support machine at the city's Alder Hay hospital but died. He was fourteen years old.

Another form of abuse common among Liverpool addicts is psilocybin, extracted from what are known on the street as 'Magic Mushrooms'. The proper name is Liberty Cap, and it was known by the Greeks – who used it for its hallucinatory effects – as 'ambrosia'. Siberian tribes, Aztecs and North American Indians used it before going into battle.

Skelton calls 'conservative' an estimate of 1500 addicts in the Liverpool area and 1600 in the Wirral district, and is trying to set up a 'safe' house to which children could come for a residential period to wean them away from drugs. The Mersey-side drugs squad consists of a total of twelve officers.

Liverpool is not, however, just a drug-consuming city. With its closeness and frequent ferry service to Dublin, it is also a transshipment point to the Republic of Ireland. Where the Dunne family live.

3

They have always been criminals, the Dunne family. During the Republican unrest that brought the Irish Free State to full independence in the thirties, the grandfather shot dead three men – one his brother-in-law – and fled to England. And the father – whose name is Christopher but who is always known as Bronco – killed the man he thought was paying too much attention to his deserted mother and served eighteen months for manslaughter.

There were sixteen children and eight of the brothers spent time in the now disbanded industrial schools, the Irish equivalent of a reform institution. They were custodial places run by the church for boys with criminal convictions and habitual school truants. They were renowned for violence.

It was in the industrial schools that the Dunnes served their apprenticeship in crime. They learned well. Only John and Ann remained straight, moving to England and marrying. The others also went to England, at various times. Shamie was jailed there. So were Charlie and Robert, Mickie and Larry and Vinney. Like the industrial schools, prisons are good training schools and it was in English jails that the boys first heard about drugs and the huge sums of money that could be made trading in them. They were still learning.

When their sentences were served they returned to Dublin and around 1972 formed a criminal co-operative, equally dividing among themselves the proceeds of their armed robberies.

Bronco, bulbous-nosed and pouch-eyed, publicly acknowledges that he knew his sons had established themselves as armed robbers, sometimes from banks. 'I quite admired them for it,' he says.

But bank robbery was more dangerous – and less financially rewarding – than the other money-making scheme they had learned about in British jails, so increasingly they concentrated upon drugs.

Cannabis was the beginning, for sale around the Dublin area and as middlemen purchasers for the IRA which, as the staunch Republican their grandfather had been, they supported loyally. By 1977, Gerard, Frances and Henry had convictions for possession. And by 1977 the family realised there was more money still in heroin. They were to become the Republic's biggest traffickers.

Their organisation was loose-knit and effective because of it. They co-operated as a family for overall finance and occasionally for supply, but each individual created his own network of customers and supplied them from the international traffickers he had come into contact with during his instruction periods in one of the British jails.

Each made efforts to distance himself from the streets – and therefore arrest – by establishing an army of middlemen pushers. Larry emerged as the largest supplier from Bray to Dun Laoghaire. Between the rest of the family Dublin was apportioned with the precision of a military operation, each taking responsibility for an area of the city and not encroaching upon another brother's territory. Council estates in Dublin – Rutland Flats, Teresa's Gardens, Sheriff Street, Dolphin House, Bridgefoot Street, Oliver Bond Flats and St Michael's estate – all developed serious heroin addiction problems through the activities of the Dunne brothers. Michael – himself a heroin addict – lived at Fatima Mansions and joined a concerned residents' group trying to eradicate the problem from their block, at the same time continuing to trade in the surrounding streets and developments. The IRA behaved in exactly the same way. Police know that the Republicans heavily involve themselves in anti-drug associations throughout Dublin, to gain support and respect from the uncommitted southern Irish. John Noonan, a Sinn Fein activist, became chairman of a residents' committee formed to drive drug dealers and pushers from the Tallaght district of the city. Christy Burke, a community worker for Sinn Fein and a candidate for the party in local elections, was among a group of residents who banded together in late 1983 to drive dealers from the Hardwicke Street council flats.

Effective local anti-drug action groups have now been formed all over Dublin: as well as in Tallaght they exist in Ballymun, Teresa's Gardens, Dolphin House, Bridgefoot Street and in the Aughavanagh Road district of the Crumlin.

The Dunne family supplied the Crumlin area where – in February 1984 – the Head Brother at the Scoil Iosagain Primary School actually saw women supplying heroin to children at the school gates from perambulators. So shocked was the priest, Brother Kenny, that he called a meeting of residents of the Lower Crumlin. Five hundred people attended and subsequently established surveillance groups who lit tar-barrel watch fires to monitor roads in the area, exchanged information with each other by walkie-talkie radios and even stopped and searched cars they suspected of carrying pushers and drugs.

A public march was also organised, led by schoolchildren. Nearly seven hundred people paraded through the streets of the district stopping at houses in which pushers were believed to live and chanting for them to get out. Following that protest march, over a thousand people turned up to a meeting at the Scoil Iosagain school when the names of pushers were publicly announced. Some of the accused people actually got up on to the platform of the gymnasium either to apologise and promise reform or to deny the accusation. The anti-heroin committees of Teresa's Gardens and Dolphin House have also marched publicly upon the homes of people they know – from street information – to be pushers, and in February 1984 the residents of the Cloonmore district broke into a squat in which one pusher was known to be living, emptied all his furniture onto the pavement and drove him out of the area.

The Dunne family employed prostitute couriers for drug-buying missions to Amsterdam and Paris and developed a third route – through Spain – which was later to become particularly important for Larry.

On the streets their organisation became known for supplying good gear, sometimes as high as twenty per cent pure even after being cut with caffeine or Bob Martin's flea powder for dogs, or barbiturates. The average price was £10 a hit. A standard dealer purchase, for onward sale on the street, was thirty bags.

They did not restrict their operation to Eire: the Dunne family became the main conduit for drugs that crossed the border into Northern Ireland where they were traded by the IRA for arms and cash. By 1979 Sir John Herman, the Chief Constable of the Royal Ulster Constabulary, was warning that Northern Ireland had become a major drug transit route. What he did not say was that the IRA were the profiting middlemen. 'Like toll-keepers' was how one enforcement official described the operation.

At first the Dunnes did not parade their wealth ostentatiously. Larry went on living at 20 Carrickmount Drive, on the council estate of Rathfarnham. Henry had a corporation flat off Thomas Street. Vinney – more normally known by the nickname Boyo – lived in a council flat in Teresa's Gardens. Shamie lived in Herberton Road, Michael at Fatima Mansions.

It was inevitable, of course, that they would become ostentatious. Henry bought his wife, Mary, a racehorse named Roebuck Lass. In January 1982 it won the Thomas Grant Fletcher Perpetual Memorial Cup at Navan. The prize money was no more than £1000, but the odds were seven to one and the Dunnes won heavily. Henry exchanged his Thomas Street apartment for a house in Rutland Avenue and spent an estimated £30,000 on extensions and installations, including a private bar in a party room and a sauna.

Vinney bought a house in Weavers Square – close to the building housing a youth development project that was later to feature in a survey of drug addiction in Dublin – and imported marble from Rome for some of its more flamboyant improvements.

By 1980 the Dunne family in Dublin had the sort of reputation that Capone had achieved sixty years earlier in Chicago. Entire meetings were devoted to discussion of the Dunnes' activities by representatives of the Eire government and law and drug enforcement officers.

Chicago had Eliot Ness. Dublin had an inspector named Denis Mullins. A dedicated anti-narcotics campaigner, in 1967 Mullins single-handedly created a drug squad after personally encountering drug-addicted children as a beat copper and managing to persuade an initially doubtful authority that there was a need. For many years his work went unrecognised, he was under-staffed and under-financed, but the situation changed when official concern about the Dunnes reached the Dail. Mullins – who was by now working with Inspector John McGroarty and an expanded squad – was told to fight the Dunnes.

They finally smashed the empire.

In October 1980 Larry Dunne was arrested and charged with possession and intent to supply cocaine, heroin and cannabis with a street value of £60,000. In the same month, Collette Dunne was charged with possession and intent to supply cocaine. Henry Dunne was arrested and charged with using a firearm to prevent arrest in May 1981. That same year Christy Dunne was charged with robbery. In August 1982 Michael Dunne was charged with possession and intent to supply heroin with a street value of £1500 and his wife, Dolores, with heroin possession. Three months later Robert Dunne and his wife Theresa, and Ellen Dunne – under her married name of Tighe – were charged with heroin possession and intent to supply. Valerie Dunne, the wife of Shamie, was arrested in 1983 and charged with receiving stolen jewellery which the prosecution alleged had been used in drug-purchasing transactions. In July of the

71

same year Shamie Dunne was charged with possession with intent to supply £400,000-worth of heroin.

This series of arrests did not, however, stop the Dunnes' activities because of the naïveté – some enforcement officers used the word stupidity – of the Dublin courts. There were protracted judicially-delayed periods – some a year or more – of bail, during which the family continued trading. So flagrant was their disregard for the law that there were further complaint meetings between the government and law enforcement authorities.

After his 1980 arrest, for instance, Larry was able to remain on bail until 1983. And to keep his passport, which proved useful. During those three years he moved from his small council house in Carrickmount Drive into an exquisite property in Woodside Road, in the exclusive residential district of Sandyford at the foot of the Dublin mountains, with a stunning view of Dublin Bay. The purchase price was £100,000. He paid in cash.

Larry's first trial came up in April 1983. The Garda – the Republic's police force – later learned that the jury's failure to agree was because one of the jurymen had been bribed, although the evidence was insufficient to bring a prosecution. A new trial was set for 21 June. The Dunne family were not able to get to the new jury. Larry sat in the dock during the morning hearing and at midday formal application was made to Mr Justice James McMahon to extend Larry's bail throughout the luncheon adjournment. The police – misguidedly, as they later conceded – did not object. From the courts Larry walked to a public house called The Quill, where friends were waiting with a change of clothes. He switched suits in the lavatory and drove to the international airport at Shannon. From there he is believed to have flown to Frankfurt, then moved on to Malaga in Spain where he is – at the time of writing – still living.

The Dunnes are familiar with Spain, a transit country for much of their marijuana from Morocco and heroin from Turkey. The warrants for their arrest date from a raid upon a Malaga apartment by Spanish police in March 1982.

They just missed Shamie Dunne. But they arrested a woman they believe to be his mistress, also his wife, Valerie, and associates Seamus Nutterfield and Peter Doran. The charge was possession of heroin and stolen jewellery found with them in the apartment. The total bail was set at £40,000 and paid from Dunne resources held in a Spanish bank. Two days later all four of them skipped bail. The women returned to Dublin where Valerie was subsequently arrested in 1983. Her husband's mistress is still free, residing in the Rathmines area of the city. Doran is still free, too, living in the United States. Seamus Nutterfield was subsequently arrested in London, not for the Spanish offence but for attempting to sell heroin to an undercover police officer. He was jailed for five years.

Larry Dunne's trial went on, even though he fled from the Dublin Court. He was found guilty of the offences with which he was charged, the maximum sentences for which were fifteen years in jail or a £2500 fine, or both. But Section 28 of the Irish Misuse of Drugs Act says that before a defendant is sentenced, he must undergo a medical examination. As Larry is unavailable for any such examination, he remains unsentenced.

At the height of the Dunnes' influence there were an estimated 5000 addicts in Dublin, a city with a population of 525,800. The Dunnes were the major suppliers but there were others as well. One was a man named James William Humphreys, a notorious London gangster who made a fortune from pornography and whose evidence – in an attempt to mitigate the length of his own jail sentence – led to the conviction and jailing on charges of corruption of a number of Scotland Yard officers attached to the Obscene Publications Squad. After his release from jail – with maximum parole – Humphreys went to Ireland with his wife Rusty, a former Soho stripper. In the somewhat prophetically named village of Hospital, in County Limerick, he set up the country's largest amphetamine factory where he produced millions of pounds' worth of drugs which he marketed not just in Ireland, but worldwide. On one occasion he and his associates – Donal Ryan and Michael Ridgley – fled from the factory, leaving behind over a million pounds' worth of amphetamine powder drying in the sun because they thought the approaching helicopters formed part of a police raid. There *were* police in the helicopters. American security men, too, guarding that most fervent anti-drug campaigner Richard Nixon, who was being transported to a nearby mansion for a visit during a stop-over in Ireland. Humphreys and the other two men remained away from the factory for a week, awaiting the announcement of a mammoth drug seizure. When they finally ventured back they found that their amphetamine powder – unruffled by the down-draught of the helicopters – had remained undetected in the vats in which they had spread it before their flight. Only now it was dry and ready for manufacture into tablets, or direct distribution in base form.

'It became their favourite joke,' said a narcotics agent when we met in Dublin. 'For them it was funny. The joke was on us.'

Only Donal Ryan was seized by Inspector Mullins' squad – which like the British Customs has nationwide jurisdiction – during a subsequent raid on the Hospital installation in December 1979. Humphreys and Rusty – named for her flowing Titian hair – escaped to Mexico, where they are both still living in the luxury financed by their drug-trafficking activities.

The success of the enforcement campaigns against the Dunnes and the Humphreys was impressive, but regretfully it did nothing whatsoever to diminish the addiction problem in the country as a whole or in Dublin, a city which, proportionally, has as serious a heroin problem as New York. Heroin is as freely available today as it was when the Dunnes were trading unimpeded, still at minimum ten per cent purity, still at £10 a hit. Cocaine is a growing market, twenty-five per cent pure on the street. LSD is £5 a shot, the same price as a pill of dipipanone, a drug that made an early appearance in Ireland as part of the drug scene.

*　　*　　*

74

Ma Baker ensures the availability of a wide variety of drugs. Ma Baker is a pseudonym in which – with the classic criminal's need for self-glorification – she delights, reminding her Guinness-drinking friends, who include the Dunne family, of the famous matriarch who led a US crime family in America in the thirties. Actually the name of her American heroine was Barker.

Ma Baker's real name is Marie Nolan. At the time of writing she is forty-five years old. She was born in Birmingham but moved to Dublin in 1942. She is separated from her husband but like the Dunne family has organised her heroin trade through her own family of seven sons. One son has been accused of murder but was acquitted after four separate trials. The boy became addicted to heroin during the extended period of his court hearings. Two other sons have been accused of drug-related charges. A nephew has been charged with heroin possession, with intent to supply.

Nolan also uses small children – usually boys – to distribute her heroin. Her Fagin squads are changed too frequently for police and welfare officers to recognise them.

She distributes the drugs from the council flat in the Crumlin area where she lives. On several occasions police have been aware of her organising strong-arm gangs to protect her business.

Violence in the heroin trade is of increasing concern to the police. Although the various residents' associations throughout the city have had impressive successes driving dealers and pushers out, there are indications at the time of writing that the dealers are fighting back. Death threats have been issued against members of the Ballymun and Tallaght anti-drug committees. In February 1984 Joe Flynn, who had played a prominent part in the efforts to clear Teresa's Gardens of pushers, was shot in the legs with a handgun. The same month Francis Storey – involved in the attempt to clear the heroin traders from council flats in Hardwicke Street – was blasted in the legs with a sawn-off shotgun. The cartridges were blanks.

Necessarily protected, I toured that area. Word of our

75

presence went from balcony to balcony through the Rutland
Flats and Teresa's Gardens, with their graffiti-smeared
walls and hostile, sullen faces. Moores, the chemist's shop
in the Teresa's Gardens complex, is a bunker of a place,
after so many drug-seeking break-ins, with all the windows
bricked up and a padlocked steel-reinforced gate where once
there was a doorway.

'They still get in,' I was told. 'When they're desperate
they will do anything.'

And when that desperation finally turns into despair they
go – sometimes – to the only treatment facility available,
the drug dependency clinic attached to Dublin's Jervis
Street Hospital. There are nine beds available for in-
patient treatment in a city with over five thousand addicts,
some of whom are as young as ten.

I met Dr Brian Foley at Jervis Street. Before we could talk
he had to make one of those nine beds available for a wan,
chalk-faced girl who could have been as young as eighteen
or as old as fifty. The waiting-room chairs at Jervis Street
are like those in most waiting-rooms, made of hard wood,
and she found it painful to sit, Dr Foley explained. She'd
been diluting her heroin with vinegar or lemon juice,
because the acidity gives the injection an extra buzz. It also
ulcerates and the girl's buttocks, genitalia and thighs were
split and suppurating. They would try to treat her with
methadone, over a week to fourteen days, and they would
have to determine, during that time, whether she was psy-
chiatrically ill as well. If she were – and that was so in a lot
of cases – then they'd have to treat her on that basis too. But
because of the demand, as an outpatient. Drug addiction in
Ireland was an acute epidemic, said Dr Foley. And rising by
the month.

It is an opinion supported by several social investigations
conducted in the country. For the Medico Social Research
Board, at the request of the Irish Department of Health, Dr
Geoffrey Dean carried out a survey of southern Ireland in
1982-3 and wrote in conclusion that Ireland was 'faced with
a drug misuse problem that seems to be uncommonly close

to crisis point'. He recorded one particular meeting with a Dublin teenager who was unemployed, living in a slum, the child of a broken home, unloved, without hope or vision, for whom drugs were the only way of escaping the reality of his existence. A. E. Housman gave the child words to speak, said Dean, words that summed up the drug-abuse problem among children in Ireland:

> And how am I to face the odds,
> Of man's bedevilment and God's?
> I, a stranger and afraid
> In a World I never made.

Dean attempted a survey never before tried anywhere else in the world, taking a small but representative community and gauging the prevalence of heroin abuse by questioning the users themselves – 'not captive patients in a ward, but free-living young people, used to evading authority in any form'. And people, he recognised, who were 'notoriously unreliable'.

The community chosen was the Mountjoy A ward of Dublin. Without disclosing the identities of the interviewees to Dr Dean and his team, the master list was checked by the Jervis Street dependency clinic who confirmed that more than three-quarters of those who agreed to be questioned were on their books. The results were compared to a similar but less detailed enquiry made in three districts of New York – Bay Ridge, Bedford-Stuyvesant and Fort Greene – in 1970. By percentage statistics, the situation among youngsters in Dublin was worse than it was in the American city regarded throughout the world as having the most serious heroin problem – and that in a year in which the effects of the Vietnam war on the use of narcotics in the USA were so much in evidence. The greatest prevalence was among teenagers in the fifteen-to-nineteen age group. In Bay Ridge, a 99.5 per cent white district of middle-income families, the percentage figure of heroin users was 2.22. In Bedford-Stuyvesant, with an 84.4 per cent black population, it was 7.2. And in Fort Greene, with a 56.4 per cent

77

black population, the percentage was 7.55. The figure for Dublin's Mountjoy area was 11.9 per cent. For people within the twenty-to-twenty-four age range, the Dublin figure was 8.64 per cent, Bay Ridge 2.83 per cent, Bedford-Stuyvesant 11 per cent and Fort Greene 10.64 per cent.

Dean found that it cost an addict between £100 and £200 a day to maintain himself in heroin on the streets of Dublin. Apart from heroin, the enquiry established that Diconal, cannabis, Palfium, morphine, cocaine and Tuinal were also in use. One interviewer encountered four boys, aged from ten to twelve, all of whom said they had skin-popped on at least four occasions and had distributed or sold drugs for older people. They thought everyone did it.

Dean wrote: 'It is difficult not to think that these young people in North Central Dublin are the victims of society. They live in a dirty, squalid, architecturally dispiriting area; education seems to provide no mode of escape; unemployment is to be their almost inevitable lot; their parents are quite often separated or else dead; abuse of alcohol is a common problem; crime the societal norm; imprisonment more likely than not; heroin-taking is regarded as commonplace by quite young children; current treatment and rehabilitation facilities seem to hold little in the way of answers to their heroin abuse.'

The chief investigator for the enquiry was Father Paul Lavelle, who was sent to America by the church authorities to study and compare the problems of New York and San Francisco. For him one of the conclusions of the report must have been particularly depressing. According to Dean: 'The one source of some deeper philosophy of life than to live from hand to mouth, evading reality with drugs and crime and drink, is the Catholic Church; but despite the presence of some excellent priests in the area, religion appears to have little or no influence on these young people.'

Another survey, reported in the *Irish Medical Journal* in July 1982, covered a larger number of children, a total of 5178 aged twelve to eighteen-plus, attending ten secondary, four vocational, one comprehensive and one community school.

Compared to a study conducted in 1970, there was a fourfold increase among boys and girls over sixteen and girls under sixteen who said they had taken drugs other than those prescribed by a doctor. Marijuana was more prevalent than heroin. The survey found greatest evidence of abuse among children under sixteen, indicating the need for an improvement in drug education in schools.

Dean ended his 1983 report with Housman again. When he wrote the lines, the poet was thinking of Wales, not Ireland.

Perhaps they were applicable beyond both countries.

The lines Dean chose were:

This is the land of lost content
I see it shining plain,
The happy highways where I went
And cannot come again.

4

In America, as in most other countries, in the days when cocaine was refined from the coca plant, and the opiates (morphine and from morphine, heroin) from the opium poppy, the drugs produced were regarded as the wonder elixirs of their time. Morphine was the drug used to ease the suffering of the 470,000 wounded on both sides of the American Civil War and so extensive was the resulting morphine addiction that it became known as the 'soldier's disease'. The cure for that, determined the doctors of the time, was at hand: cocaine.

By the early 1900s there were in the United States more than fifty thousand over-the-counter medicines, tinctures and potions containing addictive drugs. Dr Agnew's Catarrh Powder, for the treatment of the common cold, contained ten grams of pure cocaine to the ounce. One of the ingredients of Adamson's Botanic Cough Balsam was a new drug called heroin: the manufacturers assured buyers it was non-addictive. In Dr Brutus Shiloh's Cure for Consumption, heroin was mixed with chloroform. Kohler's One Night Cough Cure was a mixture of morphine sulphate, chloroform and cannabis indica which was enough to cure anything in one night. Sears Roebuck, the mail-order firm, listed in their catalogue a two-ounce bottle of laudanum for eighteen cents. The one and a half pint bottle was a bargain at two dollars.

In 1886 Dr J. C. Pemberton blended caramel, cola nuts and coca leaves into a brain tonic to cure headaches and melancholy and called it Coca-Cola. Coca, with its cocaine alkaloid, remained an ingredient until 1903.

Dr Pemberton was not the only entrepreneur to realise the advantages of cocaine as an ingredient. In the mid-1880s Angelo Mariani, born in Corsica but living in Paris, used the drug in a tonic mixture and modestly called it Mariani wine. The Tsar and Tsarina of Russia used it. So did Britain's Queen Victoria and US President William McKinley, actress Sarah Bernhardt and hundreds of other customers, including Alexandre Dumas, Emile Zola, Thomas Edison and Jules Verne. In 1898 Pope Leo XIII awarded Mariani a gold medal as a 'benefactor to humanity'.

Doctor-author Sir Arthur Conan Doyle was a user of cocaine and invested his most famous fictional character, Sherlock Holmes, with the habit – by injection. And Robert Louis Stevenson wrote *The Strange Case of Dr Jekyll and Mr Hyde* in just one week, working constantly under the effect of the drug.

Opium-smoking and consequently opiate addiction became known throughout the United States at the beginning of the twentieth century through the many Chinese and Asian immigrants. But it was not until after the Spanish-American War of 1898, when America took over the governing of the Philippines, that any attention was focused upon the problem and that resulted from the personal appeal by the Episcopalian Bishop of the Philippines, the Right Reverend Charles Brent, to the United States to curb the trade in opium.

Even before the opium-prohibiting conferences in Shanghai in 1909 and The Hague in 1911, America had two anti-opium laws – the Narcotic Drug Importation Act and the Opium Exclusion Act, both of 1906 – but US Secretary of State William Jennings Bryan did not consider these were sufficient to fulfil United States obligations to the new international treaty. Jennings Bryan was a little ahead of his time as a staunch prohibitionist and he zealously campaigned for new legislation. The result was the Harrison Narcotics Act, which was signed into law by President Woodrow

Wilson on 17 December 1914, and became the linchpin of American drug policy.

In essence it seemed a valuable piece of legislation, committing America to the terms of the Hague agreement. The chief intention was to stop the sale of drugs from grocery stores and mail-order catalogues and to place addicts properly in the care of the medical profession, whose members were required to pay an annual registration fee of one dollar for the right to prescribe. Such prescribing – 'in the legitimate practice of his profession' – would, of course, be listed and records kept.

It didn't, however, work that way. The problem was that the Harrison Act was a tax law, its implementation controlled by the Secretary of the Treasury, its jurisdiction vested in revenue agents who had no medical qualifications. Further, no one on Capitol Hill was in any doubt that prohibition was the ultimate aim of the Harrison Act. The Congressman after whom the legislation took its name wrote in a report of the 'desperate need for Federal legislation to control our foreign and inter-state traffic in habit-forming drugs, and to aid both directly and indirectly the States more effectually to enforce their police laws designed to restrict narcotics to legitimate medical channels'. Later the report says, 'There has been in this country an almost shameless traffic in these drugs. Criminal classes have been created and the use of drugs with much accompanying moral and economic degradation is widespread among the upper classes of society. We are an opium-consuming nation today.'

Responsibility for implementation of the Harrison Act rested with a section of the Treasury called the Miscellaneous Division, aptly named because its other duties included oversight of oleomargarine, adulterated butter, processed cheese, mixed flour, cotton futures and playing cards. Initially the department employed 162 agents who attacked their new duties with determination: in 1915 they achieved 106 convictions and increased that to 663 the following year. By 1917, when America entered the First World War, opium supplies were so diminished that there was a shortage of bona fide medical supplies.

As with the American Civil War, the medical use of morphine and heroin during the brief United States involvement created further addicts; but by 1919, in spite of the prevalence of the 'soldier's illness' among homecoming combatants, the drug worrying an America entering the conflicting extremes of the anything-goes Jazz Age and the moralistic attitude of absolute prohibition did not come from the coca or poppy plant. It was – and remains – a drug worse than any of their products. Alcohol.

In October 1919, the American Congress – overriding a veto from the president – passed the Volstead Act, also designated as the responsibility of the Treasury Department, initiating the era of alcohol prohibition. Two months later, the Revenue Bureau set up its Prohibition Unit, to control both narcotics and alcohol. It was composed of 960 agents, 254 inspectors, 170 narcotics specialists and inspectors and 21 men responsible for internal security.

Standard equipment, issued after an agent had been sworn in, included a badge (designed by the agents themselves and more appropriate for the uniform of a Wild West sheriff), hand grenades, a machine gun and a 45-calibre automatic pistol. Some of the pistols were actually ordnance still in storage from America's war with Mexico. To go with the pistols and machine guns there were three thousand rounds of ammunition.

It was the age of the bootlegging gangsters epitomised by Al Capone – a cocaine user – and of the rise to power of the Mafia, who retained their links with the manufacturing homeland of Sicily, realising that drug-trafficking was potentially a highly lucrative trade.

Prohibition was the watchword of the political day and because power to enforce the Harrison Act was vested with the wrong department, the initial concern over the medical treatment of addicted patients was further cast aside. The first head of the Narcotics Division was a former pharmacist named Levi G. Nutt, forced into resignation in 1929 because of the friendship of his son Rolland with Arnold Rothstein, a narcotics trafficker. Nutt, a hard-liner at the office if not at home, disdained addiction maintenance except for the old and medically proven incurable. By the end of 1921, Nutt managed to close forty-four treatment clinics. Battered by the assault from prohibition-minded agents armed with grenades and .45 pistols, the medical profession surrendered. On 8 May 1920, the House of Delegates of the American Medical Association resolved, 'that heroin be eliminated from all medicinal preparations and that it should not be administered, prescribed nor dispensed; and that the importation, manufacture and sale of heroin be prohibited in the United States'. Within three years, in December 1923, the Surgeon General of the US Army prohibited heroin, with the order to destroy all existing stocks. And in 1924 the Surgeon General of the US Navy issued a command order, 'I have the honor to inform you that further issues of heroin to the US naval service have been prohibited.'

On 26 May 1922 the Narcotic Drugs Import and Export Act was passed by Congress creating the Federal Narcotics Control Board, composed of the Secretaries of State, Treasury and Commerce. Also known as the Jones-Miller Act, its purpose was to prohibit opium imports other than for medical purposes and to limit exports to nations without an adequate licensing system. Two years later, it was amended to outlaw completely the manufacture of heroin within the United States. Onto the drugs stage during this period strode an outspoken, determined politician named Steven Porter, chairman of the House Committee on Foreign Affairs. His argument – still echoed and disputed today – was that narcotics must be controlled at source, not at the point of demand: he stormed from the Second Geneva Convention of November 1924 because the opium-producing nations were arguing – as they still do today – that control at the point of demand would automatically eliminate the source of supply.

Typical of the attitude of the period was a radio speech by Richmond Hobson, an anti-narcotics crusader. In an era when radio held the power that television has today, Hobson told listeners, 'Most of the daylight robberies, daring hold-ups, cruel murders and similar crimes of violence are now known to be committed chiefly by drug addicts, who constitute the primary cause of our alarming crime rate. Drug addiction is more communicable and less curable than leprosy. Drug addicts are the principal carriers of vice diseases and with their lowered resistance are incubators and carriers of the streptococcus, pneumonia, the germ of flu, of tuberculosis and other diseases . . . upon this issue hangs the perpetuation of civilisation, the destiny of the world and the future of the human race.'

By 1929 the Narcotics Farm Act was passed, establishing treatment facilities for addicts at Fort Worth, Texas, and at Lexington, Kentucky. It is ironic that twenty-five years later America's Central Intelligence Agency, believing that LSD was the mind-control drug they were so eagerly seeking, persuaded Lexington director Dr Harris Isabell to experiment with it upon patients supposedly undergoing detoxification from narcotics.

On 1 July 1930, narcotics control gained independence by having its agents re-established under the Federal Bureau of Narcotics, although it was still attached to the Treasury. Its commissioner was an autocratic prohibitionist named Harry J. Anslinger who created a fiefdom matched only by that at the FBI of another survivor autocrat, J. Edgar Hoover. Like so many of his successors, Anslinger believed in eradicating the drug problem at source and his prolonged tenure at the Bureau of Narcotics was marked by the number of overseas visits he made. He cultivated information and intelligence links between source and destination, and the comparison of seizure figures during his early years in office with previous interceptions makes his policy appear the right one.

The reality was that organised crime had by now fully appreciated the cosmic profits to be made from drug-trafficking and consolidated its power: a shipment intercepted was easily replaced from the ever abundant supply. It still is today.

International trafficker Solomon Gelb sold to Al Capone's gang: Anslinger led the arrest of several of Capone's lieutenants but failed to catch Capone. Louis 'Lepke' Buchalter –

dubbed Public Enemy Number One – arranged the import of more than $10,000,000-worth of heroin into America and ran an organisation that became known as Murder Incorporated, the enforcement arm of the Mafia. He was to enter history as the only organised crime figure ever legally executed. Lucky Luciano controlled distribution. The Luciano Family were known as the '107th Street Gang' and dealt in heroin from 1915, the date of Luciano's first arrest for possession of the drug. Before forming his own 'Family', he worked for Mafia chieftain Giuseppe 'Joe the Boss' Massaria and in 1928 he murdered narcotics trafficker Arnold Rothstein. He was acquitted of the murder charge and ran a drugs empire in Manhattan until he was finally arrested and imprisoned at the beginning of the Second World War. Luciano's drug contacts with the Mafia in Sicily and Italy were well established and he found a way to utilise them to his advantage by facilitating the Allied invasion of Sicily and Italy. The deal guaranteed his parole and deportation to Italy in 1945. Until his death in 1962 Luciano organised from exile a billion-dollar narcotics industry.

Marijuana emerged onto the drug scene in the 1930s when the words 'reefer' and 'mooter' entered the lexicon for the first time. Marijuana was described as a killer drug, a verdict to which few medical authorities would subscribe today, and in 1937 the Marijuana Tax Act was passed, designed like the Harrison Act as financial legislation, to be enforced by the Treasury Department. Enforcement agencies found financial legislation more effective than most other laws in bringing organised mobsters to justice.

As early as 1927, in a test case, the US Supreme Court ruled against self-confessed bootlegger Manly Sullivan that criminally earned money was taxable. Sullivan had refused to file an income tax return under the Fifth Amendment of the American Constitution, arguing that to declare money illegally gained was incriminating. The Supreme Court disagreed, decreeing that there was no reason 'why the fact that a business is unlawful should exempt it from paying taxes that if lawful it would have to pay'.

This was the ruling that led to Al Capone's imprisonment. Capone was involved in two hundred gangland killings and several times indicted, once for over five thousand prohibition violations. The charges were always dismissed or witnesses murdered before they could testify. Capone never had a bank account, never signed cheques or receipts and never bought property in his own name: everything was paid for by cash, from a strongbox kept under the bed of the Chicago hotel in which he usually lived. He was eventually jailed for eleven years in 1931 on twenty-two counts of tax evasion, calculated on the basis of his net worth and expenditure: investigators even included the towels that were sent out to launder in their assessment.

The Second World War created a legitimate demand for opiates, as had the first world conflict. Anslinger anticipated this, stockpiling a three-year supply of raw opium in Kentucky's Fort Knox along with the nation's gold. It was insufficient. Cultivation of the opium poppy was therefore permitted in the United States, but only by strictly enforced licence issued by Anslinger himself according to the terms of the Opium Poppy Control Act of 1942.

In his annual report for that year, Anslinger revealed that while the war had closed the traditional illegal trafficking lanes from Europe, Mexico had stepped in to fill the demand for heroin. It was Luciano who set up the Mexican connections: imprisonment had done nothing to diminish his control of the trade. It rarely has, for any well-organised trafficker.

War has few benefits but of necessity it spurs invention. Towards the end of the Second World War, cut off from all opium supplies, Germany ordered its scientists to find a morphine substitute and in the laboratories of I. G. Farbenindustrie, at Höchst am Main, they created methadone. This was not the only drug discovered or created through the exigencies of war. By 1945 there existed a number of preparations unknown or unthought of six years earlier. And those synthetic drugs began to flood the illicit market.

So concerned was the United States by the evidence of

synthetic drug abuse that in 1948 a protocol was sponsored through the United Nations to bring them under the same international controls as morphine and other narcotics. It was signed by nearly all the earlier signatory nations, including the Soviet Union.

There was further concern as organised crime tightened its grip upon the lucrative business and a Senate enquiry established by Congress under the chairmanship of Senator Estes Kefauver predictably confirmed the link between the Mafia and the drug trade.

There developed in America during the 1950s two opposing attitudes towards drugs. The medical profession called for an attempt to differentiate between the addict and the trafficker, at that time liable to the same criminal legislation. The New York Academy of Medicine wanted addicts to be treated as in Britain, as people who were ill rather than as criminals. The American Bar Association and the American Medical Association both agreed, calling for a relaxation of the laws as they applied to users.

But this was the period of political aberration in America, a time when Senator Joe McCarthy – an addict as well as an alcoholic, who was supplied with morphine as a hypocritical favour by Anslinger himself – was determined to protect his country from the threat of communism, both real and imagined. America wanted protection from everything and Representative Hale Boggs provided it. In 1951, the Boggs Act superseded the Harrison Act and put mandatory minimum penalties upon the American criminal statute book. First offenders were imprisoned for two to five years. The sentence was five to ten years for the second offence and ten to twenty for the third. First offenders stood no chance of a suspended sentence or probation: this failed to take account of the fact that they were often addicts selling on a small amount to support their habits and if they weren't, the courts were perfectly able to determine otherwise. A provision for treatment, rather than imprisonment, would have been a better attempt at cure but no such provision was made. The Narcotics Control Act of 1956, also sponsored by Boggs, along with Senator Price Daniel, was even harsher. Sale or smuggling was punished by a minimum of five years, with twenty as the maximum. Second offenders faced ten to forty years and an adult selling to anyone under eighteen could, upon the recommendation of the jury, be sentenced to death.

The American Bar Association and the American Medical Association refused to change their attitude, establishing a committee to study both the criminal and medical aspects of the drug problem. Newspapers devoted only small paragraphs to the creation of that committee, while the headlines came from the Mafia convention in November 1957 in Apalachin, upstate New York. Hosted by Vito Genovese, of the New York family, and attended by other Mafia mobsters like Carmine Galente, 'Big John' Ormento and Natale Evola, the purpose of the conference was to organise the multi-billion-dollar-a-year drug traffic countrywide. Instead they and thirty-four other Mafia figures were arrested and indicted by a Federal Grand Jury on charges of conspiracy to smuggle one hundred two-pound bundles of heroin from Europe, via Mafia-controlled Cuba.

In 1958, the joint committee of the America Bar and Medical Associations produced an interim report which advanced the medical argument that while law enforcement was necessary in controlling narcotic drugs, attention should also be given to developing techniques to prevent or cure addiction.

Anslinger caustically replied to the committee, 'I find it incredible that so many glaring inaccuracies, manifest inconsistencies, apparent ambiguities, important omissions and even false statements could be found in one report on the narcotics problem.'

The following year the trial of the Mafia figures arrested after Apalachin eventually came to the courts. Genovese was jailed for fifteen years and fined $20,000. So was Joseph Dipalermo. Salvatore Santora received twenty years and twelve Mafiosi received lesser sentences; twenty of those who had attended the Apalachin meeting were found guilty of conspiracy to obstruct justice. Joseph Valachi was arrested and jailed for twenty years for the violation of narcotics laws and shared a cell in the Atlanta Federal Penitentiary with Genovese, who put out a contract on his life because he thought Valachi was going to 'sing like a canary'. Valachi bludgeoned to death with an iron pipe the man he feared to be his executioner and then did precisely what Genovese had feared. He made his revelations in 1963 before the Senate Subcommittee on Organised Crime and Narcotics, and identified something called La Cosa Nostra as the governing body of crime. It was the autocratic and rarely disputed FBI Director J. Edgar Hoover who insisted upon the title: the Mafia, he decreed, did not exist. Today, in American law-enforcement circles, organised crime is still referred to as being under the control of La Cosa Nostra or LCN.

On 30 March 1961, in New York, seventy-four nations – America included – signed what is known as the Single Convention on Narcotic Drugs, which embraced the conclusions reached by the conventions held over the previous fifty years to discuss international narcotics.

The following year the American Supreme Court made an important judgment supporting the earlier efforts of the country's Bar and Medical Associations, striking down a Californian statute that made addiction a criminal offence, because it was unconstitutional under the Eighth Amendment. It was the beginning of a gradual – and not always universal – change in attitude away from the previous hard line advocated by people like Anslinger.

President Kennedy, like most of his predecessors and all of his successors, entered the Oval Office intending to attack the drug problem. He convened a White House conference on Drug Abuse under the chairmanship of his Attorney General brother, Robert. Quoting Thoreau, Robert Kennedy declared, 'There are a thousand hacking at the branches of evil to one who is striking at the root. We have not been striking at the root.'

In 1963, the President's Advisory Committee on Narcotics and Drug Abuse was established and began trying to reorganise America's narcotics agencies. Taking the lead provided by the Supreme Court the previous year, the

Committee declared in its first report that while traffickers should be tracked down and punished by federal authority, addicts should be treated as sick people and rehabilitated – by force if necessary. It also recommended that the Federal Bureau of Narcotics be transferred from the Treasury to its more logical home in the Department of Justice, although this did not happen until 1968.

In 1946, America had been concerned by the influx of a handful of synthetic drugs developed in wartime. By the 1960s the pharmaceutical industry had developed stimulants and depressants, uppers and downers, creating a Technicolor sweetshop for the peace-loving flower children. The greening of America was the green of marijuana crossing the Mexican border. A grubby suburb of San Francisco called Haight-Ashbury became the Mecca, and LSD – which by now the CIA had reluctantly concluded was not the mind-control drug they were looking for – appeared in Los Angeles and became popular with the hippies who decided it was the mind control they certainly liked.

These new drugs were not controlled by the Single Convention, so in 1966 the Drug Abuse Amendments Legislation was introduced to govern depressants, stimulants and hallucinogenic drugs. It gave the Food and Drug Administration police powers, and to exercise them it created a new enforcement arm, the Bureau of Drug Abuse Control. Lyndon Johnson then proposed that the Federal Bureau of Narcotics and the Bureau of Drug Abuse Control should be merged to form one single department, the Bureau of Narcotics and Dangerous Drugs. Neither bureau liked losing its independence and the merger was an uneasy one, just as the grouping today of a far greater number of hitherto independent bodies to tackle the common enemy of drugs is marred by petty jealousies, demarcation disputes and squabbles.

John E. Ingersoll, a former police chief, was appointed director of the newly combined bureau and it was during a trip to Europe soon afterwards that he encountered an attitude that has irritated and frustrated Washington for decades – that the problem of drugs was one peculiar to America and not of any outside concern. This was certainly the attitude in France, even though the factories and laboratories of Marseilles had for a long time been refining the heroin that was later to feature in *The French Connection*. The insularity vanished when a sudden glut of user-size packets of heroin began to be seized upon the streets of Paris. The CIA strenuously deny planting the packets, but I do not believe their denial.

With the possible exception of the present incumbent at the White House, Richard Nixon came to office more vehement than any president before or since in his declared determination to control his country's drug problem. There are some in Washington who still consider that he grossly exaggerated the heroin situation in order to appear a resolute chief executive attacking an evil everyone recognised and wanted confronted. Nixon called drug abuse the 'rising sickness in our land' and sent a special message to Congress insisting that, 'Within the last decade the abuse of drugs has grown from essentially a local police problem into a serious threat to the personal health and safety of millions of Americans.'

The day after that message – 15 July 1969 – Attorney General John Mitchell suggested modernising all existing drug statutes and legislation, splintered and fragmented through fifty different regulations. Fifteen months later, Congress approved the Comprehensive Drug Abuse Prevention and Control Act, an important feature of which was that as well as regulations and enforcement, there were provisions for treatment, rehabilitation and education. Title 11 – the enforcement provisions – was known as the Controlled Substances Act and established five schedules classifying controlled substances in order of their relative potential for abuse. The contentious mandatory minimum sentences of the two Boggs Acts were abandoned.

The following year, concerned by the continuing rise in the official – irrespective of the unofficial – number of addicts throughout the country, Nixon told Congress that drug abuse was becoming a national emergency 'afflicting both the body and soul of America'. On 17 June 1971 he made an Executive Order, establishing within the White House a Special Action Office for Drug Abuse Prevention. Its function was to organise treatment, rehabilitation, education and research over a three-year period. Dr Robert DuPont, the appointed director, said the intention was to make care for addicts 'so available that no one could say he committed a crime because he couldn't get treatment'.

The international campaign against drugs was at the same time gradually gathering momentum. The Convention on Psychotropic Substances – a global effort to control stimulants, depressants and hallucinogenic substances – was signed in Vienna on 21 February 1971 and a year later, on 25 March, 115 countries signed a protocol amending the earlier Single Convention on Narcotic Drugs of 1961. The United Nations created a Fund for Drug Abuse Control, to devise crop substitution and rehabilitation programmes in source countries.

In Washington, to co-ordinate US efforts against drugs overseas, Nixon set up the Cabinet Committee on International Narcotics Control. And in answer to demands that more be done to combat drug-related crime on American streets, in January 1972 he created the Office of Drug Abuse Law Enforcement, by Executive Order. The president had earlier blamed inter-bureau jealousy and multiple authority as a hindrance in tackling the problem; but this new proliferation of agencies was creating precisely the difficulties of which he complained. To co-ordinate collection, analysis and dissemination of drug intelligence, another department was established, called the Office of National Narcotics Intelligence.

Richard Nixon, who was much given to sports metaphors, demanded a 'game plan' from Roy Ash, whom he chose as Director of the Office of Management and Budget during his second, Watergate-burdened term of office. Ash presented the president with three options from which to formulate a policy. The first was to put drug enforcement back under the

93

control of the Treasury Department, where it had been until 1968. The second was to make it the responsibility of the FBI, whose director, J. Edgar Hoover, had always rejected involvement because he was aware of the enormous profits involved in the trade and feared corruption of his fiefdom. The third was to create yet again an entirely new body, under the control of the Department of Justice. Nixon chose this third option, consolidating all the anti-drug agencies 'under a single unified command', and calling it the Drug Enforcement Administration. He told Congress, 'This administration has declared all-out global war on the drug menace.'

Six months later he announced confidently, 'We have turned the corner on drug addiction in the United States.' He was wrong, but based his pronouncement on excessively optimistic reports from those upon whom he relied for drug information. Robert DuPont, for instance, said something similar in a speech to a national conference on methadone maintenance the same year and asserted that within the Washington DC area, the attempt to end the epidemic of heroin addiction 'appears to be drawing to a successful conclusion'.

Washington became a different, more subdued political capital after the humiliating departure of Richard Nixon and the scandal of Watergate. In 1975 President Ford issued a report in which it was conceded that, contrary to the earlier claims of success, drug analysts had begun to realise 'that conditions were worsening and that the gains of prior years were being eroded'.

In a statement to which drug prevention experts the world over are increasingly subscribing, the White House said prophetically, 'We should stop raising unrealistic expectations of total elimination of drug abuse from our society. At the same time, we should in no way signal tacit acceptance of drug abuse or a lessened commitment to continue aggressive efforts aimed at eliminating it entirely. The sobering fact is that some members of any society will seek escape from the stresses of life through drug use.'

The ascendance of Jimmy Carter to the presidency of the

United States was hopefully welcomed by many as the arrival of long-awaited liberalism, and in hindsight viewed by most as lacklustre.

In August 1977 Carter suggested to a surprised Congress that simple possession of up to an ounce of marijuana – obviously for personal use – should be dealt with by fine rather than by imprisonment, a penalty that was frequently counter-productive with young people, labelling them with the stigma of jail and introducing them into a hardened criminal environment. Five months earlier, in March, British-born Dr Peter Bourne had been appointed Director of the Office of Drug Abuse Policy to co-ordinate the various drug abuse programmes. When the Office was abolished following reorganisation a year later, he remained as presidential adviser on the subject. Bourne supported – naturally enough – the president's idea of liberalising the attitude to marijuana but was less enthusiastic about the use of the substitute methadone for maintenance purposes, which he regarded as 'defeatist'. He did not consider the control and treatment efforts had failed completely, but neither had they succeeded as well as they should have done. Nor could he any longer believe in a final solution. In 1976 he wrote, 'It is now clear that opium has only been grown in a tiny fraction of the places in the world where it could grow and that as long as there is a market in the world and immense profit to be made, traffickers will always be able to find sites for cultivation despite our most vigorous efforts to suppress it.'

During Carter's term of office various members of the White House were accused of cocaine and marijuana abuse. One open accuser was Dr Bourne, who himself resigned – rather than embarrass the president by remaining in his job – after making out a prescription in a fictitious name for methaqualone, one of the most common street-traded drugs, for a White House assistant who complained of sleep difficulty. While Bourne may have been professionally indiscreet, he brought a change of attitude to Pennsylvania Avenue. But although the budget for all drug-abuse programmes for the last year of the Carter administration was $902,160,000

(£425,471,000) and the wider use of marijuana for the treatment of such complaints as glaucoma – licensed now in thirty-three states – was encouraged, any concerted drug policy foundered after Bourne's abrupt departure in July 1980.

No other president has spent more money, created more task forces, allocated more men or given greater priority to the problem of drugs than Ronald Reagan. Nancy Reagan has committed herself personally to the programme and vice President George Bush is in charge of the task forces. Reagan's philosophy was summed up in a statement he made in October 1982: 'The time has come to cripple the power of the mob in America.'

That time came for the New York families in February 1985. After a five-year undercover operation, the FBI swooped on men they claimed were the Godfathers of the New York Mafia and also comprised a 'commission' which adjudicated on Mafia matters and divided the billions of dollars a year amassed between them. Indicted on charges of 'criminal enterprise' were Paul (Big Paul) Castellano, the 69-year-old brother-in-law of previous Mafia Godfather, the late Carlo Gambino, and his successor as the Gambino chieftain; Aniello (Mr O'Neill) Dellacroce, Castellano's underboss; Antonio (Fat Tony) Salerno, 73, Godfather of the Genovese Family; Antonio (Tony Ducks) Corallo, 72; Salvatore (Tom Mix) Santora, 69, and Christopher (Christy Tick) Furnari, 70, of the Luchese Family; Carmine (The Snake) Persico, 51, boss of the Colombo clan, together with under-boss Gemmaro (Jerry Lane) Langella, 44, and Ralph Scopo, 55, and Philip (Rusty Phil) Rastelli, 67, head of the Bonanno Family.

Manhattan's US Attorney, Rudolph Guiliani, euphorically described the hitting of the five New York families as 'probably the worst blow' the Mafia had ever experienced since its establishment in America. Other enforcement authorities were not so sure. One agent told me, 'They're bruised but not mortally wounded. The mob is the mob: they can recover, even in New York.'

That mob consists of twenty-seven Mafia families. Five of them are concentrated in New York, the heroin capital of America: they are Bonanno, Luchese, Gambino, Genovese and Colombo. Just over the river in New Jersey, it is the Cavalcante Family. In New England, the Patriarca; Philadelphia, Bruno; Rochester, Russotti; Pittston, Buffalino; Buffalo, Magaddino; Pittsburg, La Rocca; Cleveland, Licavoli; Detroit, Tocco; Florida, Trafficante; New Orleans, Marcello; Milwaukee, Balistrieri; Madison, Caputo; Chicago, Aiuppa; Rockford, Zammuto; St Louis, Trupiano; Kansas City, Civella; Denver, Smaldone; Los Angeles, Brooklier; San Francisco, Lanza. There are also families in Springfield and San Jose.

In addition – but not in competition because there are profits enough for everyone – twenty-four families operate from the Colombian cities of Medellin, Cali, Barranquilla and Bogota through organised cells within America. So does an established Mexican family headquartered in Detroit. And Japanese, on the West Coast.

Despite all Reagan's committed efforts, the then head of the Drug Enforcement Administration, Francis Mullen, conceded in a review of the first year's combined activity that the battle had ended in a draw.

That – like estimating interception at ten per cent – was a mistaken conclusion.

5

The one they call Amilcar killed twenty people, maybe more: detectives will never have a definitive body count and they know it. The machine gun was Amilcar's favourite weapon and he prided himself on his style, confronting his victims face to face, never using bombs or speeding getaway cars, like some of the other assassins, as if they were afraid.

The killer known as El Loco – The Crazy One – murdered fifteen. He preferred the machine gun, too, and he never ran either, not until he was sure his mark was dead. They always were because he was very good.

'Abnormal period,' recalled Arthur Nehrbass, Senior Commander of the Organised Crime Bureau of Florida's Metro-Dade district. 'Very abnormal. Things are better now, though.' *Only* ninety people had been murdered in the six-month period prior to our meeting in an office festooned with memorabilia of a lifetime of law enforcement, until 1980 as an FBI agent.

In 1981, 618 people were slaughtered in the district, 136 of them for drug-related reasons. The mortuaries were unable to house all the corpses and used refrigerated trucks to accommodate the overflow, causing outraged citizens to demand action from Washington. The following year Nehrbass was pleased with the statistics of 531 murders – 121 drug-related – which represented a 25 per cent drop. The figure of 90 was for the first six months of 1983.

The efforts to secure assistance at national level began before then. In 1980 the state's attorney general, James Smith, told Senators in Washington, 'Through an accident of nature and geography, Florida has become an international port of entry for most of the illicit drugs entering the United States. We now accept as fact that the drug business is, indeed, the biggest retail business in Florida.'

Law Enforcement Commissioner James York supported that opinion. He reported that the 1978 estimate of the gross value of marijuana and cocaine entering Florida exceeded $7,000,000,000 (£3,664,000,000). In the first nine months of 1979 there were 986 murders. And smuggling and violence was on the increase.

Money that created as early as 1978 a cash currency surplus of $3,200,000,000 (£1,675,000,000) was brought into banks for deposit in boxes, brown paper bags and suitcases. Economist Charles Kimball insisted that the economy of the entire state depended upon drugs money which, if cut off, would create a real estate recession. Forty per cent of all properties worth $300,000 (£156,000) or more were purchased through offshore, drug-supported corporations. By the end of 1979, $1,500,000,000 had been invested by unidentifiable offshore drug' companies in the Florida county of Broward alone. Yet these figures failed to concern many people in Washington.

It was in November 1981 that the Greater Miami Chamber of Commerce – knowing their own law enforcement agencies were overwhelmed and desperate for some federal intervention – formed an organisation called Citizens Against Crime. To join it they invited representatives of the Latin Chamber of Commerce, on behalf of the town's Hispanic business leaders, and of the Miami/Dade Chamber of Commerce for the black community. The representatives they elected to take their case to Washington were Alvah Chapman, proprietor of the newspaper chain which owns the *Miami Herald*, and former astronaut Frank Borman, chairman of Eastern Airlines, both highly influential individuals. During a meeting with vice President George Bush and President Reagan's then counsellor, Edwin Meese, they managed to persuade the White House administration to acknowledge the critical state of affairs

99

and an appropriately dramatic and public response was made. On 21 January 1982 the Federal Bureau of Investigation – resolutely debarred from narcotic work by J. Edgar Hoover – was for the first time in American history put in charge of the country's anti-drug campaign, previously the responsibility of the Drug Enforcement Administration. On the same day as that announcement by Attorney General French Smith, Francis (Bud) Mullen was recommended by President Reagan to be Acting Administrator of the DEA. Mullen was Executive Assistant Director of the FBI.

There followed an effusive effort to show that the Enforcement Administration was not being relegated, although this was in fact the case. In a speech more reminiscent of a retirement eulogy than the inauguration of a new venture it was supposed to be, French Smith said, 'The DEA, of course, will continue its fine work in the field of drug enforcement. For years, the Drug Enforcement Administration has done fine work at home and abroad. The DEA has accomplished a great deal. I want to praise our DEA agents once again as I have on many occasions in the past for their bravery, hard work and many successes over the years. I am confident that an infusion of FBI resources to supplement those of DEA will aid immeasurably the national drug enforcement campaign.'

Mullen came nearer to voicing publicly what many were thinking privately when he said, 'I think what is happening sends a clear message to DEA, to the public, and the message is not that you have not done the job, but that you have been asked to do a big job and now you are going to get some help.'

Before the January announcement, there had been a six-month experimental period, with FBI and DEA working together on a number of drug cases. The Attorney General said, 'I can't say that a merger is not a possibility in the future. We are sufficiently pleased with the way it has worked over the past six months to want to give this organisation, this arrangement, a long-term trial.'

There are enforcement officials in Washington who confidently expect that merger to take place, one of whom told me, 'If history is any indication of what will happen, I give it about three years before somebody says, "This isn't working: we've got to have mergers." Who's going to come out on top of that merger is up for grabs at this point.'

In February 1982, also as a response to the request for help from Chapman and Borman, the South Florida Joint Task Group was created. Vice President Bush was named as the man in charge, though in practice the responsibility devolved on Bush's Chief of Staff, Admiral Dan Murphy. One of Murphy's first actions was to create a 'war room', a radar facility at Miami International Airport specially designed to detect unidentified incoming planes which could be intercepted by law enforcement aircraft. Then he effected an amendment of the Federal Aviation Administration regulations which decreed it was not necessary for aircraft flying at less than 180 knots to file a flight plan.

To Florida, with its 395 miles of coastline and 6000 miles of inland waterways, were drafted over three hundred additional law enforcement personnel, extra DEA agents to work with extra US Customs Service and Coast Guard staff to bring cases for extra prosecutors to bring to trial. The FBI's involvement in this initial task force was limited to a four-man liaison group, although they had overall control.

Congress amended a law that had existed since the American Civil War – called Posse Comitatus – preventing the American navy and military from enforcing civilian criminal law. This enabled Admiral Murphy's force to utilise Air Force AWAC radar surveillance planes, military satellites and high-flying U-2 spy planes to track smuggling boats and aircraft and to locate the cultivation plantations in Latin America. Special equipment was installed in the aircraft identifying those plantations, including an optical scanner built by the Daedalus Co. for NASA. The scanner, which is linked to a Linton 72R computer programmed with the wavelength characteristics of the coca and marijuana plant, responds to five lightwave bands on a visible and non-visible spectrum. A rotating mirror sweeps an area eight miles wide on the ground: at thirty-five thousand feet it can concentrate upon an area roughly eight yards square. It is coupled to an aerial survey camera and an inertial navigational system.

Although subsequently disputed, the results of the task force's efforts were undeniably impressive. In the first nine months of its existence, federal agents made over eight hundred arrests, seized nearly $13,000,000 (£7,428,000) in assets – including 122 vessels – and prevented an enormous amount of cocaine, marijuana and methaqualone from entering the USA. Methaqualone, whose most common trade name is Quaalude – 'ludes' on the streets – is also manufactured as Mandrax, Spoor, Parest and Optimil. A non-barbiturate, it has a sedative or hypnotic effect and is also supposed, by its devotees, to be an aphrodisiac.

Within weeks of its creation, on 9 March, Customs at Miami Airport detected the biggest cocaine shipment ever impounded, 3906 lb mixed with a clothing shipment and transported from Bogota, Colombia, by a plane belonging to Tampa Airlines, a cargo firm. The value of that one seizure was put at $1,300,000,000 (£742,000,000). The next month 515 lb of cocaine, worth $166,000,000, were seized at Bimini when a Cessna 402B aircraft was detected by the radar installation at Cuba's Guantanamo Bay and intercepted by Miami-based aircraft. On 3 December 1982, 700 lb were taken from a 176-foot freighter called the *Mar Azul* in Miami Harbour. This was the largest seizure ever made from a commercial vessel, with a value of almost $214,000,000.

Marijuana seizures during the early months of the Florida crackdown were equally impressive.

On 1 April 1982, Customs boarded the 65-foot trawler *Misfit*, Florida-bound in the Windward Passage, and found 70,000 lb of the drug, valued at $54,400,000. The amendment to the Posse Comitatus law was cited in the seizure of a 150-foot coastal freighter 400 miles north of Puerto Rico, again heading towards Florida, the first detection traceable to an initial sighting and alert from a US naval vessel. Concealed inside a bolted compartment of the vessel was almost 103,000 lb of marijuana, valued at $76,656,000. In November 1982, again north of Puerto Rico, 61,500 lb of the drug was found in the 130-foot vessel *Shooting Star* and a month later, five miles south of Fort Myers, Florida, another 56,000 lb, this time in three smaller vessels.

Between 15 February and 30 September – the seven-month monitor period for the task force – a total of 1,700,000 lb of marijuana was intercepted by the federal enforcement agencies on its way into Florida, representing a 35 per cent increase over the corresponding period the previous year. The total cocaine seizures amounted to 6565 lb, making a significant increase on the Florida city and county police charts: 679.5 lb had been intercepted in 1982, against 164.3 lb the previous year.

Amilcar – Rafael Amilcar Rodriquez – a Venezuelan-born revolutionary who has become a millionaire through his drug dealing, was in custody before the official creation of the Florida force that was brought into being in order to curb the activities of people of his kind. So, too, was El Loco, whose real name is Jose Ramon Ruiz. But there was nevertheless a decrease in the number of drug-related murders, although Commander Nehrbass reports that the Mafia have moved heavily into the state and extortion-type bombings are not infrequent.

The Reagan administration entered office with a firm commitment to attack organised crime and through 1982 the success of the Florida operation – and the resulting national approval – showed that drugs were politically the right focus for that attack.

In addition to the personal crusade undertaken by his wife, in June 1982 President Reagan appointed as his presidential adviser on narcotics Dr Carlton Turner, a scientist who had done research work on marijuana at the University of Mississippi. Turner's instructions were to devise a national strategy to mount a drugs war.

In October Reagan declared the Florida successes were such that he had decided to create twelve additional task forces to cover the entire country. It was on that occasion that he talked of crippling 'the power of the mob in America'.

When the Attorney General asked for an additional $130,000,000 (£74,285,000) to finance the programme, the supportive but cynical Senate Appropriations Subcommittee reminded French Smith that only the previous year the White House administration had reduced the budgets of law enforcement agencies and that personnel in those agencies had dropped by over nineteen thousand since Reagan took office. Despite that criticism, Congress allocated an additional $127,500,000 to carry the programme through what was left of the fiscal year.

French Smith's real success was not, however, persuading Congress to grant the extra money: it was the way he persuaded them to make the allocation not to individual components of the task forces – DEA, FBI, Customs, Internal Revenue Service, the Marshals Service and the Bureau of Alcohol, Tobacco and Firearms – but *en bloc* to the Department of Justice which the Attorney General controls. In January 1984 French Smith resigned as Attorney General, to return to private legal practice in California. In April he withdrew that resignation, however, during an enquiry into the financial rectitude of the man President Reagan named as his successor, counsellor Edwin Meese. Despite the uncertainty, the Attorney General's office retained control over the country's drug programme.

There was already infighting. DEA resented the FBI takeover and complained that the supposed co-operation wasn't working. Bureau Director William Webster admitted limiting the Enforcement Agency's access to FBI files, justifying it by saying, 'Intelligence information is like toothpaste. It's hard to get back in the tube once it's out.'

There was deeper friction between Customs and DEA. Friction, too, between the Internal Revenue Service and other agencies. And the Treasury Department, which includes Customs and IRS, fought with Justice, the controlling department for the FBI.

No one liked the power that the financial control gave the Attorney General. And that included a lot of politicians. They tried to take it away. Towards the end of 1982, Congress passed a composite crime bill, partly intended to create an office of National and International Drug Operations and Policy, whose director would have held cabinet rank and authority over all the agencies involved in the narcotics crusade. The Attorney General fought against losing his power and won. The President refused to sign the drug czar into law.

The political friction between Congress and the White House was matched – or even exceeded – by the friction between Congress and law enforcement.

The cause was an FBI operation which became known as Abscam – 'Ab' for the first two letters of Abdul Enterprises, 'scam' as in sting or confidence trick – and deeply embarrassed both the Senate and the House of Representatives. It lasted eighteen months, was orchestrated from lavish houses in New York and Washington and yachts in Florida, and it finally implicated in bribery-for-favours investigations Harrison Williams, a New Jersey Democratic Senator; John Jenrette jnr, South Carolina Democrat; Michael Ozzie Myers, John Murtha and Raymond Lederer, all Democrats representing Pennsylvania; Richard Kelly, a Florida Republican; Frank Thompson, a Democrat from New Jersey and John Murphy, a Democrat from New York.

Mullen was Assistant Director of the FBI during the Abscam probe. In his proposed transfer to the DEA, Congress – who had to approve the President's appointment – saw a way of hitting back at the Bureau. Repeatedly – to the amusement of the traffickers and the embarrassment of the agencies – he was summoned back to Capitol Hill to appear before carping approval hearings which had little to do with his capabilities as administrator of the drug agency but everything to do with Washington politics. For

105

twenty months after Reagan's first proposal, the word 'Acting' had to appear before Mullen's title, which was finally confirmed in November 1983. Mullen occupied the position – and had the title – for less than two years before retiring, to make way for his deputy, John Lawn, to succeed him as the DEA chief.

That same obstructive Congress – with some justification – criticised the President's claims of a breakthrough in the drugs war. In a speech in Miami in November 1982, Reagan had said, 'There is no question that the South Florida task force has been a clear and unqualified success. Since its inception, drug-related arrests in the area covered by the task force are up twenty-seven per cent. Drug seizures are up about fifty per cent. The amount of marijuana seized has increased by thirty-five per cent, the amount of cocaine by fifty-six per cent.'

In January 1983 the General Accounting Office – the watchdog body of Congress – issued a report damning those statistics, insisting that the separate agencies were claiming the same seizures, which meant there was double counting. It cited as an example that largest-ever cocaine seizure, 3906 lb in Miami on 9 March 1982. Customs had included it in their figures. So had the Drug Enforcement Administration.

The report pressed for the appointment of a drug czar to reduce the internecine warfare and said, 'Several DEA and other agency officials told us that even though the task force has caused many traffickers to curtail or move their smuggling operations, it is doubtful whether the task force can have any substantial long-term impact on drug availability.'

That availability is traditionally measured by street price: high for scarcity, low for plenty. In June 1982 the prices of cocaine, marijuana and heroin were lower than they had been two years earlier.

The White House, naturally, rejected the criticism, asserting that it applied to a period prior to that of the greatly increased anti-narcotics campaign. Dr Carlton Turner insisted that cheaper street prices did not indicate greater availability but less demand. To support that opinion – which is not shared by enforcement agencies – the presidential adviser said five independent surveys showed there were 2,400,000 fewer Americans using marijuana in 1982 than there had been in 1980. He told me, 'In 1978 we had one in nine high school seniors using marijuana on a daily basis, an average of 3.6 joints per day, which meant they were stoned from the time they got up to the time they went to bed, so they couldn't learn. Now that is one in sixteen.'

The extent of the marijuana usage in schools can be gauged by considering the results of an examination (Scholastic Aptitude Tests) which is taken by high school seniors entering college. From 1967 to 1982, the SAT verbal results dropped by forty per cent and by twenty-five per cent in mathematics tests.

Dr Turner also had evidence to suggest that there were 1,100,000 fewer people using hallucinogens in 1982 than there had been in 1980. And 200,000 fewer using cocaine. Heroin users numbered the same, but they represented only half a per cent of the population. He said, 'I am optimistic that society in America is changing. It no longer has an insatiable desire. It's made its mind up, damn it, we're going to do something about drugs.'

Statistics can always be manipulated to support the argument of their presenter. Turner's should be balanced by additional figures from other sources. While it is true that drug use among the country's teenagers has decreased, there is evidence of growing abuse among the middle-aged, middle-class society.

In 1962, government statistics claim that only four per cent of people between eighteen and twenty-five smoked marijuana. In 1982, it was sixty-four per cent. A pound of Colombian marijuana in 1982 cost between $450 and $600 (£257 and £342). Home-grown sinsemilla – it means seedless in Spanish and is very strong – cost $1,500 to $1,900 a pound. Seizures rose from 1,935,206 lb in 1981 to 2,814,787 lb in 1982.

The US Customs seizure figure for marijuana for 1983 was 2,714,571 lb. In 1984 it rose slightly, to 2,926,192 lb. And in the first quarter of 1985 it reached 721,901 lb. Comparable figures for Customs seizures of other drugs all show a rise. In 1983, 20,136 lb of cocaine were seized while being smuggled into the United States. The figure for 1984 was 33,080 lb. In the first three months of 1985, 10,446 lb of cocaine were intercepted. In 1983, in 310 seizures, the Customs stopped 652 lb of heroin. The following year, with 424 seizures, the amount was 718 lb. In the first quarter of 1985, with 100 interceptions, 147 lb of heroin were stopped.

In 1982, twenty-two million Americans used cocaine at some time. A survey carried out early in 1984 by the *Ladies' Home Journal* returned findings that almost a third of American women under twenty-five had taken cocaine and more than six out of ten had tried marijuana. The street price of cocaine was down to £22.49 a grain, from £25.48 a year earlier, and the purity was up to 13 per cent, against the 1981 purity level of 11.6 per cent. Seizures nearly tripled, from 4353 lb in 1981 to 12,535 lb in 1982.

In 1982 heroin cost on the street £78.40 a grain against £86.18 in 1981, and the purity had increased from 3.9 per cent to 5 per cent. Seizures almost doubled, from 332 lb in 1981 to 608 lb in 1982. There are 492,000 known heroin addicts in the United States but the true figure is much higher.

In addition, there are an estimated 1,200,000 Americans using hallucinogenic drugs like LSD, mescaline and peyote.

The National Institute on Drug Abuse maintains a country-wide monitor on twenty-six metropolitan areas. In the first nine months of 1982, 9139 people were admitted to 820 hospital emergency rooms suffering heroin overdose, constituting a one-third increase over the corresponding period in 1981. In the same areas over the same period of time, 4615 people were admitted for emergency treatment for cocaine overdosing, this figure being more than the total for the entire previous year. The 820 hospitals used for the

NIDA surveys represent less than twenty per cent of America's hospital facilities.

Between May and October 1982 the Drug Enforcement Administration carried out a hospital survey in six major cities. Over the same period in 1981, New York showed a 36 per cent increase in emergency-room admissions for cocaine overdosing, Boston 46.4 per cent, New Orleans 52.9 per cent, Miami 71.5 per cent, Philadelphia 83 per cent, and Los Angeles 90.4 per cent.

Most of the cocaine overdose victims needed hospital treatment because they had graduated from inhaling the drug to injecting it as a liquid into the vein, sometimes adding heroin to that liquid ('speedballing'), or smoking it in a heated, refined form ('freebasing').

In 1981 there were 927 deaths through heroin addiction. In 1982 there were 924 deaths and in the first ten months of 1983 there were 592.

The seizures did nothing to reduce the incoming tide of drugs, not even that much-publicised interception of 3906 lb of cocaine. An agent told me, 'We were cock-a-hoop over that: sure we'd blocked the supply. Which meant that almost immediately the street price should have rocketed. It didn't. There was a hiatus for a couple of days and then everything went on as normal. Which means the bastards in Colombia provided another matching batch from their stockpile.'

Dr Turner is not depressed by views contrary to his. Not only does he believe the drug-taking trends of America are being reversed but that they can be reversed further. The most innovative of his ideas was inspired by an investigation that showed pressure to start drug-taking began in American schools as early as the fourth grade, among nine-year-olds. Working with the Customs authorities and the Department of Education, Turner evolved the concept of a comic book carrying a warning message and printed a million copies for circulation throughout the fourth grade in schools all over the country. By mid-1984, there were five million copies in print. At the beginning of the book there is a personal letter over the facsimile signature of Nancy Reagan, next to a logo of the White House.

The letter says:

Dear Friend,

Don't let anyone tell you that you can't be a hero. You can – and you are about to learn how.

Picture yourself in a battle. In fact, it is one of the most important battles our nation has ever fought. You are right in the centre of combat. Sounds incredible? It is all part of being a hero.

Is this an imaginary battle? Not at all. Many young people are already in it and they would do anything to be on the winning side. But they've learned about it too late.

The battle is against drug abuse. Declare that you will stay drug-free. At any cost. You're guaranteed to win. And you'll be a hero – to your mother and father, family and friends, but most of all, to yourself.

There's a lot more to it and you'll learn about it as you go along. The President feels as strongly as I do about winning this battle. His Drug Awareness Campaign put this material together and generous corporations paid for it. It was done especially for you. We hope you will give being a hero your very best effort.

The declaration the First Lady invites comes at the end of the comic, laid out in quasi-legal format. Each child is invited to commit itself in writing against drugs before a witness who attests the declaration. Directly above is an example of the commitment expected from the nine-year-old which says: 'I declare that I am aware of the dangerous effect of drugs. I am responsible for myself and will never use any unlawful drug. You can count on me to live by my declaration and share my declaration with my family and friends.'

Beneath the suggested promise is the proviso, 'Remember: a declaration is a very strong statement. It's not just repeating something you've already heard. It's thinking hard and being really honest about what you say.'

Dr Turner said to me, 'That's a dramatic thing for nine-year-olds to declare, to sign a document that they will not use drugs. This approach educates them about drugs. It sends them a very clear message. It also ties the family in. And that's important.'

The campaign does not limit itself to nine-year-olds. Turner – who is derisive of earlier government educational efforts which partitioned drugs into hard or soft categories – takes the message to children even younger. For tots in the waiting-rooms of doctor's surgeries there are colouring-books pictorially illustrating the anti-drug message for those even too young to read the written word.

Nor is the campaign directed solely at the young. Throughout the professions and their official publications, Turner is expanding and explaining the government's efforts against drugs. He claims to have convinced the entire ecumenical community of America to join the narcotics crusade and told me confidently, 'Throughout the United States through 1984 there will not be a single city or town that will not have a billboard or someone talking about drugs.' He is also addressing the non-civilian population.

During Jimmy Carter's administration it was estimated that 20 per cent of US troops in Europe were using drugs. By 1984, following an official survey carried out by the Department of Defence, that figure had risen to 31.4 per cent. Cannabis was the drug most widely used but nearly one in twelve servicemen questioned admitted abuse of LSD and cocaine as well. One in ten admitted working under the influence of drugs. In 1980 – the last year for which worldwide figures are available – of the 5324 servicemen transferred from nuclear weapons work, 1726 were guilty of drug use. There are 30,000 Americans based at 100 military sites in Britain. Their responsibilities include the supervision of cruise missiles and nuclear-equipped bombers and submarines. In 1983, 455 were accused of drug offences and 409 were dealt with by US and not civil courts. The majority were discharged. In 1984 American officials admitted that LSD was being used aboard the USS *Huntley*, a supply ship at the Scottish nuclear submarine base at Holy Loch. In 1981, a fireman aboard the USS *Holland* at the same base trafficked LSD, cocaine and amphetamines. At the time of writing, 14 servicemen have been discharged for drug use at Greenham Common, the controversial Berkshire base. In 1981, urinalysis showed 19 of the 30 men enlisted at the US missile research base at Hickham, Hawaii, had smoked marijuana and after a plane crash on the American aircraft carrier *Nimitz* in May 1981, autopsies showed 6 of the 14 men who died had marijuana in their systems. At American Air Force bases and aboard some US ships – the aircraft carrier *Independence* is one – dogs are permanently employed sniffing for drugs.

Dr Turner said since the Reagan administration took office, drug abuse in the navy has been cut by sixty-two per cent – as a result of their campaign and its accompanying slogan, 'not on my watch, not in my Navy'. The Marines boasted a reduction of fifty-eight per cent. In the air force the statistical drop was twenty-six per cent and in the army, twenty-two per cent. Dr Turner is confident that those figures will continue to improve.

With no political alternative – but with fair logic – Turner argued against the concept of a drugs czar. To give a man sufficient authority to make demands upon the agencies of other cabinet members made him the equivalent of deputy president. And America already had a Vice President – 'doing a phenomenal job' – combatting drugs. And the President himself was just as firmly committed to the campaign. Ronald Reagan, asserted Turner, was the drugs czar. There was no need for another. There was no mention of the Attorney General.

'It's sort of like a war,' said Turner, expanding his philosophy. 'If you've got a commander in chief running a war and he's got a general out there who's not doing his job, you don't redefine the war so that the general can do his job. You fire the general. I think the administration's approach to the idea of a drugs czar is that the bureaucracy would be counter-productive.' He dismissed the Congressional insistence upon a cabinet-ranking controlling administrator as a political ploy, as he did a certain calculated exaggeration of America's drug problem – the measure adopted by the various enforcement agencies to protect their budgets. He conceded it was an unacceptably large problem but considered it would be possible to achieve his ambition of a generation of drug-free young Americans.

Turner's is a lonely optimism.

Some drugs do appear to be less abused than they were. During 1981 and 1982 the use of a drug affecting the central nervous system – PCP or phencyclidine – approached epidemic proportions in America and to a lesser extent elsewhere in the world. Its proper use was for the sedation of animals by veterinary surgeons. Known more commonly as Angel Dust it is snorted, swallowed or injected but the most popular way of ingesting it is by smoking it in a cigarette made from either parsley or marijuana. It can induce a coma or violence, sometimes death. By 1983, however, its popularity in America had tapered off, which was encouraging for enforcement agencies, although history shows that drugs tend to have a cyclical rise and fall in favour. Marijuana use by teenagers also dropped, as Turner claimed.

In May 1983 Mullen, Congress's political pawn, told the House Select Narcotics Abuse and Control Committee that, despite these favourable trends, 'Our drug abuse problems will remain as long as there is a world glut in narcotics and dangerous drugs.'

There is no sign of that glut diminishing. Heroin producers have stockpiles and cocaine smuggling is on the increase. Throughout America there are clandestine laboratories producing methamphetamine and although it showed some decrease, methaqualone is still entering from Colombia. Abuse of non-amphetamine stimulants like Preludin and Ritalin and a slimming drug called phendimetrazine is also increasing. Talwin, an analgesic, and pyribenzamine, an antihistamine, are being combined and sold on the streets as 'Ts and Blues', and in many cities throughout the country the combination is so popular that it is replacing heroin. Another cocktail is the mixture of codeine and glutethimide, known on the street as 'Fours and Doors'. The use of Dilaudid, a synthetic opiate, has also substantially increased.

Enforcement agencies are also concerned by the rapid growth of 'look-alike' drugs, and the difficulty of asserting any form of control. Look-alikes are tablets or capsules resembling the controlled drugs but containing non-prescription, over-the-counter preparations. Caffeine is the most common. While the placebo is harmless, the danger of look-alikes is that the user manages a psychological impression of a high and can then quite easily overdose when, instead of being cheated by look-alikes, he manages to obtain the real drug and takes it in the same quantity as the placebo.

Although there has been a decrease in marijuana smoking, the same does not apply to its cultivation within America. From statistics returned from every state in the union, the DEA calculated that more than two and a half million plants had been destroyed in 1982 – more than the agency previously believed to exist in the *entire* country.

Mullen told Capitol Hill politicians, 'Public officials at all levels are being corrupted by drug money. We have reports of rural sheriffs and police officers accepting payments of $50,000 or more merely to "look the other way" while traffickers make a single landing at a makeshift airstrip.

'Clearly the violence and corruption attending the illicit drug business threaten the very foundations of our system of law and order.'

In July 1983 the President announced the creation of a twenty-man commission on organised crime, chaired by 73-year-old Judge Irving Kaufman from the New York Appeals Court, whose purpose is to hold hearings throughout the country and then recommend ways to curb the syndicates. The initial budget of $500,000 (£328,947) was taken from the already agreed task force allocation, but the administration wants separate funding for the

$2,500,000 the Commission's investigations cost in 1984.

Conceding that the government 'cannot stop or abolish the human impulses that make racketeering profitable', the President considers it possible nevertheless to 'break apart and ultimately destroy the tightly knit regional and national networks of career criminals who live off these activities'.

There is yet another factor which has to be considered in measuring the effect of narcotics upon America. Government monitoring agencies – particularly the Department of Health and Human Services – have estimated conservatively that drug use in the factory and office is costing the country $25,000,000,000 (£17,240,000,000) a year. Between 1967 and 1981 America's manufacturing output increased by 39 per cent. During the same period, the figure for Japan was 209 per cent, for France 98 per cent, for West Germany 90 per cent and for Great Britain 57 per cent. Roger Smith, chairman of General Motors, has been quoted as saying that absenteeism, much of it due to drug and alcohol abuse, costs his company $1,000,000,000 every year.

Conscious of the staggering drain of lost production, companies throughout America have set up five thousand assistance programmes to help their workers combat drug abuse in the workplace. There are also a growing number of private programmes including Cocaine Anonymous and Narcotics Anonymous groups, both modelled on Alcoholics Anonymous. Similar to the declaration that schoolchildren are invited to complete in the back of their anti-narcotic comic is a contract used by the Addiction Research and Treatment Services Clinics in Colorado. Users seeking help conclude with the clinic a written undertaking that if they revert to drugs, the addiction clinics have the right to inform their employers of their dependency.

Such private programmes are necessary in America because the funding for treatment and education programmes has actually been reduced, while enforcement expenditure has soared. In 1980 government funds of $458,000,000 (£197,000,000) were available; by 1983,

115

only $206,000,000. Methadone is most widely used in the treatment of heroin addicts, but of the known 492,000 addicts only 65,000 are thought to be under any sort of methadone programme.

The twelve task forces established following the success of the Florida experiment will not, according to FBI Director William Webster, precisely follow the southern state model, which is based upon interdiction. Instead they intend to concentrate on long-term investigations into organised crime and the involvement of foreign cartels in narcotic dealing. Webster is well aware of the size of his task: in April 1983 he told a conference in Missouri, 'The impact of drug-trafficking on American society today can be described as nothing less than a national menace – capable of eroding the foundation of our society. And I am not given to over-statement.'

The additional drug budget of $127,500,000 allocated in 1983 rose to $160,000,000 in 1984, to allow for 1260 extra enforcement personnel and 340 extra prosecutors. Most importantly it enabled the FBI to install for the first time, although not before time, special digital radios which are secure from eavesdropping criminals. Those radios – coupled with the FBI's expertise in wire-tapping, an art previously unfamiliar to the DEA – are being utilised by the countrywide network of task forces.

Webster talks of 'significant inroads' being made into organised crime, which he refers to as 'this previously almost untouchable area'. Fourteen leaders of the leading Mafia families throughout the country have either been convicted or put under indictment. Two hundred lesser 'soldiers' were convicted in the first nine months of 1983. The controlling families in Kansas City, Philadelphia and Cleveland were badly hit. So was the Genovese Family of New York. Indictments were returned against Santos Traf-ficante, godfather in Florida, and Joseph (Joe Bananas) Bonanno, godfather of one of the New York families, was convicted on a narcotics-related charge. 'Big' Paul

Castellano, godfather of the Gambino Family, was arrested in March 1984, and charged with twenty others from the family with twenty-five murders, extortion and drug-trafficking. One of the murder victims was his son-in-law, Frank Amato, who had cheated on Castellano's daughter.

According to the latest Justice Department figures available, from early 1983 to 21 March 1984 a total of 1841 people were indicted on narcotics charges and nearly $50,000,000 (£34,482,000) seized in cash and property.

Despite these apparent successes, there were contradictions concerning the operational status of the task forces, which the President promised would be fully equipped and ready to go by January 1983. That promise appeared to be confirmed in June by D. Lowell Jensen, the associate attorney general representing the department that persuaded Congress to allocate the additional $127,500,000. Jensen assured a committee of that Congress that each of the twelve task forces was in operation and that more than two hundred high-level drug-trafficking enterprises had been identified and were under investigation.

Attorney General French Smith insisted, 'The programme is on schedule.' But it wasn't.

In May 1983 – a month before Jensen's assurance – his own department admitted that only $7,000,000 of the $127,500,000 had actually been allocated. And only 500 agents, lawyers and support staff had been assigned to the new anti-drug squads, not 1600 as intended. The main cause of the delays was interagency rivalry, each task force division competing to attract additional personnel. In April 1983 Webster assured the Texas conference of judges, 'Just two weeks ago I had a conference for all field commanders, both of the FBI and DEA, and it was almost impossible to tell who was on which side of the house.'

Lowell Jensen said the delays resulted from the necessary care that had to be shown in selecting permanent replacements to 'back fill' vacancies created by the existing and trained personnel who were being assigned to the task forces. And care was imperative because of the high level of corruption among public officials.

In 1982 six Florida homicide detectives were convicted of drug-related offences which involved the policemen providing protection for the racketeers and extorting drug debts on their behalf. Ten policemen were convicted in Chicago, where extortion was again involved. In Henry County, Georgia, the chief of police, the sheriff, the probate judge and the manager of the airport formed a ring to provide a safe escort service for drug traffickers landing at the local airfield. That safe escort extended to protecting their journeys to Atlanta and back to the airport. David McCain, a former Florida Supreme Court judge, is a fugitive, on the run from a charge of conspiring to smuggle thirty thousand pounds of marijuana into Louisiana from Colombia.

The extent of the problem was summed up by Cary Bittick, a former Georgia sheriff and Executive Director of the National Sheriffs' Association, when he said, 'How long does it take for a $9000-(£5921)-a-year sheriff or deputy sheriff to save $50,000 that he can pick up in one evening or one week by looking the other way or being somewhere else when drugs are passed?'

Increasingly enforcement agencies throughout America are not considering narcotics in isolation but carrying out statistical researches to establish a link between drug use and other crime. A study by the US Department of Justice showed that one third of the 12,000 state prison inmates around the country were under the influence of drugs when they committed their offences. Other studies have indicated that 50 per cent to 60 per cent of all property crimes are drug-related. A consensus of those surveys was that every year drug-related crime touched one third of all the households in the country. According to figures produced by the National Institute on Drug Abuse, male addicts were responsible for 42,000,000 crimes, which represented a yearly cost of $12,000,000,000 in lost property. The National Institute conducted one study in Baltimore which found that just 243 male heroin addicts were responsible over an eleven-year period for 500,000 crimes.

The FBI Director has openly admitted that the huge drug-connected crime rate is undermining the confidence of Americans in the ability of the government to maintain law and order. It has led to an increasing number of Americans arming themselves for personal protection, and to Senator Joseph Biden, a Delaware Democrat who was one of the most prominent advocates of a drugs czar appointment, expressing the opinion that, 'We're reaching the breaking point.'

Congress's General Accounting Office had already reached that conclusion. The critical 1982 report judged that, 'Current federal resources have been inadequate to stop or even substantially impair drug smuggling.'

To illustrate that inadequacy the watchdog body revealed that the total budget for the narcotics campaign in 1981 was $533,000,000. They estimated that a further $2,000,000,000 would have been necessary just to stop 75 per cent of the marijuana getting into America via the Caribbean.

Defeating all efforts to make it otherwise, America remains a marketplace for narcotics. There are parts of New York which are literally that.

6

All markets are dirty, but usually there is some colour and variety as well. But not in a very specialised market in New York, where there is only one product. Drugs.

It is a slum of a place, a stink of sewer streets and shuttered, decaying buildings, stretching from New York's 14th Street right down to Canal Street and then across, through A, B and C Streets to East 1st Avenue, the area known as the Lower East Side. Lower originally meant downtown but not any longer. Today it means low: as low as you can get.

There are a few passing similarities to other marketplaces in the world, for instance the noise and the bustle with which the pitchmen proclaim the attraction of their wares. And they shout quite openly, detailing the brand names which are all of significance to the discerning customer. 'ET' is one, named after the film's lovable space character. 'OD' suggests a grim sense of humour in a place where humour is entirely lacking. '·357' is the calibre of a gun – there are a lot of those around – and 'good pussy' has the obvious sexual connotations in a place where a lot of women addicts have to work as prostitutes to support their habits. '24/7' boasts satisfaction twenty-four hours a day, seven days a week.

Forty per cent of America's heroin addicts – 197,000 of the 492,000 – live in New York. This is where they shop, twenty-four hours a day, seven days a week.

Every corner of the market has its steerer, easy to spot from his mace of office – a baseball bat or a golf stick – a weapon of protection for the functions he performs. The steerer runs supplies from the stash to the vendors because vendors don't carry large stocks; it's too easy to get robbed. So on the supply runs, and also when he's transferring money, the steerer risks attack from penniless users. It is also the steerer's responsibility to protect his turf from encroachment by other steerers, which he does with the jealousy of a jungle animal. And he is never afraid to make violent use of his weapon.

The steerer's most important function, however, is designated by his title – to steer eager customers to eager sellers – and the mace of office is his recognised form of identification. Customers sometimes need identification as well, particularly if there are two of them, which is how the police operate – for corroboration – although a police bust is little more than an irritating interruption to business. If he's doubtful about his potential customer, the steerer asks him to bare his arms, to show the familiar black track marks or the sores of a hypodermic needle.

The honest, the respectable and the frightened are getting out of the Lower East Side as quickly as they can and the dealers are promptly moving into their houses, barricading the doors with steel bars and steel mesh and cutting hatchways to which the steerer – once he's satisfied – guides the addict. The customer passes his money – ten dollars – through the hatch and the invisible supplier, protected by his barrier, returns the 'dime' bag.

Sometimes the street doors are sealed and barricaded completely and then the steerer explains a different system. Following his shout, a bucket or basket is lowered from an upstairs window. Into the container the buyer puts his money. Once the purchase price has been checked – always, naturally, money first – the sachet is lowered to the customer.

Sometimes protection is actually provided by the civic authorities! To prevent vandalism – and occupation by dealers – the Manhattan Housing Department breeze-block all the doors and windows of abandoned houses, creating a supposedly impenetrable wall. The dealers gain access from adjoining or rear buildings and the sealed wall only becomes impenetrable to the drug officers of NYPD's Ninth District. Just one breeze block is carved out from the inside, creating the 'window' through which the deals are done.

When I toured the market I saw where the block had been cut from a wall decorated by a garden-scene mural, after the housing department had apparently sealed off the building. Three men came with me for protection, all enforcement officers, all armed, guns in ankle holsters or trouser waist-bands. Despite this we rarely stopped the car, and then only very briefly, because we were in a four-door Ford, an obvious police vehicle. And an obvious target.

'They don't care, these bastards,' said one of my companions. 'If we stopped too long they'd know we were just watching, maybe setting up a bust but not intending to do it, not yet. So they'd surround the car. Rock it. Maybe turn it over and if the gas spilled, fire it. Bastards, like I said. Mother-fuckers.'

There's another form of attack on a loitering car: from the abandoned kitchens redundant refrigerators and cookers are hauled to the top parapet, usually five or six storeys high, and dropped, crushing the vehicle and the people inside.

I witnessed two busts by the Ninth Precinct drug officers, street-wise and street-dressed in stained headbands, stained jeans and stained workshirts, which is how they'd made it past the baseball bats and golf clubs. The dealers and the steerers emerged smiling, with their arms handcuffed, and the other steerers in the hostile-faced crowd smiled back, knowing the joke and enjoying it.

My companions knew it, too, but they didn't think it was a joke. The officer next to me said, 'That's three hours' official paperwork, maybe four. In an hour those bastards will be bailed on charges they won't surrender for and be back here, trading just like they were a little while ago. Nothing but an irritating interruption. Mother-fuckers.'

The two others with us, who'd seen it all before anyway,

weren't watching the arrests but looking around and above us, alert in case of attack. Because we weren't part of the official scene we were vulnerable, a possible retribution target. After only minutes at each bust we moved on. I asked the men with me how long I would be safe outside the car and they laughed at the naïveté of my question. It was daylight, after all. Less danger by day than at night. And a lot of people on the streets were wearing collars and ties. It is a mistake to imagine that heroin addiction is the poor man's kick: Wall Street is close and they do heroin there, too. Alone I could have made it, even escaping the track-mark check. The danger would have come after I'd scored and had my packet because after getting his fix, an addict runs the risk of attack by a moneyless addict. Later, through a one-way mirror system in a specially adapted vehicle, I saw men dressed like I was score easily. Fashion-dressed girls, too.

'Secretaries, personal assistants, chicks like that,' said my agent companion. 'Puts out pussy, maybe. Maybe her salary is good enough. Maybe her guy funds her to do the buying run.'

There is a bizarre order about everything, the addicts with the forced calmness of desperation and the steerers and the vendors with the smooth control of traders assured of a sellers' market. It is a market that looks after its customers, as good markets always do. The discerning know what the brand names signify but the packets are usually colour-coded, too, marked with tape to indicate purity or place of origin, Iran or Afghanistan or one of the Asian source countries. Despite the colour boasts, the heroin here is cut to the ultimate degree. Three per cent is the average purity: sometimes three and a half per cent. Ten per cent is a rarity. It's higher in Harlem, Manhattan's other heroin market. The average there is six and a half per cent.

Customer service on the Lower East Side doesn't end with the colour-coding. Throughout the rabbit-warrened, decaying houses there are shooting galleries for addicts overdue with their fixes, unable to wait until they get back to their own places, guided there by the steerers. The shooting galleries stink, like the cesspools they literally are; the rooms are completely bare except for the urine- and shit-soaked mattresses to doze on after the hit. There are bottle-caps in which to heat the heroin and a hitter to do it for you if you don't know how or are too bad to do it properly. He carries works, too, a needle and a hypodermic and a rubber tube band, to bring up the vein if you're mainlining. The needle and the hypodermic will have been used before, of course, many times, which is how the sores of septicaemia and the hepatitis start. These are the risks the addicts accept, like getting mugged by other addicts or stealing or selling their bodies to get through another day.

The agents I accompanied had all been involved in narcotics enforcement for several years and were cynical of any effort to clean up the Lower East Side. 'We could arrest a hundred sellers today and by tomorrow there'd be another hundred to replace them,' said one. 'And at street level anyway they're only punks, despite the effort to seem otherwise, users themselves selling on to support their own habits. A good ninety per cent of those we arrest beat the rap anyway. And we rarely get to within a million miles of the people who matter, the important ones in the Bonanno or Luchese or Gambino or Genovese and Colombo Families. Occasionally, maybe. But not often enough.'

New York's heroin addicts don't all live on the island of Manhattan, of course: along every street we travelled there were cars with out-of-town licence plates. New Jersey and Brooklyn were common but there were a lot of places further upstate, sometimes into New England. I watched an attractive girl of maybe eighteen, wearing designer jeans, get out of a car with Boston plates and familiarly approach a steerer carrying a golf club. From the greeting he knew her, and gestured further along B Street to a door reached down three or four steps. There were others ahead of her, waiting in a patient line. She joined them, dipped briefly out of sight when her turn came, and re-appeared within minutes carrying a bundle, a bulk buy of ten packets. There might have been more in her handbag.

'Shopping run,' said one of my companions. 'She'll sell on when she gets back to Boston, to support her own needs and the cost of the trip down. Wonder why she came all the way down here. There's plenty available in Boston. Seems like she does it all the time, from how she knows her way around.'

She waved to the steerer on her way back to the car and he waved in return. She could have been buying groceries from a friendly corner store except that buying groceries would probably have taken longer.

Rudolph Giuliani, the US Attorney for the Southern District of New York, and before that an associate attorney general in Washington closely involved with the creation of drug task forces, says he considers heroin abuse and trafficking in New York are practically at an emergency level. He added, 'I think it is fair to say that if we could tomorrow eliminate Mafia heroin-dealing in New York, you could reduce heroin throughout the nation to a very acceptable level.'

Enforcement officials have discovered that a barter trade has arisen between New York and Florida, dealers exchanging heroin for cocaine and vice versa. Dr Carlton Turner said this indicated that they were winning their war, because the dealers were being forced to exchange the drugs they couldn't sell.

I couldn't get any agent working on the streets to agree with this interpretation during my time on the Lower East Side. I was told it indicated that the dealers are becoming even better organised and better supplied and have reverted to the easy barter arrangement to spread heroin into the cocaine-dominated southern state and bring cocaine up into New York, to meet an ever-increasing demand for that drug in and around Manhattan. Although heroin is the predominant product on the Lower East Side, cocaine is as easily available.

Through the one-way observation mirror I saw a boy of about fifteen emerge from the same dealer who had supplied the girl from Boston. He opened his cocaine sachet quite openly in the street and snorted with the professionalism of a hardened user. There was a professionalism, too, in the way he nodded approval at the strength. Three others standing with him, awaiting his judgement, descended to make their purchases. On this occasion the boy had tested the product for his companions' benefit, but during the 1970s period of the French Connection, when the Lower East Side started developing into what it is today, this was frequently the way the big importers from Italy tested the purity of a drug on its arrival in New York. From the Lower East Side one of the importing families would pick up a recognised addict and experiment to establish the percentage he could endure, then use him as a guinea pig for the newly arrived shipment. If he died, I was told, that was good, because it showed the heroin was high-grade material, far beyond the addict's tolerance. There was no danger from the law in these experiments: addicts lying dead in alleys were a common enough sight. And there were always plenty to choose from, whenever a new consignment arrived.

'There still would be today, if there hadn't been progress,' one agent told me. 'Now the dealers have "hot boxes" – specially designed testing containers into which the drug is put and then heated through the known burn-off temperatures of the refining and adulterating chemicals and ingredients.' 'Hot boxes' are very accurate, working to laboratory standards, so this is obviously a more efficient testing method than was used previously. And a live addict is a customer. A dead one isn't.

Maintaining and increasing the level of sales is, after all, the ambition of every business.

The creed, in fact, of Hollywood and America's crucible state, California.

7

When his addiction became so bad he was daily shooting cocaine, heroin and morphine as well as taking Dilaudid, John Phillips, who founded the Mamas and the Papas group and composed the 1960 standards like 'Monday, Monday' and 'California Dreamin'', never bothered to take the needle from his arm but taped it there permanently, his vein always open, ready.

He didn't – couldn't – compose, not by then. His only interest was in drugs, in maintaining a permanent high. It was costing him $1,000,000 (£431,034) a year but he didn't care. Any more than he cared that he had to sell houses to raise the money to buy the drugs. And cars, including four Rolls Royces, one of which was worth $80,000 but which he sold for only $24,000, eager for a quick buck for a quick fix.

His third wife, Genevieve, was addicted, just as badly. So was his brilliantly promising actress daughter Mackenzie Phillips, who achieved instant stardom in 1973 with *American Graffiti* and sustained that promise in the CBS hit *One Day at a Time* until she was fired because of drug abuse. By then she'd spent $400,000 and become known in Hollywood as another Judy Garland. Today she finds that difficult to comprehend.

Drugs have been an integral part of life in the world's film capital since before Judy Garland's time, since the early 1920s. And they still are, despite the denials and the efforts to make it seem otherwise.

Cocaine is the favourite but the use of heroin is increasing.

127

And all sorts of pills. Elvis Presley sought out J. Edgar Hoover in Washington and according to a later Bureau memorandum asked, 'How can I help the FBI stop the drug traffic among young people?' Presley died in 1977, aged forty-two, grotesquely bloated, incomprehensible in speech and song and wearing a nappy because of the incontinence caused by his addiction to amphetamines, barbiturates and sedatives. After his death his doctor, George Nichopoulos, admitted – before an examining medical panel that temporarily suspended his licence – that in the twenty months prior to the singer's death he had prescribed ten thousand pills.

Richard Watkins, a West Coast-based insurance adjuster for Lloyds of London, claims that the increasing use of cocaine on film sets has forced some companies to introduce into their production policies exclusion clauses that can be invoked when shooting is interrupted or delayed by a star's habit. An enforcement official told me that some insurance companies have lists of actors and actresses known to use drugs and premiums are adjusted accordingly for films in which those stars appear.

Julia Phillips – no relation to John Phillips – publicly admits having spent more than $1,000,000 on cocaine during a glittering Hollywood career in which she produced movies like *The Sting*, for which she won an Academy Award, and *Close Encounters of the Third Kind*. She snorted at first but then graduated, like everyone else in Hollywood, to freebasing, ingesting a purer form of the drug by holding an extraction pipe over a flame to burn away the hydrochloride salt. Alcohol is sometimes used instead of ether as a solvent. Richard Pryor, America's most highly paid and successful black comedian, almost burned himself to death in June 1980 when the rum ignited in his pipe and set him alight while he was freebasing. He later admitted his dependency on cocaine in a warning sequence in his movie, *Live on Sunset Strip*. 'It's an addiction,' he says, 'a monster. I finally got to the point where the drug dealers refused to sell me cocaine. They said, "Man, you're killing yourself." '

Speedballing is another way of using cocaine: it means injecting a mixture of cocaine, which gives a high, and heroin, which gives a low, so the effect is that of a roller coaster. Another American comedian, John Belushi, died in March 1982 after speedballing in a Los Angeles motel room.

Freebasing so badly affected singer Natalie Cole, daughter of Nat King Cole, that Los Angeles Superior Court agreed that her mother, Maria, should take over the administration of her estate. Linda Blair, critically acclaimed star of *The Exorcist*, was arrested and charged by Florida police for conspiracy to deliver and distribute cocaine. Oscar-winning actor Richard Dreyfus was accused of unlawful possession of a controlled substance when cocaine was found in his convertible Mercedes after a crash in Los Angeles in October 1982. 'I've been there. I've done it all,' admits Sammy Davis jnr, who now lectures to youth groups and the military on the dangers of drug and alcohol excesses. Cocaine caused a split in the marriage of Jeff Wald to Australian-born singer Helen Reddy. Wald said, 'In Hollywood it is easier to get cocaine than a loaf of bread. For a loaf of bread you have to wait until the supermarket is open. For a gram of cocaine the supermarket is always open.' Christopher Lawford, son of actor Peter Lawford – who was himself admitted in 1983 to an alcohol and drug rehabilitation clinic in California where Elizabeth Taylor, Johnny Cash and actor Tony Curtis have been treated – was charged in 1980 with unlawful possession of heroin. The same year one of Senator Edward Kennedy's nephews, Christopher, resigned his job on the Senator's ill-fated presidential campaign after being charged at Aspen, Colorado, with trying to obtain pills by pretending to be a doctor.

Singer Johnny Mathis kicked a pill habit which began, he admits, from tour exhaustion and visits to 'a very famous New York doctor whom I won't name, who gave me treatment twice a week'. The doctor's name, in fact, was Max Jacobson, who in 1975 had his licence revoked after a two-

and-a-half-year investigation by the New York State of Regents, the medical disciplinary board, which found, among other accusations, that Jacobson had endangered patients' lives by amphetamine injections.

One of those patients was US President John Kennedy. The late president's nephews, Robert and David Kennedy and Sargeant Shriver jnr, have all been arrested and charged with drug offences.

In February 1984 David Kennedy jnr, who resigned his job as an assistant district attorney in Manhattan after twice failing his law examinations, pleaded guilty in Rapid City, South Dakota, to heroin possession. Two months later he was found dead in an hotel room at Palm Beach, Florida, near the Kennedy winter compound in which his grandmother, Rose Kennedy, was staying. She was not told of her addicted grandson's death.

Kennedy had been speedballing a mixture of cocaine and Demerol, a painkiller containing N-acetyp-aminophenol. Found in the hotel room were 20.05 grains of cocaine with a purity of seventy per cent. Investigators calculated that Kennedy overdosed because he did not know how strong it was. Those same investigators, who arrested two bellhops for drug-selling, also sought to interview a thirty-year-old dealer named Harry Wollkind – a well-known social figure in Palm Beach – who in March 1983 supplied a fatal cocaine dose to millionaire William Wendell Ylvisaker, a twenty-three-year-old friend of Prince Charles. In 1982 Ylvisaker had captained a polo team that defeated Prince Charles's team at Smith's Lawn, Windsor, and had been presented with the victor's cup by the Queen.

Julia Phillips, who admits herself that she looked like 'someone out of Dachau', was cured of her heroin dependency by Hollywood psychopharmacologist Dr Ronald K. Siegal, who treats many leading figures – businessmen as well as entertainers – in California. He estimates that freebasing addicts spend from $2000 to $12,000 (£1142 to £6857) a week on cocaine, but in spite of those figures, Hollywood resents the accusation and bitterly denies a greater incidence of drug abuse than any other section of affluent American society.

In 1981 that resentment figured large after a cover story published by the small but influential *TV Guide*, claiming – on the basis, sometimes, of unsupported facts – that Hollywood was awash in drugs. From Washington the House Select Narcotics Abuse and Control Committee convened hearings on the West Coast and in April they crossed the continent to attend sessions at which they wanted – and expected – stars to appear.

Hollywood's reaction was to ignore and deride the visiting politicians. Kim Fellner, a spokesman for the Screen Actors' Guild, protested, 'We are tired of people always starting their investigations with Hollywood just because it is prominent and will generate publicity. We know that alcohol and drug abuse exists in our industry, but in no greater proportion than in the rest of society.'

Actress Cathy Lee Crosby, who the previous year testified before the Committee and invited a Hollywood visit to correct 'the false picture that the majority of celebrities are drugees', cancelled a promised reappearance and protested at 'media hype and sensationalism'. And Lou Asner, who portrayed news editor Lou Grant in the television series of that name, openly accused the visiting Congressmen of attempting a repetition of the mid-fifties McCarthy witch-hunts and called them 'highly ridiculous and stupid'.

The accusations were rebutted by one of the Committee members, Los Angeles Representative Robert Dornan, who said that any media hype had been generated by Cathy Lee Crosby and Asner, 'trying to get themselves publicity'.

The only publicly recognisable personality who did attend the Los Angeles sessions was Greg Morris, a star of the television series *Mission Impossible*, and he reiterated the views expressed by his colleagues. Before giving his testimony, Morris repeated the accusation of a witch-hunt and said the Congressmen were alleging 'by innuendo, that Hollywood is a cocaine-influenced industry'.

Not so, insisted the Committee chairman, Brooklyn Democrat Leo Zeferetti. He assured his hostile witness, 'We didn't come to the industry to create a McCarthy-like era of interrogation of individuals but to get expert, professional guidance on how to educate and influence the public.' From the questioning it seemed Zeferetti was unaware that the black actor had personally appeared in four anti-drug educational films, one of which was called *H is for Heroin*.

And while these short-lived hearings were being held, NBC, America's oldest television network, was working on their most ambitious educational effort to date, an hour-long special called *Get High on Yourself* for which they sacrificed $2,000,000 (£956,937) in advertising revenue. The producer was Robert Evans, whose previous films included *Chinatown, Love Story* and *The Godfather*, and his decision to make the film was the result of his appearance in a New York court in July 1980, when he pleaded guilty to agreeing to buy for $19,000 (£8189) five ounces of cocaine. Judge Vincent Broderick deferred judgement and offered Evans the chance of erasing his record after a year's probation if he would use his 'unique talents where others have failed in this horrible thing of drug abuse by children'.

Evans's immediate response was to spend $400,000 of his own money on a television spectacular featuring stars like Bob Hope, Burt Reynolds, Cheryl Tiegs, Tracy Austin and John Travolta. Actor Paul Newman – who created the Scott Newman Foundation to prevent drug and alcohol abuse in memory of his son who had overdosed – also took part. So did comedienne Carol Burnett, who has openly admitted and discussed the marijuana and cocaine dependency of her daughter, Carrie. Evans's co-producer was Cathy Lee Crosby.

The keynote of the production was a jingle composed by Steve Karmen, composer of the 'I Love New York' theme, regarded by advertising executives as one of the most successful promotional tunes ever created:

You can be somebody with a plan of your own,
You can say no and you won't be alone.
You can make yourself get higher than you have ever known,
By making up your own mind,
Doing things your own way,
Setting up your own style,
By being yourself.

When NBC broadcast their spectacular, *Get High on Yourself*, they not only forfeited their advertising revenue, they spent a further $1,000,000 on public service announcements promoting an anti-drug campaign. In April 1984, one of their vice presidents, Jay Rodriguez, announced that the Corporation was preparing a third prime-time special for transmission later in the year.

Actress Michele Lee, who portrays a reformed drug addict on CBS's programme 'Knot's Landing', told US Congressmen of the formation of an organisation called Entertainment Industries' Council for a Drug Free Society. Composed of producers, writers and actors, the Council plans to make prime-time shows for adults, portraying the evils of drug-taking.

And Jean MacCurdy, Vice President of Programming for cartoon-making Hanna Barbera productions announced that a cartoon series featuring anti-drug heroes Teen Titans was being created for an estimated children's audience of 15,000,000.

Dr Turner, the presidential drug adviser, has praised NCB for taking 'a very positive role in deglamorising drugs', followed by ABC, with CBS 'sort of lagging behind'. He is critical, however, of America's top Hollywood-based chat show host, Johnny Carson, who frequently seeks laughs from drug references. At the 1981 Oscar presentation ceremony, for example, he said, 'The biggest moneymaker in Hollywood last year was Colombia. Not the studio – the country.'

Turner's dismay at Carson's humour reflects the attitude of all anti-narcotics campaigners who recognise the immense influence wielded by the stars, whether on large or small screen. 'Stars are paid millions of dollars a year to endorse bona fide, legitimate products,' one rehabilitation official said to me. 'And they know it works, because otherwise they wouldn't be paid those millions of dollars. So when the hell are they going to realise the damage they do by making cheap, throwaway cracks which glamorise drug-taking?'

Despite the plethora of Hollywood denials that they are no different from any other rich ghetto, major film studios are showing increasing concern about the abuse of narcotics. At the beginning of 1983, estimating that sixty per cent of film-set absenteeism was being caused by drugs or drink, MGM, 20th Century Fox and Burbank Studios decided to participate in a course established by the Motion Picture and Television Fund to train supervisory staff to recognise people affected by drugs or alcohol. The first company to implement the programme was 20th Century Fox, whose Employee Relations Director, Bob Holmes, said, 'Whether you snort it, inject it in your arm, drink it or pop it, substance abuse is an enormous problem that can't just be swept under the rug.'

In addition to the training course, the Fund persuaded all major studios to put an advisory pamphlet on drugs in employees' wage packets. It included a telephone number through which anyone would be guaranteed confidential counselling.

It was to such counselling services that producer Dick Ebersol referred the new and existing cast of 'Saturday Night Live' when they arrived for the start of a new series in January 1985. Failure to seek help, warned Ebersol, would lead to suspension. 'Saturday Night Live's' most famous alumni was John Balushi but it was not the memory of Balushi's death that prompted the warning from Ebersol. Instead it was the sentencing – confirmed upon appeal – in England of actor Stacy Keach, for attempting to smuggle into the country £3,000 ($2,500) of cocaine hidden in a shaving foam dispenser. Keach was jailed for nine months, which meant CBS had to take out of its schedules the Mike Hammer TV series in which he stared. Dozens of technicians and other film workers were made jobless.

134

Increasingly in Hollywood enforcement agencies and treatment centres are encountering addicts who have taken their heroin not in the usual way – by injection – but, like cocaine, by cutting and chopping it with a razor blade into a series of lines on a smooth surface – glass or marble – and then snorting it through a rolled-up, high-denomination dollar note or a specially made nose-tube. One treatment expert said, 'There is a deep belief out here that by snorting heroin and not injecting it, there is no risk of addiction. That you can't become addicted that way. But you can.'

The heroin that is smoked in Hollywood is called Persian Tan. Experts who testified before the thwarted Congressional enquiry assessed its purity, in some cases, as high as seventy to a hundred per cent, with a then street price of around $600 (£287) a gram. Mexican heroin was also available, with a purity as low as seven to eighteen per cent, at a street price of $10,000 (£4,784) an ounce.

Another drug which became popular on the Hollywood streets during 1981 initially defied analysis by drug enforcement chemists; it was called China White. Thirty people died from overdosing before the DEA laboratory on the outskirts of Washington DC recognised it as the methyl analogue of fentanyl, an analgesic.

By 1985 it was to develop into a nightmare for enforcement agencies. The verbal shorthand was designer drugs. It designated a laboratory-produced drug 1,000 times stronger than heroin, the amount needed to produce a better-than-heroin euphoria so small that the active dosage amounted to only 50 micrograms, so small that it fitted to a pinhead and was undetectable in any laboratory with apparatus unable to test to parts per billion or per trillion.

Scientists (enforcement agencies calculate there may only be two or three, working out of one or maybe two laboratories) simply slightly alter the molecular structure of fentanyl and produce something that is not only 1,000 times stronger – and cheaper – than heroin, but perfectly *legal*!

An enforcement official explained to me: 'Even if we managed to locate the laboratory and raid it, it is doubtful under the law whether we could bring a successful prosecution. To be an illegal drug, it must be described and listed as such under the Controlled Substances Act. We've managed to get two fentanyl derivatives proscribed and in April 1985, the newest variant, 3-methyl-fentanyl, was added. But even though we've managed to reduce to 30 days the time it takes to get a drug listed, these chemists – if indeed it is more than one man – can just make another slight change to the basic drug and carry on without any risk of arrest.'

There could, some experts calculate, be as many as 200 variations.

Although concentrated around the Bay area of San Francisco, the synthetic heroin is being moved into other states. At the time of writing 90 people have died through overdosing, unaware of just how incredibly strong the laboratory drug is. Two of these were in Oregon and one in Arizona, the remainder were in California.

Officials estimate that one fifth of California's heroin addicts are, by choice, using the fentanyl derivative rather than normal heroin. So concentrated is the synthetic drug that the chemists in two weeks can produce 200 grams or sufficient – with the reduced amount necessary – for 4,000,000 doses.

Synthetic heroin is not the only designer drug available on the streets of California. In 1982 a group of underground chemists in the northern part of the State tried to design a copy of Demerol. They overheated the experiment, however, and produced a drug known as MPTP. It gave its users Parkinson's Disease. Twenty people were permanently afflicted and doctors expect 500 more who used the tainted batch to develop the disease during their lifetime.

So concerned are the enforcement agencies that they have promoted newspaper and television reports, to warn street users. 'Even though these people know they are risking death – some people were actually found with the needle still in their arms – they won't stop,' said one agent, wearily. 'It's a new and better high and so they want it.'

Neither do enforcement officials expect the runaway

demand for cocaine to diminish following reports that it is more deadly than heroin. A controlled study carried out in California and published in July 1985, in the American Medical Association journal, disclosed that of twelve rats wired to unlimited supplies of cocaine, eleven were dead in thirty days. It had, the journal reported, obvious implication for human beings and Dr Ronald Siegal, of the Los Angeles School of Medicine, said 'Cocaine produces a more tenacious dependency. With unlimited access you will reach toxic levels faster.'

Of eleven rats wired to unlimited supplies of heroin, only four died during the same test period.

Since 1977 – when it published its findings that cocaine was a relatively safe recreational drug when snorted – the US National Institute on Drug Abuse has changed its mind. A fresh study, entitled 'Cocaine: Pharmacology Effects and Treatment of Abuse', claims half the users of cocaine risk becoming physically dependent. The Institute further says, reversing its previous opinion, that cocaine can produce all the symptoms of physical addiction, going beyond the accepted view until 1983 that it was merely psychologically addictive.

George Halpin, DEA regional director for eight western states, told the Senate Subcommittee on Alcoholism and Drug Abuse, 'Los Angeles has a reputation as a big consuming town, much as Miami does as a source town. This city is flooded with drugs – cocaine, PCP and marijuana are everywhere, dangerous drugs are readily available and the use of heroin is increasing.'

California is the leading American state for the cultivation of marijuana. There are illicit plantations in all of the country's fifty-eight counties but the largest are in Mendocino, Humboldt, Lake and Del Norte. The Californian brand of the drug is the particularly potent sinsemilla: the average yield of a single plant is a pound, sometimes more, sufficient for 1500 hand-rolled joints. Growers will pay $1800 to $2000 a pound for buds. By comparison, the Chardonnay grape, the basis of the state's supposed major industry, sells for less than $1000 a ton. The illegal marijuana industry is a bitterly competitive one, with growers employing armed guards to protect their crops against raids both from enforcement officials and other growers: in the first nine months of 1982 there were four marijuana-related murders.

The synthetic drugs most common in Hollywood, Los Angeles and San Francisco are Quaalude, Preludin, Tuinal, Ritalin, Biphetamine and Dilaudid, the choice of heroin addicts if they cannot get heroin. Enforcement agencies and police drug squads believe that a large number of West Coast physicians are employed in what are known as 'script mills', literally prescription factories masquerading as clinics from which addicts can go to approved and receptive pharmacies and have their prescriptions made up without any fear of interception or arrest. At least a hundred of these pharmacy-linked script mills exist in the Los Angeles area alone.

A report assembled by California Attorney General John K. Van de Kamp, based on 1983 statistics, which were the most recent available, estimated at the beginning of 1985 that the script mill industry in the State 'may well exceed $1,000,000,000 (£800,000,000) a year'. In May 1985, in what assistant US Attorney Joyce Karlin called 'the first time that there has been a co-ordinated effort by all involved authorities to delve into the problem and stop it', seventeen people – including seven doctors, two pharmacists, medical clinical operators and their assistants – were indicted on charges of illegally prescribing and dispensing drugs.

George Halpin said during the 1981 Los Angeles hearings, 'I sometimes feel as General Custer must have felt as he crossed the mountains to the Little Bighorn. We are overwhelmed by drug abuse in this area.' This was theatrical understatement in the light of the evidence provided by another witness, Albert Bergesen, the regional customs commissioner, who reported that during 1980 448 lb of cocaine had been seized, with a street value of $112,000,000 (£48,275,000). During the same period the narcotics division of the Los Angeles Police Department had seized an additional 183.32 lb. Applying the 10 per cent interception ratio favoured by enforcement officers, that meant that 6310 lb of cocaine entered the Hollywood area in 1980. Los Angeles police also seized 63.26 lb of heroin, compared with 42.81 lb the previous year, and almost 48,800 lb of marijuana, an increase of 1513 per cent over the previous year's interception figure, with a street value of $107,330,700. Of the 400 murders in the Los Angeles area in 1980, 132 were narcotics-related.

Three years later I was assured that the situation had deteriorated considerably.

Evidence of that deterioration came in 1985. Early that year the Los Angeles police intercepted what was for them, until that time, a record cocaine seizure, 556 lb of the drug valued at approximately $158,000,000 (£131,600,000). Announcement of the haul was made by Los Angeles police chief Daryl Gates, who knows personally of the ravages of drug addiction because of the hopeless dependence of his 29-year-old son, Lowell Scott Gates. Gates created a controversy just before the seizure announcement by acquiring for his force an armoured car with a 16-ft battering ram to smash down the fortified doors of 'rock houses', premises where pebble-sized rocks of adulterated cocaine are sold for as little as $25 each. Said Gates 'This will put a dent but not a big dent (into drug trafficking). Los Angeles is a tremendous consumption point.'

The arrested gang attempting to bring in the 556 lb of cocaine were Colombians. Gates said that from their enquiries the police estimated that until they were caught the group were bringing into California about a ton of cocaine a month!

By 1985 authorities estimated there were maybe a thousand 'rock houses' selling this vast influx of cocaine in the Los Angeles area alone. By the beginning of that year, during a twelve-month period, sixty-five people had been murdered in gang fights over control of rock houses, each of which can take between $5,000 and $10,000 a day.

One of the major cocaine suppliers to Hollywood is

identified by federal authorities as William Morgan Hetrick. A resident of Ventura County, the fifty-year-old Californian ran a company called Morgan Aviation from a leased hangar in the Mojave desert. It was a wealthy company, lavishly equipped with five aeroplanes, a fifty-three-foot yacht called *Ivory* and a forty-six-foot trawler, *Highland Fling*. But its business wasn't the aircraft repair described in its prospectus, but the importation of cocaine and marijuana from Colombia.

It was Hetrick who imported into America the cocaine that resulted in John DeLorean being arraigned in Los Angeles on a drug-smuggling charge of which, in 1984, he was acquitted by a jury who decided that the circumstances of his arrest by the FBI in October 1982 amounted to entrapment. The FBI's failed case was that DeLorean – who needed $10,000,000 in three days – intended using the cocaine to save his bankrupt sports car empire in Dunmurry, West Belfast, from closing. Produced in court was an FBI video recording made in room 501 of the Sheraton Plaza Hotel in Los Angeles in which DeLorean was seen and heard to say, 'It's as good as gold. Gold weighs more than this, for God's sake.'

Champagne was being poured when DeLorean was arrested.

Cocaine was the equivalent of champagne for John Phillips and his wife: up to half an ounce a day, every day. And two and a half grains of morphine. And heroin. And Dilaudid.

Phillips recalls, 'The only other person I ever heard about who took as many drugs as we did was Elvis.'

Elvis died. John Phillips, Genevieve and their daughter Mackenzie survived. But only just. By the time Phillips was admitted to the psychiatric hospital in New Jersey, the arms that had once cradled a guitar were useless and blackened, every vein collapsed. It was feared that he might lose the use of them, but revolutionary and enlightened treatment from a doctor named Mark Gold restored to John Phillips the use of his arms, his mind and his life, to counsel now against drug addiction. Mackenzie does the same. From unrivalled experience.

John Phillips was a consummate musician, not a Hollywood actor, but it was while working on a movie that he graduated to heroin from cocaine. And it was while he was in London, not Hollywood, composing the score for David Bowie's *The Man Who Fell to Earth*. David Bowie is another self-confessed abuser of drugs, but it was Phillips who literally fell, returning to America a confirmed addict. In New York he and Genevieve were mistakenly (some people use the word criminally) told by a doctor that cocaine was a medically recommended substitute for heroin; withdrawal – the same advice that had been given more than twenty years earlier by London's Lady Isabella Frankau. So they shot cocaine to free themselves from heroin, and because heroin was so easily available and they could afford it they shot heroin as well, and boarded the roller-coaster that stops too frequently for the ride-again ticket.

Mick Jagger – who had experimented himself – was aware of the pressure upon musicians. His friend Keith Moon, The Who's eccentric drummer, died from a drug overdose, by an ironic coincidence in the same London apartment in which Mamma Cass Elliott – the co-founder of Phillip's once famous group and, according to him, a heroin user – had died four years earlier. He was closer still to Keith Richard, the heroin-addicted lead guitarist of the Rolling Stones, part of whose sentence from a Toronto court was an order to make a public gesture, a charity concert, something akin to Robert Evans's TV film, *Get High on Yourself*. Jagger was also a contemporary of the Beatles, whose manager Brian Epstein – another drug victim – had his suits tailored with 'pill pockets' inside the jacket. And he knew John Lennon, who used every drug including heroin and was sometimes so stoned that he had to record lying on the studio floor.

Jagger became one of Phillips's closest friends, the man whom Genevieve telephoned for help whenever Phillips disappeared, which was often, and couldn't be found for days and nights. He was *always* found by Jagger, who risked arrest, accusations and mugging by going into the glass- and needle-littered shooting galleries to drag Phillips back to safety. And when Phillips, suffering from withdrawal symptoms, crashed a Cadillac and was briefly hospitalised in July 1980, Jagger looked after the Phillips's children, Tamerlane, nine, and a baby named Bijou.

John Phillips's addiction was eventually cured at Fair Oaks Hospital in Summit, New Jersey, by detoxification with clonidine and a non-addictive drug called naltrexone. He was one of the lucky ones. His cure was successful. There are still millions uncured in America where treatment is considered less important than law and enforcement.

8

Richard Nixon was the American president who determined that the answer to America's narcotic problem would be the eradication of supply, a goal towards which succeeding American presidents have unfailingly worked but been unable to achieve.

Within months of assuming office in 1969, Nixon isolated Mexico as his first target. There the drugs trade was under the control of the fifteen-branch Herrera family.

Sixteen years later, it still is.

Jaime Herrera-Navarez was the controller then, from the Mexican state of Durango, the godfather of a network of relatives which spreads through family connections to Calumet, a suburb of Chicago and Joliet, Illinois. Now fifty-six, he is still in control.

There are further relations in Chicago's Kensington district, the legitimate owners of bars, garages and restaurants where 'dirty' drug profits can be 'laundered', to become untraceable. Six separate Herrera families are among the Mexican-American population of Chicago which is numbered at four hundred thousand. According to a federal law enforcement official in Washington, the combined worth of the Herreras is incalculable, amounting to tens of billions.

Jaime Herrera-Navarez was not so well known in 1969 as he is now, but his were the trafficking activities Nixon tried to stop during his first year of office with an operation codenamed Intercept, which later became Operation Co-operation.

Intercept was just that: the posting of 2000 customs and

patrol agents along the 1700-mile border between Mexico and America for what was described as 'the largest peacetime search and seizure operation by civil authorities'.

As is so often and so unfortunately the case with planned drug interdictions, it was unsuccessful. Five and a half million American and Mexican travellers were intercepted in three weeks, without one dramatic seizure. In addition to the border blockade, which caused delays of up to half a day, towns just inside Mexico were declared off-limits to American service personnel within the area, a heavy hint of the economic pressure that could be applied if Mexico did not make some internal effort to reduce its poppy and marijuana cultivation in the ravine-split Sierra Madre, an area which is impossibly difficult to police.

Not surprisingly the operation provoked an angry response from Mexico who accused the United States of interfering in the affairs of another country when it should more properly be considering treatment of its own addict population, without whose demand there would be no supply. The irritation of the Mexican government became such that the United States Department of State warned the White House that Operation Intercept was threatening its Latin American good-neighbour policy.

Deputy Attorney General Richard Kliendienst, who chaired the interdiction effort established by his superior, Attorney General John Mitchell, explained somewhat ambiguously that the intention was neither border blockade nor harassment, but the eradication of the drugs at source. And to that end the United States offered Mexico $1,000,000 (£418,500) to wipe out the plantations.

Over the years and in spite of the increasing claims of success of a number of variously named operations, the level of that aid has grown with the tenacity of the *papaver somniferum*, the opium poppy that Washington seeks to destroy. It is estimated that the total amount of monetary aid and equipment allocated so far stands at $80,000,000 and includes forty-three American helicopters and twenty-two spotter planes. Some of these are equipped with a specialised camera developed by Spectral Data Corporation of Hauppauge, New York, capable of photograhing 1200 square kilometres a day and later identifying marijuana and opium fields from the reflection of their spectral signals. They have also employed ten specially equipped aircraft to spray the paraquat-based herbicide Gramoxone upon located plantations.

Although there appeared to be some effort to combat Mexico's narcotic industry during the presidency of Jose Lopez Portillo, it was largely cosmetic. One of the biggest traffickers – and bribed protector of traffickers – was Arturo Durazo Moreno, whose ability as election campaign manager Portillo repaid by making him Mexico City police chief. During his king-like reign, Moreno amassed a fortune. Within his 3,000-man Department for the Investigation and Prevention of Delinquency, he created a torturing, murdering vigilante squad estimated to have been responsible for at least twenty assassinations. Officially with a salary of only $1,000 a month, Moreno built two estates – one covering 600 acres near Acapulco, the other on the outskirts of Mexico City – valued at $15,000,000. When Portillo was replaced as President in December 1982, Moreno fled the country. He was later arrested in Puerto Rico and identified as one of Mexico's most wanted criminals.

In the first year of Portillo's presidency the US government said they destroyed almost 33,000 acres as a result of their paraquat-spraying campaign. In the second year they claimed a further 8200 acres and in the third, over 3700 acres. Deputy Attorney General Samuel Alba-Leyva, who was in charge of the anti-drug campaign, also announced in the first year that in addition to the crop destruction they had captured 46 smuggling aeroplanes, 575 vehicles, 3 boats, 4,000,000 pep pills and closed down 17 heroin laboratories. To illustrate the extent of the Mexican success he quoted the fact that in America the price of raw opium had risen from $25,000 (£14,367) to $100,000 (£57,471) a kilo.

145

Americans from the Drug Enforcement Administration were drafted to Mexico to help the local force of 4500 government troops and 250 Mexican agents. Alba-Leyva divided the country into twelve regions and their main target was the area identified as Zone VI, the 40,000-square-mile Sierra Madre district comprising parts of three states, Sinaloa, Chihuahua and Durango, the drug-processing capital of which was Culiacan, the headquarters of the Herrera family.

As well as being a producer in its own right, Sinaloa was at that time – and still is – regarded as one of the major conduits for the cocaine traffic of Colombia, Bolivia and Peru. There are 750 kilometres of easily accessible beach and an estimated 1400 illegal landing strips. Most of the 3000 inhabitants of its major town, Badiraguato, and the 20,000 peasants who live in the outlying villages, derive their income almost entirely from drugs.

Because of the eradication campaign of the Mexican authorities, the growers have expanded their estates beyond Durango, Sinaloa and Chihuahua to Guerrero, Veracruz, San Luis Potosi, Hidalgo, Oaxaca, Sonora and Baja California. Intelligence estimates made available to me calculate that the opium production in Mexico was sixteen tons for each of the years 1980, 1981 and 1982. One analysis reported: 'Intelligence indicates that not only is the purity of Mexican heroin up but that the price is down – this has traditionally meant that there is an abundance of heroin for distribution into the illicit market.'

By extending their production area, the traffickers have stretched the abilities of the eradication forces. Furthermore, agents have discovered that farmers have developed the practice, immediately after an aerial spray, of either scoring the mature plants to collect the opium gum before the plants die or hosing off the herbicide to diminish its damage.

The Mexicans take less care than other producing areas of the world in refining their heroin – they separate the morphine base from the opium gum by mixing it in fifty-gallon drums with water and slaked lime, not filtering it sufficiently, and their dirty brown product is known as Mexican Mud. As it is easily identifiable, US authorities have been able to determine that the amount of heroin entering the USA from this source is less than it was in the mid-seventies when it was claimed – an exaggeration, I believe – to provide eighty to ninety per cent of America's needs.

An indication of how contemptuous Mexican traffickers are of official efforts to stop them, came in February 1985. That month Enrique Camarena Salazar, a 37-year-old agent of America's Drug Enforcement Agency, was intercepted as he left the US consulate in Guadalajara by four gunmen and bundled into a waiting kidnap car. The same day, a Mexican pilot named Alfredo Zavala Avelar, who flew occasional missions for the DEA, was kidnapped.

Bribed police played down the kidnapping to local American officials, until the soon-to-retire Drug Enforcement Administrator, Bud Mullen, flew personally to Mexico and, according to an aide who travelled with him, 'started banging on desks'. The echoes didn't stop there. Attorney General William French Smith blasted off a telegram to the Mexican Attorney General so sharply worded that State Department officials warned it could upset relationships between the two countries. And President Reagan sent a personal letter to the Mexican President, Miguel de la Madrid, seeking action.

The bodies of Salazar and Avelar, tortured and badly decomposed, were found on 6 March at a remote ranch 60 miles southwest of Guadalajara. Acting on a tip, Mexican authorities raided the ranch and had to shoot their way in during a battle in which one policeman and five traffickers were killed.

A month later a man whom Mexican and American authorities described as a prime suspect in the murder was arrested in a luxury hacienda set amid a coffee plantation near San Jose, in Costa Rica. According to investigators Rafael Caro Quintero, a known trafficker, fled Mexico two days after the kidnapping of the two DEA men. He left in a private jet, despite being intercepted by officers of the Mexican federal and state police, alerted by the DEA. Quintero was carrying a Russian-made AK-47 assault rifle and was accompanied by at least twelve bodyguards. He told the blockading police he had to 'find a way to fix this' or the shooting would start. The way to fix it was to bribe the officers to let him go, which they did.

When Quintero was seized by Costa Rican authorities, with him in the hacienda was the kidnapped, 17-year-old daughter of Cesar Octavio Cossio, a rich businessman and brother of an official of Mexico's ruling political party.

The Costa Rican authorities deported Quintero back to Mexican arrest. At the time of writing authorities are also investigating Quintero's part in the unsolved disappearance in January 1985, of Americans John Walker, 36, and 32-year-old Alberto Radelat. Walker, a would-be novelist, and Radelat, a trainee dentist, from Fort Worth, were last seen going into the La Langosta restaurant, in Guadalajara. Quintero was hosting a dinner party in the restaurant that night. According to evidence obtained by Enrique Alvarez del Castillo, governor of the Jalisco State of which Guadalajara forms part, Quintero and his party thought the two Americans were Drug Enforcement agents and killed them. Their bodies have never been found. Also under investigation is the disappearance in December, 1984, of four American Jehovah's Witnesses. American officials in Mexico believe the four, who were making the traditional house to house visits to obtain converts, might also have been suspected by traffickers of being Drug Enforcement agents.

Although his arrest has curbed Quintero's activities, the Herrera family continues to operate and to profit hugely. While it is impossible for either Mexican or American officials to assess the Herrera wealth, they are believed to control banks, hotels and cattle ranches, their entire empire built upon the profit from heroin. Recognising the power of that wealth, in 1983 the then US Attorney General, William French Smith, conceded that pursuit of the traffickers, rather than crop eradication, might be a better focus for the Mexican and American authorities.

A month after the slaying of Salazar and Avelar, the Mexicans mounted a public relations exercise to show the intensity of their activities, flying journalists over an area of Sinaloa to see defoliant sprayed over supposed marijuana and poppy crops.

The purity of Mexican Mud seized on the West Coast is rising. In 1983 it was from 40 per cent to 60 per cent, compared to the 25 per cent to 30 per cent of the previous year. And Drug Enforcement officials estimated that Mexican heroin now accounts for no more than 35 per cent of the American trade. Which was roughly what it had been when Nixon began his efforts to curb supplies from Mexico, way back in 1969.

Nixon did not limit his efforts to Mexico. Indeed, there was a hiatus after the initial efforts of Kliendienst and Operation Intercept because the president determined he could achieve more dramatic and more immediate results by demanding that Turkey completely ban its poppy production. It was because of this plan that he was unfairly accused of inventing a heroin problem.

Afyon, in the Turkish province of Anatolia, actually means opium. For centuries the poppy grown in Afyon, from which the sticky gum is extracted after the unripened pod has been slit open, sustained a way of life for the peasants living there. And only since the extraction of morphine, codeine and finally heroin in the 1880s did that gum change the attitude towards the flower. Before that the cooking oil – obtained from the seed – mattered more. The husks provided food for animals. The leaves could be eaten and the stalks used for fuel. The gum also had its uses, of course. No one quite knew the reason, but it was good for illness, particularly pain. Women in childbirth frequently chewed it.

Priorities changed when the active principles were scientifically extracted. By Turkish law, farmers had to sell their opium to the government at fixed prices, for resale to the world's pharmaceutical outlets. Not all of it was actually handed over for the legitimate market, but when Nixon made his demands in 1971, the amount of heroin reaching America from the plains of Afyon was nowhere near the White House claims of eighty per cent. And the Ad Hoc Cabinet Committee on Narcotics, yet another body created by President Nixon in his anti-narcotics campaign and chaired by national security adviser Henry Kissinger – who usually delegated the task to deputy General Alexander Haig – knew from statistics that Turkey was not responsible for such high amounts. India – still the world's largest legitimate producer, and from intelligence assessments a growing conduit and black-market source – Pakistan, and the Golden Triangle countries of Thailand, Burma and Laos were all producing more.

The advantage of Turkey was that it could be pressured by the threat of withdrawal of the aid and arms supply while the others could not. So success could be publicly seen to be achieved, if the pressure were successful.

At first it wasn't. The Nixon administration and the Department of State encountered the familiar problem of a country unable to understand why it was being asked to make sacrifices and abandon a centuries-old way of life in order to solve a problem in America, thousands of miles away. It was, Ankara reported initially, 'politically impossible': farmers were, after all, voters too. And there were five hundred thousand poppy-growing voters.

Nixon was determined to win his public victory and brought pressure to bear both through NATO and through the US ambassador to Turkey, William Handley. The situation changed early in 1971 as a result of a coup by a military regime anxious not to jeopardise America's military assistance. Handley reported back to the State Department at Foggy Bottom that the new government would ban poppy cultivation if the United States would compensate them for lost income and provide agricultural expertise to find replacement crops. In 1972 Nixon achieved his success

150

at the cost of $35,000,000 (£14,000,000) compensation and instructions on how to grow sunflowers and wheat.

Heroin supplies continued to enter America unabated.

Mexico – the first object of attack – actually increased its illicit production under Jaime Herrera-Navarez' direction to fill the Turkish vacuum, despite President Portillo's claims of success. And although the heroin being produced in the Golden Triangle countries was already feeding the habits of disillusioned troops in Vietnam, there was sufficient left over to make an impact on the American market as well.

The only positive result of the ban imposed upon Turkey was to create a shortage within America of legitimately produced codeine cough medicine. This became so serious that the American Medical Association demanded White House action and in 1974 the Office of Management and Budget, whose director Roy Ash was overseeing White House drug policy, actually asked India to increase its poppy production. Additionally, America decided to experiment by growing a poppy of its own – *papaver bracteatum* – to obtain thebaine, another important opioid, for cough medication.

This state of affairs was as ridiculous as it was illogical. In July 1974 the Turkish government of Bulent Ecevit lifted the 1972 ban. In immediate protest, America withdrew its recently appointed ambassador, William Macomber, and in the same month the US Senate passed a motion to suspend all economic and military assistance, including military credit sales, if Turkey failed to take adequate steps to prevent the re-establishment of its drug cultivation.

Turkey responded by introducing strict policing of the drug-producing areas and by imposing a law forbidding the collection of the opium gum from the poppy by the traditional method of lancing, which made it easy for some gum to be retained and channelled into the illicit market. Instead the poppies are harvested intact – technically known as poppy straw – and the morphine is extracted by the Turkish factory at Bolvadin.

By 1984 the Turkish authorities had authorised controlled

cultivation on just under 134,000 acres, although it was unlikely that all of this land would be used. If it were, the crop would represent about thirty-nine tons of morphine equivalent.

The threat of the US Senate was never invoked. And in practical terms – in that it barely reduced the amount of heroin exported to America in particular and the world in general – the Turkish ban was meaningless, apart from its political benefit to Richard Nixon. Nor have I found any evidence to support the claim that during the two-year suspension the addict population of America dropped by two hundred thousand.

What I have found is evidence that while it suspended its own poppy cultivation, Turkey – with its bridge across the Bosporus forming the gateway between Asia and Europe and with an established trail of traffickers – all the time remained, and is still, an open highway for the products of other production areas, significantly the Golden Crescent and the Golden Triangle.

9

Khun Sa is a warlord, the most powerful in Asia and one of the richest in history. Combining feudal practice with modern luxury, there are harems of concubines in his air-conditioned villas, along with colour television and swimming pools, all guarded by a five-thousand-strong army.

His kingdom is the Golden Triangle and Khun Sa is a millionaire many times over because the Golden Triangle produces sixty tons of heroin every year. There is a huge local demand for opium and heroin, but there is still twenty tons for the West, enough to flood the rest of the world's illegal market. But that would be bad business – volume depressing the prices – and Khun Sa is a warlord because of his ability as a businessman. So stockpiles are kept from those twenty tons in case of poor opium harvests, as in 1979 and 1980 when there was drought. He supplies Europe with fifty per cent of the crop he allocates for export, Hong Kong with thirty per cent, North America fifteen per cent, and Australia and New Zealand the remaining five per cent. Every year.

Khun Sa worries about the weather, because it can endanger the business through which he exercises personal control over eighty per cent of the narcotics in South-east Asia. There is no other danger.

Geographically the Triangle is bounded by the meandering Mae Sai and Mekong rivers at the point where the borders of Laos, Thailand and Burma meet, creating a virtually unpoliced territory of about seventy-five thousand square miles. It is an area of breathtaking beauty, of stream-ribboned mountains, their peaks shrouded in mist, and dense, brilliant green jungles. There are few roads, paths even. But the mountain people, the Shan, the Hmong and the Ahka, know how to travel, the fathers telling their sons who in turn tell their sons when it is time for them to learn. Tigers roam, although they are fewer now than they were. Elephant and buffalo, too. Near Chiang Mai, on the Thai side of the Triangle, is the royal palace of Phu Ping – without air-conditioning or colour television – where Thai King Bhumibol escapes from the heat of lowland Bangkok.

In so large an area there have, of course, been other warlords, like Lao Su, whom the Thai police claim to have shot dead in 1983, but who is in fact thought to have been killed by his own followers after a disagreement. But fifty-six-year-old Khun Sa – who also used the name Chang Chi-fu – is the most important.

He is well known to Washington, for varying reasons. He was once an intelligence source for the CIA. While trafficking, naturally. And in 1978 he made an open approach to President Carter's administration, proposing his own solution to America's increasing heroin problem. For $30,000,000 (£15,707,000) he promised, over a five-year period, to supply five hundred tons of opium direct, enough to manufacture fifty tons of heroin. Officials of the Drug Enforcement Administration successfully argued against the deal, rightly convinced that the size of his operation would enable Khun Sa to continue his illegal trafficking regardless. He only allows thirteen tons of heroin to leave the Triangle every year. And America only consumes a total of four tons – at most four and a half – from *every* source.

Khun Sa is of mixed parentage. His father was Chinese, a colonel in nationalist Chiang Kai-shek's Kuomintang army which fled south into Burma's northern Shan states after their 1949 defeat by the communists. His mother was Shan and Khun Sa's soldiers – whose long-ago and now forgotten purpose was to fight for the region's independence from Burma – are called the Shan United Army.

It was from General Li Wen-huan, a leading commander in the Kuomintang force, that the youthful Khun Sa learned the opium trade and its many and diverse advantages. Li's forces were financed, trained and armed by the CIA to report upon communist China. Which they did. But American-supplied weaponry and expertise also enabled them to create in northern Burma the virtually independent state to which the Shans aspired and to impose upon those same Shans a tax on the opium they traditionally trafficked across the borders in Thailand. The original Kuomintang army splintered into rivalling, squabbling factions but each one continued to use the opium traffic. And the existence of such a large number of factions meant that different departments of succeeding American administrators wasted valuable resources by involving themselves in conflicting, absurdly confusing alliances.

Until President Nixon's dramatic *rapprochement* in 1972, the communist government of Peking was the American enemy and the nationalists of Taiwan were the friends. In Washington Presidents Kennedy, Johnson and Nixon declared war on drugs, while in the lush, verdant jungles of the Golden Triangle the CIA supported the trafficking Kuomintang generals – who frequently retired to Taiwan – and the opium-growing peasants whom they formed into guerilla armies to combat the growing threat of communism. As the ageing Chinese nationalist officers departed for the villas in Taiwan they had purchased with their drug profits, Khun Sa rose through the command hierarchy, juggling drugs and the CIA with the ease of the experienced conjuror he had become.

The escalating American conflict in Vietnam added to the anomalies and created an unparalleled drug-abuse problem among a reluctant, disillusioned military, abetted by the North Vietnamese and Vietcong who used the addiction as a weapon. Statistics vary: I have been told by one source that one in ten servicemen used drugs in Vietnam and by another that the figure was one in seven. In 1972 and 1973 I often sat on the open-sided terrace of the French colonial Continental Hotel in Saigon – now Ho Chi Minh City – and watched sailors, soldiers and airmen stumble glazed-eyed and zombie-like up and down Tu Do, the main street, in drugged oblivion to any reality. On a flight across the South China Sea in 1972 I sat next to a weeping load sergeant whose addicted best friend had died the previous night from injecting not the heroin he believed the ampoule contained but battery acid substituted by the communists. In 1970, more Americans were evacuated from Vietnam for drug-related reasons than for war injuries.

Khun Sa used the addiction as well as the communists. And – despite his CIA links – against them. Believing that Khun Sa's forces – and those of the break-away groups – were suppressing the growth of the Burmese communist party in the north, the government in Rangoon allowed the warlord his undisputed fiefdom. In reality, however, Khun Sa was working *with* the communists, encouraging the expansion of the opium fields for the ever-eager Vietnam market. He was also urging the Thai growers to extend their activities. At the time, Laotian production was firmly under the control of an independent trafficker, Ouane Rattikone, Chief of Staff of the Laotian army, who was also supported by the CIA.

Along the border areas and across into Thailand, around the town of Chiang Mai, Khun Sa created refining laboratories. To guarantee the uninterrupted movement of the soldier-guarded mule-trains by which the drug was back-packed through the twisting mountain paths to the Thai capital of Bangkok, he enlisted the willing support of the notoriously corrupt Thai police. When drug enforcement agents raided a laboratory on the outskirts of Chiang Mai in July 1974, they found it managed by Police Lieutenant Colonel Sawai Pudharek, the deputy provincial commander, on behalf of a group of police colonels. Pudharek escaped during his trial the following year and is now managing another laboratory, this time for Khun Sa.

In Khun Sa's border laboratories the staff is predominantly Chinese, from the Swatow region of southern China,

156

and known – because of the difficult dialect they speak – as the Chiu-chow. The Chiu-chow also run laboratories in Bangkok and, through other Swatow émigrés with whom they maintain an almost Masonic secrecy, they have created financial outlets in Hong Kong.

In August 1983 an attempt was made to penetrate that financial organisation by the authorities in Hong Kong, where the Central Registry figure of 41,906 addicts is estimated to reflect only half the true figure of opium and heroin users. That month the island adopted legislation permitting law enforcement agencies to extract from financial institutions information about bank accounts, safe deposits or other property holdings they suspected to be held or created by drug traffickers. Financial institutions refusing to comply are liable to fine and their representatives or anyone else blocking the information may be punished by both fine and imprisonment.

Khun Sa – always the good businessman – always caters for his customers. Discovering in the early 1970s that the American addicts in Vietnam disliked the coarse No.3 – smoking heroin – he insisted upon improved purification from his Swatow chemists and produced a finer, whiter powder – No. 4 – that could either be smoked or injected. It was a good investment for the future. Which came in 1975, with the ending of the Vietnam conflict.

Like a good businessman, always able to adjust to new markets, Khun Sa was ready to switch outlets when the war ended and his American market went home. He simply sent his product after them. And he found new buyers as well, throughout Australia and New Zealand. As his business expanded, so the number of his laboratories increased. Several of them are situated around Chiang Mai, Chiang Rai, Mae Hong Son and Nan. Khun Sa built his favourite house in the same area, in the village of Ban Hin Taek, where a generator provided the electricity for his air-conditioning system and his video television. For the inhabitants of the village he built a basketball court and a swimming pool.

Ban Hin Taek is buttoned against the side of a valley of great beauty but it is not the beauty that attracts Khun Sa. The village is only five miles on horseback from the Burmese border, which is useful when the Thais attack, as they do occasionally, to act out – like the charade it is – their supposed allegiance to an American government which contributes $6,000,000 (£3,947,368) a year to their anti-narcotics efforts. Or to officials of the United Nations' Fund for Drug Abuse Control, which is trying to persuade the opium farmers to switch to alternative crops, such as kidney beans, potatoes and coffee.

The last attack upon Khun Sa's headquarters was in October 1982. Nearly 2000 Thai police and troops staged an assault with bombers and American-supplied helicopter gunships and OV10 counter-insurgency aircraft. It was no coincidence whatsoever that the assault was staged when the then US Attorney General, William French Smith, and Drug Enforcement Administrator, Francis Mullen, were in Bangkok, urging greater efforts at control. Khun Sa fled across the border, as he had done in the previous attack nine months earlier when a laboratory capable of producing 55 lb of heroin a day was discovered. During that raid 900 troops, supported again with air cover, seized 10 tons of weaponry – including 700 rifles and pistols, 25 grenade launchers, 300 hand grenades, 53,000 rounds of ammunition and bazookas – and 63,000 plastic bags for the packaging of heroin. They took the colour television, too. And killed 200 of Khun Sa's soldiers.

Khun Sa re-established himself near the Burmese village of Mong Young, controlled by the country's communist party. He is particularly safe there. The communists produce three-quarters of the Golden Triangle's heroin and use it to buy their weapons and ammunition, which they no longer get from communist China. Khun Sa has exclusive rights to sell their heroin for them and it is this connection which has prompted the Rangoon government to declare him an enemy. The regime of We Nin – whose son has trafficked – accepted American aid and claims to have destroyed fifty-five thousand acres of poppies. Using American-supplied Bell Huey helicopters, they also claim to have eliminated three of Khun Sa's refineries on the Burmese side of the border, but up to the time of writing Rangoon has not put its army into the field against Khun Sa's soldiers.

The intelligence report consensus among American and Thai drug enforcement officials is that Khun Sa pays about £1333 to £1666 for the raw opium which is refined in his laboratories into a kilogram – 2.2 lb – of heroin. In Bangkok that heroin, still pure, is retailed for £10,666. By the time it reaches America – either direct, by air, but more likely via Europe and the Mafia laboratories in Sicily – the wholesale price for an undiluted shipment averages £133,300. It is then cut, with lactose, quinine, talcum powder and strychnine or even brick dust, on an average of six times on its way through the chain of dealers to the street. And there Khun Sa's original – but now much expanded – kilo sells for £1,530,000.

According to the most reliable intelligence reports, Khun Sa has returned to Ban Hin Taek, where he operates on the rigid, life-or-death rules expected of a warlord. A Thai government informant he suspected of leading troops to him in the first attack in 1982 was buried alive as an example to other villagers. Another was hanged, drawn and quartered in the main street. And when US Drug Enforcement officials offered a $25,000 (£10,775) reward for his capture in 1980, Khun Sa in turn offered bounties for any Americans killed in the Golden Triangle he regards as his own territory. Shortly afterwards the wife of United States Drug Enforcement agent Michael Powers was shot dead in the main street of Chiang Mai and Washington immediately ordered twenty American wives and children back to the safety of Bangkok.

Thailand has an incentive to move against Khun Sa and his opium growers with more vigour than it has so far shown: in a country with a population of forty-eight million it has six hundred thousand addicts, a higher proportion than the United States, and only seventy-one over-worked treatment centres. Bangkok's argument for not doing more is that the majority of the opium is not grown in Thailand at all, but across the border in Laos and Burma, over which they have no control. Certainly there is incontrovertible evidence of both extensive production and addiction in Burma: while there are thirty-eight thousand addicts officially listed on a government-maintained register, of whom thirty thousand are dependent upon opium and eight thousand upon heroin, I have been assured by Asian narcotic experts that Burma's addict population is actually nearer sixty thousand. Treatment facilities exist in twenty hospitals but a recent United Nations survey reported, 'These facilities are far from adequate and there is a high rate of relapse among persons treated.' More centres are planned by the Rangoon government.

Khun Sa and his communist supporters have devised enforcement-defeating routes to bring the chemicals necessary to refine heroin from its base into their border laboratories. When the Thais banned the essential precursor, acetic anhydride, Khun Sa switched from land delivery to the inland Burmese waterway system. A Western intelligence agency with excellent sources in the region has assured me that within the area controlled by Khun Sa there exists – along with his heroin stockpile – an acetic anhydride dump sufficient for a year's processing.

That same source estimated that 85 per cent of the Golden Triangle's opium – and therefore heroin – originates from Burma. The principal growing areas are the Shan and Kachin States, with the most intensive cultivation east of the Salween River and north of Keng Tung. In 1978–9 it is estimated that between 95 and 100 tons of opium – which would convert into a maximum of 10 tons of heroin – was produced in Burma. By 1983, the Burmese production of 500 tons was sufficient for 50 tons of heroin. Throughout 1982 and 1983 the Rangoon government destroyed about 14,700 acres of poppy fields. None, however, was in the regions controlled by the 20,000-strong army of the Burmese Communist Party and its benefactor, Khun Sa.

In a campaign designed to highlight their drive against narcotics, the Thais have passed a law imposing the death penalty for trafficking – as have Malaysia, Singapore and the Philippines – in addition to putting acetic anhydride on the same banned list as heroin. The strongest complaint in Washington is the slowness – one official called it refusal – with which the Thais are moving with their declared policy of destroying opium plantations. Dominick DiCarlo, Assistant US Secretary of State for International Narcotics Matters, a post which was created in 1972, is openly critical of the fact that the Thais have only attacked fields in ten of the three hundred villages where poppy is the crop. The Thai response to that criticism yet again echoes irritation at American interference and misunderstanding of conditions in another country.

Major General Chavalit Yodmani, Secretary General of Thailand's Narcotics Board, dismisses DiCarlo's criticism for a number of reasons. One of them is that at least fifteen thousand of the one hundred thousand hill tribesmen are opium addicts who need the poppy crop. Another is that even those who aren't addicted need it to survive, unless they are provided with an alternative income from a crop substitute, a crop that could just as easily be transported to market. Heroin is a small-volume, high-value product, easily transportable through the trackless jungles on the backs of mules. To secure a comparable return from another crop, the peasants would need lorries to carry their kidney beans or potatoes along paved, multi-laned high-ways to the towns.

There is a further problem. The Bangkok government are nervously aware of the strongly organised and motivated communist party in Burma among whom Khun Sa hides when he is attacked. And they are frightened that the communists will ship the philosophy of revolution as well as drugs across the border to tribesmen who have grown opium for centuries, don't know or care where Washington or London or Paris is, and would regard crop destruction, even with the compensation of paved roads, not as part of an international effort to curb drugs but as an attempt by central government to annihilate them. It is a message that Khun Sa is already encouraging. And the hill tribesmen – whose language isn't even Thai – believe Khun Sa, who has provided them with a living for twenty-five years, much more readily than they believe a far-away Bangkok government.

Frequently the irrigation advice they have accepted from well-intentioned United Nations agronomists has been utilised to improve the watering of their opium fields.

On Khun Sa's orders.

There are in the world three communist countries whose governments actively engage in narcotics trafficking. The biggest of these – because it is also a producer – is the closed, Pathet Lao-controlled nation of Laos. Khun Sa has good relations with Pathet Lao, as he has with the communists of Burma, and much of the Laotian heroin trade is channelled through his hands. But there are other major traffickers. One leading figure is Poonsiri Chanyasak, a drug fugitive from Bangkok who has travelled extensively in the Far East on a diplomatic passport, issued in the name of his adopted pseudonym, Thao Sethahirath, by the current Vientiane government. Poonsiri's chief associate is Iem Norasing, a flamboyant figure who drives around the capital in an imported American Ford Mustang. He runs the BGL brewery in Vientiane and a detergent factory on the Tha Deua highway, near the ferry crossing-point to Nong Khai in Thailand. Both businesses are state-owned, which brings Norasing under the control of the Ministry of Trade and Industry. In October 1977 that Ministry granted Norasing the licence to import acetic anhydride into the country.

Laos is an irrelevant signatory to international legislation which requires it to submit yearly returns of its opium production to the United Nations International Narcotics Control Board. It does not do so. Almost pathetically, the Narcotics Control Board in its most current review of the world drug situation says in a three-line entry, 'Seizure data abroad would indicate availability of opium and cannabis in the country. The Board would welcome renewal of the dialogue begun with the government several years ago.'

Vientiane says glibly that it is allowing opium poppy cultivation 'to supply the requirements of bona fide pharmaceutical industries', but gives no indication or even hint of the extent of that officially approved cultivation. International monitoring bodies estimate that Laos produces seventy-five tons of opium a year, which would refine down to seven and a half tons of heroin. The samples intercepted – No. 3 and No. 4 – have a high and therefore dangerous acid residue from the refining process employed.

Laos has known the value of opium since colonisation by the French in 1954 when the business was controlled by Regie de l'Opium, a state monopoly whose tax upon the product was one of the most important sources of income for the exchequer. In 1970 the Minister of Finance of the time, Sisouk na Champassak, told the British Broadcasting Corporation, 'The only export we can develop is opium and therefore we should increase its production and export.'

The Vietnam War fuelled not only increased production but increased export as well, and once again – amazingly – the higher demands were met with the connivance of the CIA. The finding of a later Congressional enquiry – that the Agency's involvement and awareness were minimal – is nonsense. The biggest Laotian producer during the Vietnam War was a Chiu-chow Chinese named Huu Tim Heng, holder of the American Pepsi Cola and Esso franchises in the capital, Vientiane. His stroke of genius was to make General Ouane Rattikone, the Army Chief of Staff, an equal partner. Rattikone – the holder of his country's highest decoration, the Grand Cross of a Million Elephants and the White Parasol – cultivated his contacts with senior officers in the South Vietnamese army and developed a direct trafficking chain to feed the habits of Americans who were supposed to be their allies.

The American military alliance in Laos was covert,

which is how the CIA became involved. Succeeding American presidents from Kennedy onwards refused to consider the placing of American military personnel in Laos: they decided instead that the CIA should be responsible for moulding the opium-growing Meo tribesmen into an effective, anti-communist army. The commander of the Meo forces on the Plain of Jars was an infamously corrupt general named Vang Pao, who made a fortune even before his involvement in narcotics by pocketing the American-financed salaries he should have passed on to his Meo mercenaries. Vang Pao saw advantages ahead of his superior, General Rattikone, and Huu Tim Heng in joining forces with the CIA. From his headquarters at Padong, Vang Pao and his American advisers criss-crossed the opium-growing lands of Laos as far north as Phou Fa and eastwards to Bouam Long, and by 1964 – long before the height of American involvement in Vietnam – Vang Pao captured Sam Neua province.

Wherever his influence was established – and at the height of Vang Pao's operations his influence was enormous – he convinced the CIA and their cover airline, Air America, of the need for airstrips, ostensibly to provide rice and supplies to the loyal Meos but in reality to create a means of transport for their opium. At one time there were twenty-three landing strips carved out of mountains and lowlands.

Air America wasn't the only airline using them. Corsican traffickers who had traded during the French colonisation of the country also took advantage of the improved communication facilities in small, short-hop aircraft. The CIA realised what was going on but they needed the Meos and the Meos needed their opium income. And so the Americans turned their backs and allowed their strips to be used, without landing fees. Their involvement was – briefly – even more firmly established after 1965, when the Laotian government stopped the Corsican flights because insufficient bribes had been paid. As rice and other foodstuffs *had* been landed at the airstrips, the Meos had grown opium on their vegetable plots, under pressure from Vang Pao and Ratti-kone. That additional opium had to be transported to market and Air America flew it to Vientiane and to Long Cheng where the Agency had established its Laotian headquarters.

This direct involvement, however, concerned CIA chiefs at Langley, Virginia, who determined to distance the Agency from such provable trafficking activities. To do this the CIA and the United States Agency for International Development financed Vang Pao in the creation of his own airline, which became known as Xieng Khouang Air Transport. Its aircraft – two C47s – were provided by Air America and Continental Air Services, both CIA front airlines. Vang Pao's airline probably had the most restricted route in the world, then or since: shuttling between Long Cheng and Vientiane. Not that Vang Pao wanted anything more extensive. The sole purpose, after all, was the transportation of raw opium or heroin to the heroin factory in the 555 cigarette factory in Vientiane, and he was now able to operate in a way that enabled the CIA to disclaim all knowledge of the business. Vang Pao and Ouane Rattikone had five halcyon years – years in which they made millions feeding drugs to Americans across the border in Vietnam – before the Pathet Lao became organised and crushed the Meos and government forces, both of which America abandoned as part of President Nixon's determination to achieve peace with honour in Asia.

The political philosophy of Laos may have changed, but other things have remained unaltered. The favourite product of Rattikone, Tim Heng and Vang Pao from their cigarette factory laboratory was a No. 4 heroin sold under the brand name Double U-O Globe, guaranteed one hundred per cent pure and showing the motif, rather appropriately, of two lions arguing over a globe of the world. On 20 October 1980 – a full five years after the communist take-over – a car was involved in an accident in the Thai river town of Nong Khai, just after the ferry had arrived from Vientiane. In the car was found seventeen and a half pounds of Double U-O Globe heroin.

One month later the Laotian government were invited by Thai anti-narcotic organisations to a meeting in Chiang Mai to plan interception strategy. Vientiane did not send a delegation. The problem of drug addiction, they said, belonged to the wealthy nations of the West; they had no interest or concern.

The Pathet Lao did, however, move against Poonsiri. Or appeared to do so. The Thai renegade, who built up a network of drug outlets throughout Asia, America and Europe from the Honey Club in Bangkok, established a business called Tasita Imports Ltd in rue Sethahirath in central Vientiane, selling tractors and heavy machinery. In January 1981 he was charged with bribery and smuggling goods – although not heroin – from Thailand. There was, however, no trial. At the time of writing Tasita Imports continues to operate although Poonsiri is less in evidence. Norasing, his chief assistant and the man with the right to import acetic anhydride, is still driving his Mustang around the streets of the capital.

There is no doubt among the enforcement community in neighbouring Thailand that Poonsiri's arrest – like the attack upon Khun Sa's headquarters when important Americans were in town – was a cosmetic gesture. Immigration authorities have been asked to look out for someone travelling on a diplomatic passport in the name of Sethahirath, cynically taken from the street in which he established his heroin-manufacturing company.

The 'watch list' request is another cosmetic gesture, with the make-up smudged. Poonsiri is still travelling throughout Asia, although not on the Vientiane passport issued in the name of Thao Sethahirath. Enforcement agencies from four countries are attempting to discover the fresh pseudonym on his new, official Laotian passport.

Because of its geographical location Malaysia is a major trafficking crossroads and a nation with a correspondingly serious internal narcotics problem: seventy thousand people are listed on a centralised record as being drug dependent, the majority of whom are heroin users under thirty-five years of age. I am assured that ninety-three thousand is a more accurate figure and includes extensive cannabis and psychotropic substance abuse.

In an effort to combat what was described to me by one spokesman as an epidemic, the Malaysian government have declared that treatment is compulsory and established nine detoxification centres and four institutional treatment centres: by the end of 1984 they hoped to have made nine thousand beds available for in-patients.

Acetic anhydride is banned, but despite the prohibition it continues to be smuggled in either overland or by sea. There are also indications of warlords attempting to establish themselves in the pattern of Khun Sa, to the north.

Singapore likes to think of itself as the shining pearl in a muddied Asian sea, a conveniently small island community with a personally fastidious ruler in Lee Kuan Yew and a swingeing statute book that has eradicated drug abuse within the country.

A pivot in the Asian trafficking syndicates during the Vietnam era, and later for a major Australian-based ring, internal heroin abuse has now been controlled. Rehabilitation centres with a four-thousand-bed capacity have been established and medically diagnosed abusers are compulsorily detained within them for a minimum initial period of six months – detoxification is always 'cold turkey', with no medicinal aids – with the state having the legal right to extend that incarceration to thirty-six months. Aftercare supervision from treatment centres ranges from two to four years and includes regular but random urine tests, to detect relapse. Up to the beginning of 1984, twelve traffickers – one a woman – had been hanged since the death penalty for drug dealing was introduced into the Misuse of Drugs Act of 1975. The legal definition of a trafficker is anyone arrested with more than 231 grains of heroin or 201 grains of marijuana in their possession.

The crackdown has achieved impressive results but

Singapore is still not the drug-free haven it would like to appear. There is irrefutable evidence of widespread cannabis abuse and, as the government's convincing stranglehold on heroin tightened, a number of addicts who escaped the round-up net (the codename for the addict sweep was Operation Ferret) turned to the pills that were readily available, the psychotropics. The government has now introduced computer monitoring of prescriptions in an effort to control psychotropics as successfully as they have come to control heroin.

Singapore's anti-narcotics campaign has certainly proved more effective than similar campaigns in other parts of Asia where enforcement efforts are a disaster. As one enforcement official said to me, 'What's the point of attempting control when so much is uncontrollable!'

Control *is* being attempted, but by the Yakuza. They even want to put people like Khun Sa out of business.

10

Enforcement officials – particularly the front-line US Customs Service – have produced a series of recognisable profiles in order to identify and intercept drug runners. It is a system that works particularly well with the Yakuza because of the bizarre but rigid code of ethics by which the Japanese Mafia conducts itself, quite different from any other criminal society in the world. It concerns fingers, or rather the lack of them. And tattoos. All-over tattoos. These provide clues to recognition that the authorities pursue relentlessly because of the growing belief throughout American and European control agencies that the Yakuza have the potential to take over and run the entire South-east Asian drug distribution network.

So concerned was William French Smith that he included Japan in a trip to the drug-producing countries in the Far East and persuaded the Tokyo government to explore with Washington a mutual assistance treaty to complement an already existing extradition agreement concluded in 1980. He felt the visit was necessary because intelligence reports had provided evidence that the Yakuza were already involved in trafficking in Hawaii and California and on parts of the US western seaboard, and on his return to the American capital he told politicians that they wanted to crush the growth, before it spread any further. One enforcement executive told me, 'The Yakuza are so strongly controlled and regimented it almost makes a joke of the Sicilian Mafia's code of silence, *Omerta*. If the Japanese get control of the market, it'll be a disaster.' Which is why missing fingers are useful.

Japanese authorities estimate there are a total of 2,300 Yakuza gangs throughout Japan and that their narcotics income is $2,000,000,000 (£1,666,000,000) a year.

There are families in the Yakuza, just as there are in the original Mafia. The biggest is the Yamaguchi-gumi, based in Kobe. Until January 1985, Godfather of the Yamaguchi-gumi, which controls ninety-two gangs throughout Southern and Western Japan, was thick-set Masahisa Takenaka. It took him three years to achieve the role, following the death in 1981 of the previous 'don', Fumiko Taoka. During that time, twenty people died in gangland slayings, and throughout the acting head of the Yamaguchi-gumi was Hiroshi Yamamoto. Angered at being passed over, Yamamoto called a press conference to announce his split from the Yamaguchi-gumi, to form a rival family, the Ichiwa-kai. Six thousand mobsters followed Yamamoto and police readied themselves for a fresh outbreak of gang warfare. It started on January 26, 1985, when Takenaka was gunned down at the home of his mistress, in a suburb of Osaka. Killed with him were two bodyguards. In the weeks that followed, eight Ichiwa gangsters were killed and twelve seriously wounded in a series of retaliatory gunfights. Fighting back, the Ichiwa killed three more Yamaguchi soldiers. At the time of writing police have identified fifty separate shooting incidents involving the two warring families and expect more killings until the leadership role is filled.

Another prominent family is the Matsuda-gumi. The Sumiyoshi-Rengo and the Inagawar-kai are headquartered in Tokyo. Each of the cells is controlled by an *oyabun*, a godfather to whom the soldiers of *kobun* belong. It's the *kobun* who lose fingers, the penalty for any mistake or infringement of the Yakuza law.

The amputation is fittingly ritualistic. The offending *kobun* squats bow-headed before his *oyabun* and spreads between them a square of silk the size of a handkerchief. He then lays upon the silk whichever hand he has chosen to mutilate. In the other he holds a short-bladed samurai knife. He has to sever his finger at the first joint in one sweep, showing no sign of pain, then wrap the sacrificial finger in the silk and formally offer it to his godfather. If the *oyabun* accepts it, the offence is expunged. If not, the *kobun* is expected to make the sacrifice of suicide.

The finger-severing is not the only eccentric ritual performed by the Yakuza. Another – which applies to all of them – is complete body-tattooing, the covering of the skin with a series of formalised patterns which have specific connotations within the secret society. The patterning always finishes at a line around the neck, high on the arms and sufficiently high on the legs so that normal clothing conceals the tattooing from the uninitiated. However, when a Yakuza is naked it's actually difficult to tell that he is unclothed.

Japan's second largest city, Osaka, has the highest concentration of Yakuza-organised crime groups, an estimated three hundred. Sixty-three per cent of all Yakuza income is generated by drugs, predominantly methamphetamine and amphetamines, although increasing amounts of heroin are being imported from the Golden Triangle. South Korea and Taiwan supply the stimulants.

Throughout Japan the Yakuza have successfully cultivated a Robin Hood imagery and Japanese authorities try hard to undermine the mystique, rejecting the favoured title 'Yakuza' for the more demeaning 'Boroyokudan'. The titles are taken from a popular card game, an Eastern version of blackjack or pontoon. The target score is twenty-one, known as 'good for nothing'. The government's efforts to show the Yakuza as good for nothings have only had limited success. They have had greater – but far from total – success at combating drug addiction within the country.

In the years following the war, Japan experienced an outbreak of methamphetamine abuse which analysts have described to me as an epidemic: between 1945 and 1955 it is estimated that more than two million Japanese became addicted. An unambivalent policy was enshrined in the Stimulants Control Law of 1963, which made clear the official attitude that the user was as great a threat as the supplier because he created the initial demand. Possession of narcotics carried a maximum sentence of seven years, while possession or use of stimulants or marijuana could be punished by five years in jail. That law is still valid today: the conviction rate for drug offences is estimated at ninety-nine per cent and courts rarely, if ever, allow suspended sentences. Foreigners are liable to equally stringent punishments. In January 1980 Paul McCartney spent ten days in a Tokyo jail after being arrested with a small quantity of marijuana in his possession and his release was conditional upon 'immediate deportation'. Eleven Wings concerts had to be cancelled.

Japan's first anti-drug law – in 1870 – decreed decapitation with a samurai sword as the punishment for trafficking and the government today still fights a vigorous campaign against drug abuse. It is highly critical of other countries' more lenient attitudes towards sentencing – particularly in America – and vacillating policy changes in their campaigns, concentrating sometimes on the users, sometimes on the suppliers.

Under existing Japanese legislation, a life sentence is possible for trafficking in heroin and every user arrested is confined for a minimum of thirty days for treatment. Methadone is available but is rarely employed by doctors because the Japanese believe that methadone maintenance is simply another form of drug addiction. They prefer to prescribe unaided abstinence – 'cold turkey' – as do some Western doctors.

An official with long experience of the Japanese response to drug abuse and trafficking said, 'Their greatest success has been in the consistency of their attitude, compared to other nations. The greatest fear is that the official determination to eradicate the problem of drug addiction is matched by the Yakuza's determination to expand what is already their most lucrative source of income. If they get control of the Golden Triangle, God help us!'

Further cause for alarm is the fact that the Golden Triangle is no longer the world's major supplier of heroin. That comes from the Golden Crescent.

172

11

The bazaar of Landi Kotal is a muted place, certainly by Asian standards. There are the few inevitable spice stalls, tatty, dried-out places. Guns are popular, as they always have been, some exquisitely filagreed and ornamented, others still grease-packed from the Czech factories, and they quickly sell across the border. Battery-driven video cassettes are also there, seemingly incongruous. But it is difficult to find anyone selling the expected colour-blazed silks or intricately woven shawls and it is strangely quiet, with few traders shouting to advertise their wares. They don't have to, not in Landi Kotal. Every customer knows the principal merchandise of this bazaar is ninety per cent pure heroin, cellophane-wrapped and laid out openly for inspection and purchase.

Landi Kotal is the sun-bleached gateway through the Khyber Pass, that tortuous thread of uncertain road etched into the mountains linking Kabul, in Afghanistan, with Peshawar, the provincial capital of Pakistan's north-west frontier. Geographically, Landi Kotal is part of Pakistan but it is not in fact governed by Peshawar. Nor by the national capital, Islamabad. There is no accepted law in Landi Kotal: no police force or station or court. And the Khyber Rifles know their place, which is inside the preserved Beau Geste fort from which the British once governed the area, albeit tenuously. For the Pathan tribesmen – the Afridas, the Khatake, the Wazirs, the Orakzais, the Bangash, the Turis and the Mahsuds – the gun rules Landi Kotal. As it always did, even under British rule. And before the gun it was the sword.

173

The independence of the Pathan tribesmen is officially recognised in a Solomon-like judgement from central government. Islamabad claims ownership and control of the main roads in the area while everything else – including the land through which those few roads run – is controlled by the tribesmen.

During his 1982 tour of the drug-producing areas of Asia, French Smith was determined to get as near to source as possible, and in November of that year he visited Landi Kotal, wanting to see the half-subterranean bazaar and maybe even one of the heroin-refining laboratories. Massive security was arranged but there had been insufficient discussion with the local tribal elders and the American group – which included Drug Enforcement chief Francis Mullen and Dominick Di-Carlo – were actually on their way into the town when the Pakistani authorities realised their mistake. They realised, too, that there was going to be shooting but before it could break out the trip was hurriedly curtailed and French Smith and his party were bustled away to safety. He never managed to see a laboratory.

There exist between America and the military government of Pakistan's General Zia a number of security and assistance programmes, some dating back as far as 1976. The total value of the US aid is $3,200,000,000 (£2,130,000,000) but the opium poppy-growing areas are contractually precluded from receiving assistance unless they undertake to eradicate the crops. During meetings between the Pakistani leader and President Reagan it was made clear to General Zia that in return for the subsidy, the Pakistani authorities were expected to achieve positive results in cutting the flow of drugs to the West. Officials from the Bureau of the Secretary of State for International Narcotics Matters assured me that substantial eradication was being achieved in Gadoon-Amazii, Malakand and Bunair. Working this time *with* tribal elders, in 1982 and 1983 the Pakistan government closed down forty-one processing plants, although others opened soon afterwards despite the tribal leaders' agreement not to allow replacements.

As an estimated seventy-five tons of opium were produced on the Pakistani side of the border region during 1983, it is hardly surprising that the local tribes were reluctant to relinquish control. Then, in order to impress Washington further, Pakistan arrested Sheik Jumor, a thirty-eight-year-old Pathan drug king, with contacts throughout the West, who was running six of the newly created laboratories. Officials in Peshawar jailed him for three years on narcotics charges.

In February 1985, Pakistan police arrested at his mansion in Karachi an international trafficker, Mustaq Malik. Through his dealings which stretched back to 1975, Malik had become a billionaire and was only arrested by the Pakistani authorities on information from London, where his courier associates were arrested and jailed after British Customs intercepted and smashed a £20,000,000 ($23,000,000) heroin smuggling attempt.

Still free in Pakistan – although with an arrest warrant outstanding against him – is millionaire trafficker Zulfikar Choudhry.

The limited success with eradication in Pakistan is completely nullified by the cultivation across the border in Afghanistan, which has been totally unpoliced and uncontrolled since the 1979 Soviet invasion: in the last growing period of 1984 an estimated five hundred and fifty tons of opium was produced.

International enforcement agencies fear that definite links have been forged with some London criminals and extend beyond London to New York, to the ever-active Gambino Family. It has also been established that heroin and morphine base are being smuggled to Mafia families in Sicily via Turkey. Again the Gambino Family are involved.

In Maryland, on the outskirts of New York, and at Aldermaston in the English county of Berkshire, there are forensic laboratories whose scientists can identify the source countries of heroin. From the analysis of drugs seized, Washington estimates that 60 per cent of heroin entering the United States comes from the area extending across the border into Afghanistan and Iran but controlled by Landi

Kotal. Research at Aldermaston suggests that the figure for Europe is as high as 90 per cent. Which means that the majority of America's 492,000 addicts are dependent on drugs exported from a mountain eyrie township most have never heard of. The same applies to Italy's 150,000 addicts, West Germany's 62,000, and the 66,000 British addicts. The same source supplies Iran where, despite the invariable death sentence passed upon traffickers by Ayatollah Khomeini's government, the minimum dependent addict population is estimated as 1,500,000 against other assessments of 4,000,000. Landi Kotal also caters for the needs of Pakistan's 450,000 opium users and 30,000 heroin addicts. And Afghanistan's 100,000 users.

India, the world's largest supplier of licit opium, is causing Western intelligence agencies increasing anxiety because seizures during 1983 indicate not only that the country is developing into an illegal producer as well, but that it is increasingly becoming a transit route for opium from both South-west and South-east Asia. During the first nine months of 1983 almost one and a half tons of opium were seized crossing India's north-western border. The chief source of concern is the huge stockpile of opium – sufficient for a hundred tons of heroin – at the government-run factory at Neemuch, in Madhya Pradesh, much of which could easily be diverted on to the black market. And during 1982, two clandestine laboratories were seized, one at Lucknow and the other in Varanasi, in Upper Pradesh. Both were manufacturing morphine from opium supplied not from within the country but from Pakistan.

It is not only the West and the immediate source countries which are being affected by the opium of the Golden Crescent. Like the American troops in Vietnam, the Russians are turning to drugs through disillusionment with their Asian involvement.

Surveillance of Eastern-bloc drug abuse is maintained from Vienna and I spent a day there discussing the addiction problems of Soviet troops with a number of officials, some of whom had spent time in Kabul. From the debriefing of Soviet defectors and clandestine contact with the mujahideen, the guerillas who oppose the Russian occupation, there is evidence that the Afghan fighters are fully exploiting their opium and marijuana crops. They have so successfully cultivated a drug habit among Soviet soldiers that Moscow – like Washington almost a decade before – has in some cases cut to nine months the period their military personnel are stationed in Afghanistan in an effort to reduce addiction. Intelligence officials report, however, that this abrupt turn-around policy is insufficient to prevent contamination and even exacerbates the problem by accelerating the return to Russia of a growing number of addicts, thus creating a demand upon the streets of Kiev, Leningrad and Moscow. I have also been told by a number of individuals that the extent of Soviet addiction in Afghanistan is such that it is not uncommon for Russian soldiers or airmen to negotiate the exchange of ammunition for drugs with the very people they are supposed to be fighting. One official said, 'The Afghan rebels are increasingly fighting the Soviets with weaponry every bit as good as the Russians'.' Sometimes better. The Russians neglect their guns. Having had the importance of a gun bred into them, the local population never do.

Marijuana is more prevalent than heroin or opium, although methaqualone is also in plentiful supply and widely abused. The heroin is more usually smoked – as is the indigenous way of Pakistan and Iran – than it is injected. So close to source, it is of an extremely high purity, normally sixty per cent but sometimes even as high as ninety per cent.

Like Chiang Mai in the Golden Triangle, Landi Kotal forms the fulcrum for the Golden Crescent. There are, in fact, a number of parallels between the two: for instance, the Golden Crescent is composed not just of one country – Pakistan – but areas of Afghanistan and Iran as well, arcing into the crescent that gives it its name through seven autonomous regions in a three-hundred-and-fifty-mile-long, eighty-mile-wide mountain belt. Two million people live there.

For the Golden Crescent, 1979 was a year of many changes.

It was the year in which Pakistan's President Zia banned opium production by the Hadd Order, although this was a gesture more rhetorical than practical. It was the year the Soviet Union invaded Afghanistan. It was the year the Ayatollah Khomeini overthrew the Shah, and the American embassy in Tehran was seized, putting an end to any US check on narcotics in the country.

And the combined opium production of the Golden Crescent countries was 1600 tons. That output was sufficient to manufacture 160 tons of heroin, more than any other growing area has ever produced in one year in its history; more, in fact, than the combined Golden Triangle, Mexico and Turkey have managed in one year.

The oversight agencies hoped that the Russian incursion would disrupt the cultivation potential of at least the Afghan part of the Crescent – which it did, because opium-growing is labour intensive and the defending Afghans had insufficient time to devote to their poppy fields – but the surplus from the 1979 harvest compensated for the shortfall. And that surplus – easily smuggled, easily transported – also provided the basis for a new life for the thousands who fled to the West following the demise of the Shah. And a different kind of escape for those who didn't choose to run.

Opium has been cultivated and used in Iran since the eleventh century. From then on feudal landowners were responsible for the crop until the Pahlavi dynasty seized the country in 1924 and imposed a government monopoly over cultivation and production, channelling the profits to the exchequer. Despite half-hearted attempts at control, addiction in Iran increased faster than in any other country of the world, until in 1955 the government introduced a total ban on poppy cultivation. This gave rise to the development of the smuggling routes so well trodden today, from Afghanistan and Pakistan and from Turkey, but did nothing, predictably, to curb or even control addiction.

In 1969 the last Shah re-introduced limited cultivation, in open recognition of his country's addiction problem. That was not, however, the only reason. The farmers were obliged to sell their crops to the government, ostensibly for medical use as well as for use by addicts, thus directing the profits from the cultivation into the exchequer of the Pahlavi family, who doubly benefited by having interests in the poppy fields. To assert government control still further, anyone caught illegally trafficking was liable to punishment by death.

Six hundred of the 1600 tons produced in the Golden Crescent in the year of the Shah's overthrow were estimated to have come from the government-controlled fields. That control disintegrated completely in the immediate aftermath of the Ayatollah's return to Tehran and has not been re-established, despite the large number – at least seven hundred – of executions for trafficking and the re-introduction of the cultivation ban, exempting only sufficient opium to meet the needs of the country's addicts.

A Canadian intelligence source estimated that Iran produced another six-hundred-ton opium crop in 1982. The United Nations International Narcotics Control Board learned that in August 1983, one ton of opium and more than one ton of morphine – both produced in Iran and both of eight-five per cent purity – were seized on the eastern border of the country.

The production of opium in Afghanistan is illegal, as it is supposed to be in Pakistan and Iran, but the prohibition is as meaningless as it is elsewhere. And after the setbacks of 1980 the farmers have returned to the valley-gouged area where the Himalayan Mountains merge into the Hindu Kush and are growing more actively than ever. The 1983 opium crop was expected to be in the region of three hundred tons, well up to the previous best production figures and sufficient for thirty tons of heroin. And there is no indication that the stockpiled reserves of 1979 have yet been exhausted.

Since 1979 heroin-refining techniques have become more sophisticated. Chinese chemists are now known to be working in the Landi Kotal area and in laboratories in another nearby bazaar town, Dera. Their improved efficiency is indicated in figures produced by the US Drug Enforcement Administration which showed that in 1981 – the first year that the Chinese are believed to have been fully established – eighty-eight per cent of the twelve hundredweight of heroin seized in Europe came from the Golden Crescent.

As in the Golden Triangle, the United Nations are trying to introduce a crop-substitution programme and part of the American aid package of $3,200,000,000 has been set aside for this purpose. But apart from the improved irrigation techniques which have been implemented, there is little incentive for the Crescent farmers to change from high-paying opium to low-paying wheat and maize. Particularly when any farmer who considers changing is under threat of death from the Pathan tribal elders to whom Islamabad already cedes positive autonomy.

Like the Bangkok government, General Zia has good reason to worry about the independence of his border tribesmen: perhaps more so. Divided over almost everything else, the Pathan tribes are united in their wish for continuing separation from Islamabad, to the point of regarding Peshawar as their capital. Zia knows well the nationalistic independence, as well as he knows that while the tribesmen would never become vassals or clients of the Soviet Union, they might consider asking for help if Moscow promised to show them the way to secede.

Like Laos, Iran is impervious to Western – particularly American – pressure and has a huge and increasing opium crop.

As in Burma, the appropriate area of Afghanistan is completely unpoliced, is likely to remain so and will undoubtedly increase its opium production every year, hindered only by bad weather.

There is one further connection between the Golden

Triangle and the Golden Crescent: the Turkish cities of Gaziantep and Diyarbakir. It is through these two townships, in the eastern part of the country, that the majority of land-smuggled opium and morphine base and heroin passes on its westward journey from the two principal production areas.

Some is transshipped by sea, to the Mafia refining laboratories in Sicily.

Much more is routed through a second communist country which actively participates in drug-trafficking and in the channelling and use of drugs in international terrorist activities. And which floods Europe.

12

The Vitosha is the best hotel in the Bulgarian capital of Sofia; it opened in May 1979 and is still superbly modern, offering every sort of comfort and convenience. The luxury is often a surprise for first-time visitors to a communist country who expect something more spartan. The hotel honours most major Western credit cards, there is a swimming pool, a sauna and a gymnasium, and a glittering, high-stakes casino that is crowded every night by dinner-jacketed men and bejewelled women, another cultural shock for the uninitiated. There is also a Japanese garden, though this is not as surprising as it might be in view of the fact that the hotel is Japanese-designed, part of the New Otani chain. British Airways also has a business interest.

The guide-books and brochures correctly claim that the Vitosha is conveniently positioned for all business and trade activities in the Bulgarian capital, but its siting – at No. 100 Anton Ivanov Boulevard – makes it an especially useful location for one particular business.

At No. 66 Anton Ivanov Boulevard are the headquarters of an import and export firm named KINTEX. Its literature lists trading activities in sports and hunting articles. and explosives for mining and construction work. It also deals in 'compensation and multi-lateral transactions and transit operations'.

The phrase 'multi-lateral transactions' euphemistically describes a terrorist arms-for-drugs mart and the transit operations ensure that those drugs travel through Europe legally protected from customs interception by international treaty agreement.

The Vitosha is where the deals are struck. Ironically, some of them have involved weaponry for the Japanese Red Army, whose declared aim is to destroy the capitalist system. The Palestine Liberation Organisation – for a while with drugs of its own to market – also trades there. So do the IRA; the Irish National Liberation Army; the Secret Army for the Liberation of Armenia; ETA, the Basque movement seeking independence from Spain; and the Grey Wolves, the paramilitary group of Turkey's banned National Action Party whose most infamous terrorist is Mehmet Ali Agca, the Turkish killer who attempted to assassinate the Pope in May 1981.

KINTEX is an agency of the communist government of Todor Zhivkov. Further, it is used as an arm of the Dajnavna Sigurnost, the Bulgarian secret intelligence organisation which in turn is wholly subservient to the Soviet security service, the KGB.

Testifying before a Senate Judiciary subcommittee on terrorism in April 1982, Drugs Enforcement Administrator Francis Mullen refused to identify the terrorist groups involved in KINTEX activities – he considered the information classified – but insisted there was a 'definite relationship' between drugs and terrorism. A DEA official in charge of foreign operations was more forthcoming during a long meeting I had with him a year later. He told me then that the Bulgarian government not only tolerates drug-trafficking but has for a long time been prepared to sell arms for foreign exchange to anyone who wanted to pay for them, regardless of their political affiliations. He was echoing the protest made in July 1982 by US Ambassador Robert Barry who identified the Vitosha as a drug marketplace every bit as active as the bazaar of Landi Kotal and said, 'We and other countries have provided and continue to provide specific information designed to assist in the interdiction of smuggling of drugs and arms. To date we have been disappointed at the Bulgarian response.'

One proviso stated by the communist government of Zhivkov and his Soviet controllers is that no drugs are sold during transit through Bulgaria. And if any independent trafficker attempts to ignore the official KINTEX route, his drugs are seized and sold to dealers adopting the proper procedure.

Bulgaria is obligated under international treaty to exchange drug intelligence, but ignores the regulations. America, on the other hand, complies with the treaty's requirements. Long before his emergence as the £500,000 paymaster to the would-be assassin of the Pope, the DEA identified to the Bulgarian authorities drugs-for-arms dealer Bekir Celenk, a Turk who is estimated by intelligence sources to have made £50,000,000 from his dealings. They even specified the Vitosha Hotel as his favoured negotiating place.

It was the near-fatal attack upon Pope John Paul II that briefly lifted the curtain upon the scene that drug enforcement officials had known of for years: revealing Bulgaria as the hub of a vast trafficking network. The shooting in St Peter's Square has been investigated intensively by intelligence agencies of the Vatican, Italy, France, West Germany, Turkey and America. And from my knowledge of those investigations I am convinced that the attempt was ordered by Moscow, using a subsidiary intelligence organisation to distance them from the actual crime, and that Sofia's best-known drug trafficker was coerced, by the Dajnavna Sigurnost through KINTEX, into confusing the trail. The implication of a mentally confused, already convicted killer like Agca, already on the run from a Turkish jail where he was serving life for the murder of a newspaper editor – demonstrably violent, and politically right- not left-wing – was an attempt to compound that confusion further.

Confirmation of the KGB–Bulgarian intelligence link actually comes from *inside* the Dajnavna Sigurnost via counter-intelligence director Dimitre Savov, who conceded the connection – and the Moscow instructions – to a close and trusted friend within the service, Iordan Mantarov.

Shortly after their conversation Mantarov left Sofia to spy upon the French in Paris, under cover as Deputy Commercial Attaché at the Bulgarian embassy there. Instead he defected to French counter-intelligence and suggested during his debriefing that the Kremlin wanted the Polish-born Pope killed in order to eliminate his support for the Solidarity movement.

The Kremlin involvement in the assassination attempt would have remained undetected had Mantarov not defected. And had Agca been shot immdiately after the assassination attempt, which was the original plan.

Investigators – particularly the Italians – believe Bekir Celenk paid substantial bribes to be freed from house arrest in Sofia, during which he was paraded before world television cameras to deny all knowledge of Agca and assassination plots against the Pope. But they realise the Bulgarian authorities would not have dared charge him for a subsequent, public court appearance, any more than they dared comply with Ankara's application that Celenk be extradited to them. Because any deep, independent investigation of Celenk would have disclosed too many details of Bulgaria's arms-for-drugs activities.

Even without Celenk's co-operation investigations have already proved that Agca and Celenk had several meetings at the Vitosha Hotel, where Agca stayed during his planning meetings in Bulgaria, and that the gun Agca used was probably supplied through KINTEX sources.

American Drug Enforcement officials estimate that seventy-five per cent of *all* illicit drugs entering Europe do so through Bulgaria and KINTEX. A foolproof way has been evolved to prevent discovery or interruption by any other country. Bulgaria is one of the European countries which has signed the international customs convention under which TIR-designated vehicles proceed through signatory states from point of origin to destination without further stop or search. Bulgaria has the largest TIR lorry fleet in Europe.

I was able to discuss Bulgaria's role in drugs and arms

smuggling during several meetings with a leading law enforcement official from that country. He will not be identified for fear of reprimand or disciplinary action from the government, despite the fact that he said nothing to embarrass Sofia. He denied, for example, the American claim that Bulgaria abuses the international customs convention. 'It is nonsense,' he said. 'A propaganda put out by the Americans, for what reason I do not know. Maybe they are jealous of our containment of a problem they do not appear to know how to handle.'

Out of a population of nine million, the official said there were only four hundred Bulgarian drug addicts. And that addiction is closely controlled: their prescriptions are made out on easily identifiable yellow forms that can be checked by both pharmacists and health authorities.

'The TIR agreement is to facilitate the free movement of goods throughout Europe,' said the official. 'If we were to impose the sort of checks the Americans appear to want, we would literally block the gateway from Asia. We do not consider the Americans or any other drug enforcement authority have satisfactorily made out any sort of case to prove our involvement in either drug- or gun-running. KINTEX is a reputable government agency, not a criminal organisation.'

There is an irony behind the current animosity between the United States and Bulgaria. In 1978 an international drug conference in Varna was jointly hosted by the customs authorities of both countries. By 1980, Washington had become convinced of Bulgaria's trafficking role and decided to boycott the second conference which had been scheduled for that year. Confronted with the possible international embarrassment of being ostracised, the Bulgarians offered Third World countries free transportation – on Bulgarian airlines – as an incentive to attend. Most of them did. So did the majority of Western countries, despite American diplomatic pressure to stay away.

Thomas O'Grady, now the US DEA chief in Vienna, was a delegate to the 1978 conference. 'Bulgaria appears constantly and desperately in need of foreign currency,' he said. 'Which is why we consider they have adopted the role in drug affairs that they have.'

Bulgaria was at one time a marketplace so important to the Palestine Liberation Organisation that the movement could not have survived without using it as a conduit. Following the 1973 oil crisis, Western nations reduced their demand, creating an oil glut and a drop in price. With diminished income, the oil-rich Arab countries consequently cut back their contributions to Yasser Arafat's organisation. 'At the time,' an intelligence officer with experience of the area told me, 'the world – and certainly not Israel – didn't realise what a crisis this created for the Palestinians.'

Drugs provided the solution to that crisis.

The homeless Arabs were concentrated in the Lebanon, particularly in the Bekaa Valley, the fertile agricultural area between the central mountain range and Syria, through which runs the Beirut-to-Damascus highway. Since Roman times the Bekaa has been recognised as a granary, but the predominant crop has changed: today the Bekaa is the world cultivation centre for hashish, the resinous sap excreted from the flowering top of the female cannabis plant. It can be eaten raw or smoked, or even used as an ingredient in desserts or cakes.

The capital of the Bekaa is the city of Baalbek which the Romans called Heliopolis, the city of the sun. There, in 1977, was recorded the largest and most profitable hash growth ever – a hundred thousand tons. Under the conveniently neglectful eye of Egypt's President Anwar Sadat, the majority of that incredible crop went southwards to Egypt, but huge amounts of the drug were routed through Bulgaria, some of which was refined – by chemists who had been brought into the area when Turkey submitted to US pressure in 1972 – into the concentrated but more easily transportable hash oil.

Syria's government also permitted the movement of both hashish and hash oil across the border into Damascus where

187

it was officially ignored in transit from the international airport to destinations in Asia, Europe and North America.

In the Bekaa Valley Sraune and Zahle are the main areas of cultivation. Although most of the profits were channelled away from the growers – partly to purchase weapons – the Palestinians were sensible enough to leave cultivation in the expert hands of the thirty 'families' in the area who have farmed hashish for generations. Predominant among those families are the Jaffa, which maintains its own paramilitary army of three thousand equipped with two privately-owned tanks. The Palestinians demanded taxes on the family's production but respected its independence, as did the Syrians when they crossed into Lebanon to take control. Throughout the successive civil wars that have pummelled the country into increasing chaos, the hash fields of the Bekaa, an area of seventy square miles sweeping southwards towards Deir Zeinoun, have been protected by invaders and defenders alike: they provide an income too important to be interrupted by something as transitory and as inconvenient as war. Before the continuing and near-devastating conflicts were fought out on its soil, thirty per cent of Lebanon's foreign currency earnings came from hash.

During the fighting that drove the Palestinians out of the country, not only were Syrian tanks positioned in the Bekaa to protect the hash fields but Soviet-supplied SAM-6 rockets as well. And a proportion of the thousand Iranian Revolutionary Guards who volunteered to fight were appointed drug guards. The Jaffa family received particular protection from the Syrians, even though they have their own tanks, because their chemists are more expert than those in other laboratories in the area at refining the hash oil.

As in Sofia, there is a particularly smart hotel in Baalbek where the drug transactions are carried out – the Palmyra Hotel, the verandah of which looks out over the Roman-built Temple of Jupiter. It was at the Palmyra that the PLO forged their Bulgarian links and established not just a source of income but a source of arms. After their invasion of the

Lebanon to crush the PLO, Israeli intelligence sources said eighty per cent of the 'huge hoard' of captured weapons and ammunition originated from the Bulgarian port of Varna on the Black Sea, the venue for two anti-narcotics conferences.

The 1982 report of the United Nations International Narcotics Control Board said of the Lebanese wars, 'Traffickers have exploited the difficult situation in the country to expand the illicit cultivation of cannabis and the production of resin which dominates the illicit traffic. Multi-ton consignments leave Lebanon by ship and smaller quantities by land route.' One of those land routes leads southwards towards Israel. There, fearful of a 'violent outbreak' of drug abuse, Professor K. J. Mann, Chairman of the Inter-ministerial and Interinstitutional committee on the Problems of Drug Abuse, has proposed the formation of a national drug authority in order to co-ordinate an anti-narcotics policy.

By international standards, drug-trafficking in Israel is comparatively small, a £65,000,000-a-year business. In the absence of any reliable surveys it is difficult to gauge the true extent of the country's drug problem but it is estimated that there are between three thousand and five thousand addicts, the majority of whom are members of the street gangs in major cities like Jerusalem and Tel Aviv. In addition, according to the 1982 report of the Institute of Applied Research, three per cent of the four million population has used hashish at least once and two per cent use it frequently. Enforcement officials consider that Israel's geographical location, particularly its proximity to the cannabis and hashish production centre in the Lebanon, gives serious cause for concern about the possible escalation of drug abuse.

Professor Mann's group, the Drug Abuse Committee, has consequently urged the government to develop wide-spread educational programmes in schools, workplaces and even in homes, and to establish treatment centres throughout the country. They believe mental health centres concentrating upon addiction problems are needed in Jerusalem, Tel Aviv, Haifa, Acre, Ashdod-Ashkelon, Ramla-Lod and Beersheba, and youth guidance centres in Jerusalem, Tel Aviv and Haifa. Special out-patient clinics for treatment and rehabilitation already exist in Jerusalem, Tel Aviv, Haifa and Acre but they consider such facilities should be extended to Ashdod-Ashkelon, Ramla-Lod and Beersheba. In total Professor Mann and his experts would like to see thirteen mental health centres, eleven guidance clinics, thirteen special treatment and rehabilitation out-patient clinics and the establishment in one of Israel's principal towns of a therapeutic drug-free community.

While the addicts of Europe and the gun runners of Bulgaria provide a more lucrative market, Israel will remain of negligible importance to the international dealers.

The European market is of far greater significance.

13

The Netherlands have taken a cautious step in the direction in which other governments fear to tread and now make marijuana available to teenagers at certain youth centres throughout the country. Lawyer Roelof Manschot, of the Dutch Ministry of Justice at The Hague, told me, 'We want to get rid of this impression that Holland is the international paradise for addicts.' The Dutch believe they can achieve this by providing limited amounts of marijuana legally and consequently keeping youngsters away from the areas where they might, under black-market pressure, succumb to harder drugs.

Manschot added, 'We do not feel too comfortable about it. We are not missionaries claiming our vision is the right vision. Ten to fifteen years ago we went through the experience which the rest of Western Europe is undergoing today. We had the hippy explosion and the revolt of the young not just from our own country but from every other country as well. The wreckage remains, in our towns; eight hundred of the heroin addicts in Amsterdam are Germans.

'Our policy towards marijuana is not one of legalisation. It is one of recognising the difference between hard and soft drugs and trying to prevent a further escalation in the country. By making cannabis available in the controlled way we do, we feel it may be possible to keep them from turning to hard drugs.'

The forerunner of the 1978 bill permitting sales of marijuana at youth centres was legislation, passed in 1976, making it a misdemeanour rather than a felony to carry up to one and a half ounces of the drug for personal use. The Dutch also considered legalising heroin, making it available to known addicts on a maintenance system, to undermine their dependence on the black market, but in April 1983 the Welfare, Health and Culture Secretary, Joop van der Reijden, informed parliament that the proposal was not going to be pursued. In a letter to the government's drug policy committee he wrote, 'According to the available information, the risks involved in the issue of heroin are too great to start experimenting. The advantages and drawbacks are still inestimable. We must first make [further] enquiries.'

In defiance of the decision made by the national government, in December 1983 the city of Amsterdam – the country's drug capital and home of ten thousand of its twenty-five thousand known addicts – decided to initiate an experiment and issue the drug to a selected three hundred addicts, both to maintain them and to assess the expected drop in the crime by which they financed their habit. The Amsterdam Council argued to The Hague that the idea was valid on medical grounds in that it would make the life of the selected few – to be extended if the scheme proved successful – a little more bearable.

The proposal was refused by central government which has even, on occasions, changed its mind about the selling of cannabis from youth centres. When the city council of Enschede, five miles from the border of West Germany, authorised the sale of marijuana in November 1982, it little anticipated that word would spread across the border (advertisement was strictly prohibited) and that hundreds of Germans would arrive to buy supplies. There was an international outcry, led by West Germany, and the Enschede store was closed within a month. Manschot commented, however: 'Repression by itself doesn't end any problem and certainly not that of drugs. We are trying to find a different route.'

This fresh approach drew David Mellor, the Home Office minister, to visit the Netherlands in August 1984, to study the effectiveness of the Dutch attitude to drugs.

Another step taken by the Dutch government in their anti-narcotic campaign was the expulsion of the Chinese community, which at its height numbered more than thirty-five thousand and had been largely responsible for cultivating Holland's drug problem, concentrating their trafficking activities in Amsterdam's red light district of Veedik. However, the openings left by the Chinese were immediately occupied by Pakistanis and the Turkish guest-workers.

Known as *Gastarbeiter* in West Germany, their principal country of employment, the Turks have not only cultivated the heroin market to the extent that there are sixty-two thousand addicts in West Germany but have also engineered the development of a financial support structure for a leading terrorist group, the Grey Wolves, to which Mehmet Ali Agca, the Pope's intended assassin, belonged.

There are 1,500,000 *Gastarbeiter* in West Germany, including an estimated 18,000 members of the Grey Wolves, the paramilitary enforcement group of the Turkish Federation embracing almost 100 right-wing groups. The total membership of the Turkish Federation – which is banned by the Ankara government – is thought to be 50,000. A monthly levy of £4 is imposed on each of the members in West Germany.

'That's £71,280 a month – £855,360 a year – all to finance terrorism,' a Bonn police officer told me. 'It all comes from drugs.'

Bonn enforcement officials have liaised closely with US authorities and from the exchange of intelligence information they are convinced that the Grey Wolves have made extensive use of the Bulgarian trafficking route to bring drugs into West Germany. The leader of the Turkish Federation is Alpaslan Turkes, who controls the organisation from prison. It was he who, in 1979, appointed Musa Cedar Celebi – chairman of the board of two Frankfurt companies later accused by German authorities of smuggling – leader of the Grey Wolves in Germany. After the attempted assassination of the Pope Celebi was extradited to Italy, where the authorities alleged he was the man who offered Mehmet Ali Agca around £500,000 to shoot the Pope. West German intelligence agencies have established that following Celebi's extradition in May 1983, the Grey Wolves held a conference in Stuttgart and appointed Ali Batman as his successor.

The West German government is fully aware of the connection between international terrorism and drug trafficking and has made its Wiesbaden-based anti-terrorist squad responsible for narcotics as well.

Helmut Butke, from the Ministry for Youth, Family Affairs and Health in Bonn, told me: 'My government regards the drug problem of our country very seriously . . . there is particular concern that it appears to be every year upon the increase. A trafficker can receive up to fifteen years' imprisonment. Maybe a third of people arrested in possession of a small amount of cannabis will be allowed off with a caution. The remaining two-thirds are brought before the court. Seventy-five per cent of them are sentenced to a period of probation, with a condition that they work upon some community project.'

Interior Minister Friedrich Zimmerman refers to his country's drug problem as 'worse than terrorism'.

America is also deeply concerned at the drug addiction problems throughout Europe – and particularly West Germany – because of the vulnerability of US troops. As long ago as 1978, Representative Lester Wolff, then Chairman of the House Select Narcotics Abuse and Control Committee, said that the ten to twenty per cent of the two hundred thousand troops on hard narcotics in Europe was the equivalent of almost two divisions 'incapacitated by hard drug use'. He compared the drug situation among US military in Europe to that in Vietnam: 'They had spare time, free time, they didn't have an idea of their mission and there was an availability.'

Spare time – and the boredom resulting from it – is blamed for the development of drug abuse among British servicemen, particularly in Germany, where they work nine-to-five hours with weekends free and are within easy reach of any drugs, either in Germany itself or by taking a short car journey to the Netherlands. So serious is the problem of abuse considered among service chiefs that the Defence Ministry is establishing a special drug squad. Already – copying the American navy's slogan poster – the RAF have devised a pictorial warning. It is an RAF roundel with a hypodermic syringe scoring the bull's-eye, coupled with the warning 'You are today's target.' The illustration accompanies a one-and-a-half hour lecture and film show which all new recruits have to attend. It is shown at RAF installations around the world. Chiefs of all three services intend introducing random urine tests to detect drug abuse.

Austria – with its heroin addict population estimated at ten thousand, marijuana as the most widely abused drug and hallucinogens also readily available – is now considered an important transit route for drugs entering the whole of Europe. And the government is under pressure from international law enforcement agencies to improve its interdiction.

United Nations' surveys have proved conclusively that trafficking, and therefore drug-taking, is on the increase in Europe. In 1981 and 1982 eighty tons of cannabis were seized by enforcement officials, and in 1982 more than one ton of heroin was intercepted, a quarter of which was impounded on one single occasion by Dutch officials. In the same year 7.85 cwt of cocaine were seized; in the first nine months of 1983, the figure was 10.60 cwt. In addition, LSD, amphetamines and methaqualone or its look-alike are all freely available.

I have heard the estimated official figure of 250,000 heroin and opiate addicts in Europe dismissed as laughable by European enforcement experts convinced that a more likely figure is nearer 2,000,000.

Fifty per cent of the cocaine entering Europe from Latin

America is thought to pass through Madrid's Barajas Airport which averages four hundred flights a day, the majority from South America. Customs officials complain to international authorities that they have insufficient means to check incoming cargo and passengers properly.

Spain's attitude towards drugs confuses some international agencies. During the crackdown of the Nixon era General Franco – who disliked the idea of a hippy trail developing through his country from Morocco – introduced swingeing laws, imposing severe penalties on personal users and traffickers alike, with a minimum sentence of six years and a maximum of twenty. Since 1977, however, the Spanish attitude has softened and in 1983 a law was passed making it legal for a person to have up to three and a half ounces of cannabis for his or her personal consumption. This has provoked some criticism from international authorities but I believe that the ambiguities in the marijuana legislation will shortly be amended by the Madrid government which, according to one of its narcotics officials, has no intention of relaxing its attitude towards drugs. In March 1984, in fact, following a spate of ten deaths within three months from heroin overdoses, the Spanish cabinet decided to reverse some of the liberalisation promised by Justice Minister Fernando Ledesma in a 1982 election manifesto. Crime on Spanish streets soared after that liberalisation. In April 1984 south London businessman Gordon Maclachlan was severely slashed in a fight with two Spanish heroin addicts in Torremolinos. At the beginning of September three stiletto-wielding heroin addicts stabbed to death twenty-five-year-old London typist Miss Linda Bradley in a handbag snatch in the same city. Miss Bradley's companion, Mrs Christine Batty, twenty-eight, and also from London, received serious knife wounds to the liver. At the end of the month, forty-three-year-old David Mathieson, from Fife, was knifed to death in front of his wife and two children when he tried to stop three men, who had tried to ram them in a car, stealing the handbag of his wife Sheila. Their children, David, fourteen, and fifteen-year-old

Angela, watched their father bleed to death at their feet.

The British embassy issued 'don't carry valuables' warnings to British tourists and concerned Spanish travel authorities demanded a special crime squad for Torremolinos to protect holidaymakers against drug-related street attacks. Such protection already exists – of necessity – in Benidorm. Twelve thousand police operated in Spanish resorts in 1984.

Within days of the murder of Miss Bradley, British hitchhikers Diane Bond and Claire Soper were blasted by shotgun-carrying bandits who robbed them just outside the Spanish capital of Madrid. Francisco Gabea, Deputy Director General of Tourism, directly blamed drug addiction for tourist crime.

After the March 1984 cabinet reversal, Interior Minister Jose Barrionuevo – a political opponent of Ledesma – declared: 'The government is prepared to rectify its mistakes.'

In France – where, until his suicide in Marseilles jail in August 1984, the illicit trade was masterminded by Mafia chief Gaetan Zampa – the Paris drug squad has been increased by fifty per cent to deal with increasing narcotics abuse. Opiate abusers number approximately fifty thousand, of whom eighty-five per cent are between the ages of fifteen and twenty-five. France has rejected any thought of decriminalising soft drugs and there are educational programmes warning schoolchildren of the dangers of abuse.

After Zampa's suicide, a bloody battle broke out in Marseilles for control of the narcotics market in France. Chief contestants were Francis (Belgian Frankie) Vanderberghe, who was released a month before Zampa's death from a twelve-year jail sentence imposed for his part in the original French Connection, and 54-year-old Jacques (Mad Jacques) Imbert. By March 1985, twenty-three underworld figures were slain in the battling for control of a billion francs a year business.

Sweden's attitude towards drugs has changed in the light of an increasing number of addicts. Until 1980 the authorities did not consider marijuana a particularly serious problem, but that year sixty-four thousand cases of possession were recorded and the government realised they had a near epidemic on their hands, involving children as young as twelve years old. The minimum jail sentence for marijuana-trafficking was increased from one to two years and extra funds were allocated to the police to finance their campaign against drugs, psychotropics as well as opiates.

The use of psychotropics is also increasing in Denmark, another country which condones the personal use of cannabis.

The attitude is different in Italy which, because of the control exerted by the Mafia, is regarded internationally as a special situation. Private cannabis-smoking is ignored, even in the streets, and within parliament there is a lobby – led by the Partito Radicale – to legalise the drug. The American DEA have helped to assemble a special anti-narcotics unit, the Gruppo Misto Intervento, from police forces within the country, and they also advise the three agencies with jurisdiction in drug matters, the State Police, the Guardia de Finanza and the Carabinieri. Of Italy's 150,000 addicts, the official estimate is that 11,000 of them between the ages of 18 and 25 are on heroin. It has been suggested to me that a more accurate figure would be 50,000.

Yet in 1980, Health Minister Renato Altissimo caused uproar in parliament by suggesting that heroin should be made available free to addicts to destroy the black-market trade in the drug. That trade is organised principally by the Mafia.

And Tom Tripodi knows how powerful they are. 'They'll kill me if they want to,' he told me. 'There's nothing I can do about it.'

14

Tom Tripodi *looks* what he is, a tough cop; he is a huge, bull-chested figure of a man, the clipped, street-wise American accent overlaid with the lilting Italian he speaks fluently, and if he hadn't chosen to be a real cop, he could have made a fortune on the screen. He's a rare cop, too. One of the few ever to have had a contract put out on his life by the Mafia and still be alive. He's the only survivor from the recent operation which earned the Mafia public hatred. Every other leading figure involved has been murdered.

So concerned were the Drug Enforcement Administration, for whom Tripodi is an agent, that they offered to provide him with a completely new identity – passport, bank account, social security number, credit cards – and house him under that new name in any part of America he chose. Tripodi refused. 'You can't escape from a Mafia contract, not really,' he told me. 'Changing names and houses would have been ridiculous. I'm trained – before the Drug Administration I was a CIA agent – and in a neighbourhood and an environment with which I am completely familiar, I'll notice anything strange. Anything to react to . . .' He paused and then added, '. . . I hope.'

So Tripodi lives in a Washington suburb, works in a Washington office and spends every spare moment fishing. 'I'm good at catching things,' he admits modestly.

In 1978 Tripodi was the DEA agent in Rome when the Italian authorities first decided, under pressure from Washington, to move against the Mafia. The outcome was Operation Caesar, a two-pronged investigation designed to attack the drug-trafficking from Sicily to America, and to probe the financial links in the drug business between the two countries. The investigation continues but the highlight came in June 1983 when sentences totalling four hundred years were passed against sixty-five members of the three leading Mafia families in Palermo – the Spatola, the Gambino and the Inzerillo.

In attempts to stop those sentences ever being passed the Mafia shot down hundreds of people, including politicians, police chiefs and judges. 'I don't know why they haven't hit me,' said Tripodi. 'Maybe I've been lucky. Although luck doesn't usually come into anything to do with the Mafia.'

It was in 1977–8 that American scientists realised from their analysis of intercepted heroin that chemists believed to have been put out of business by the smashing of the French Connection in 1972 were working again. And that because the seized drugs had come from Sicily, not Marseilles, those chemists had crossed the border.

In September 1978 Tripodi was ordered from Rome to Palermo. His Italian counterpart was Giorgio Guiliano, the deputy chief of the State Police in Sicily's capital. 'He was a brilliant policeman,' recalled Tripodi. 'One of the best I've ever worked with.'

The respect was mutual. Together the two men set about achieving what no one else had ever been able to do: breaking the Mafia. Tripodi had all the information from American investigations into the French Connection which was not, as was implied in the film of that name, a single smuggling attempt but a whole series. He was able to identify a chemist named Ishmet Kostu, a Turk who *was* involved with the Frenchman portrayed in the movie, Jean Jehan, and Tripodi and Guiliano also suspected the involvement of a second French chemist. Andreé Bousquet. By June 1979 – with eight laboratories located – they felt they had sufficient evidence to make their first arrests.

The swoop upon a hundred people began at 5 a.m. one Saturday. By 10 a.m. Guiliano told Tripodi, 'Word is that the Mafia have put out a contract for you.'

From that moment, an enormous police operation was mounted to keep Tripodi alive. The American was based at the Politeamo Hotel in Palermo. A system was immediately established whereby he would telephone Guiliano fifteen minutes before he left it, for *any* reason, to specify the route to his destination. Never, under any circumstances, would he deviate from that route.

Whenever Tripodi left the hotel his car was covered by an unmarked police car front and back and he travelled within a cavalcade of four or five protective vehicles. Still Guiliano was dissatisfied. The following Tuesday he moved Tripodi to another, more secure hotel: the Villa Igeia, a castle, with protective perimeter walls eight feet high. The arrangements for Tripodi's movements remained the same, though he rarely left his base. On the occasions he did, it was usually to eat with Guiliano and his wife and they were always accompanied by eight or nine bodyguards.

This was still not enough for Guiliano. The next weekend he told Tripodi that despite every protection he did not think he could keep him alive and urged him to communicate his fear to Washington. Tripodi was immediately recalled; smuggled – under heavy police guard – to Rome and from there directly back to the American capital where the offer of the new identity was made.

Guiliano and his squad continued to investigate the Mafia in Sicily, island of more than a hundred murders a year. Their initial findings – though minimal by comparison with what was later to emerge – were startling: the Mafia had extended the supply side of their billion-dollar connection beyond Sicily into mainland Italy and were importing and utilising French expertise.

No special equipment is needed to refine heroin from morphine – just running water, a fire and containers – but the precursor, acetic anhydride, produces a particularly unpleasant and therefore easily identifiable smell. The Mafia overcame that. In Italy Guiliano's men found three laboratories built by Sicilian brothers Marco and Orazio di Maggio, one in a castle tower at Cereseto, sixty miles from

Milan, another in a nearby farmhouse, and the third in the basement of a Milan house. The Milan installation had tiled walls, proper laboratory apparatus and – to get rid of that smell – extensive drainage and air-conditioning.

Not all the products from the Maggio laboratories were sent to America: a considerable proportion helped create the heroin epidemic which has enveloped Italy and given it an addict population which, at 150,000, is the highest in Europe today.

Pia was one of them. She is currently undergoing a fourteen-month cure and rehabilitation course, away from Italy, because her wealthy industrialist father realised that any effective treatment would be impossible in a country where drugs are so freely available.

'I'm frightened to go back, when I finish,' Pia told me. 'It's so easy to get, so tempting. I don't want to start again but I'm not sure if I am strong enough.'

Twenty-three now, Pia was fourteen when she started on heroin, smoking first but then very quickly mainlining. By the time the Mafia established their laboratories in Milan, she was an eager client.

'All my friends were addicts, like me. Most still are. My brother, too,' said Pia. 'Streets were littered with kids dozing off their fix: hypodermics crunched under foot as you walked.'

Milan isn't the only city in Italy with an addict population visibly obvious on its streets. Rome is another. So is Verona where, in October 1982, twenty thousand people marched through the streets in a public demonstration against what their protest banners described as 'merchants of death'.

In Sicily Guiliano identified one of those merchants: Leoluca Bagarella, the Mafia Capo of Corleone, the city which gave its name to the godfather in the movie of that name. Guiliano personally led a raid on one of Bagarella's houses, near Palermo's railway station. Bagarella had fled, for a freedom that was to last for a further six months, but Guiliano found a photograph of twelve Mafia capos at a planning meeting similar to that hosted in Apalachin in 1957 by Vito Genovese. And from documents found with the photographs, Guiliano deduced that the subject of the meeting was the same as it had been in New York twenty-two years earlier: worldwide control of drugs.

Guiliano believed he was close to a break-through. So did the Mafia.

Every professional, no matter how expert or careful, makes mistakes. Guiliano had regrettably created a routine of leaving his Palermo home promptly at eight forty-five every morning and taking coffee at the nearby Bar Lux. On the morning of 19 July 1979 – six weeks after he and Tripodi initiated the first of their arrests – just as Guiliano was leaving his home, he received a telephone call.

From the speed with which he left the house, his wife later told detectives she assumed the call had come from an informant, arranging a rendezvous. The call *had* been to arrange a rendezvous, although not with an informant. Investigations established that Guiliano arrived at the Bar Lux and ordered his customary expresso but sat more alertly than usual, as if expecting someone. When no one joined him he appeared to become impatient. He stayed longer than normal, eventually rising and going to the counter to pay for his coffee. As he did so a man entered the bar from behind the policeman. The assassin fired eight bullets, three into the head, five into the body.

Police later interviewed thirty people whom they were positive had seen the killing. Each one of them insisted he had seen nothing.

A much-respected judge and member of a parliamentary anti-Mafia commission, Casare Terranova, fifty-eight, was appointed investigator of Guiliano's killing and instructed also to continue his enquiries into the Mafia control of the heroin trade. He began work on 26 September 1979. He arrived at his new office early that first day and immersed himself in the records Guiliano had left of the investigations up to the time of his assassination. On his way home for lunch, his car was caught in a traffic jam. Armed motorcyclists pulled up on either side of his open-windowed vehicle and trapped him in crossfire. As with Guiliano, they fired eight times. The judge died instantly.

Twelve eyewitnesses were interviewed. Not one of them had seen anything.

Carabinieri Captain Emanuele Basile was appointed to take up the investigation and proved to be as dedicated as Guiliano had been. It was Basile who established a vital link in the chain between Italy and America: members of the ground staff of Alitalia at Rome and Kennedy Airports who despatched and collected unaccompanied baggage packed with consignments of heroin. Basile also suspected that the huge profits from the transactions were being laundered in Sicily through investment in billion-lire property developments of hotels and high-rise apartment blocks. That suspicion was confirmed at the 1983 trial of Rosario Spatola, the Mafia building contractor through whom the money was channelled into bricks and mortar. When the properties were completed, they could either be left to accumulate value or sold for 'clean' money.

Basile never lived to witness that trial, however. In spite of the warnings provided by the deaths of his two predecessors, on 4 May 1980 he made the same sort of mistake that had cost Guiliano his life, walking unprotected to the police barracks in the town of Monreale with his four-year-old daughter. As Basile passed a bar, three gunmen emerged and shot him dead; the child, miraculously, survived.

Thirteen eyewitnesses were interviewed. Not one of them had seen anything.

Gaetano Costa was Palermo's chief prosecutor, the man who originally created the indictments for Operation Caesar and who issued separate charges against a group of people for laundering drug money through Sicily's banks. On 6 January 1980 Costa waited on the doorstep of his Palermo home for friends who were driving him away for a winter vacation. The car that arrived contained not friends but Mafia assassins: Costa died under a hail of bullets.

Seven eyewitnesses were interviewed. not one of them had seen anything.

Basile had spoken to Piersanti Mattarella about his belief that the Mafia-run construction industry was being used to clean drug money. Mattarella was a representative of a small communist-supported minority of the Christian Democrat Party committed to oppose the Mafia. He was also president of Sicily's regional parliament. Basile had provided names to support his suspicions, heading the list with a set of companies run by Rosario Spatola. Mattarella had responded immediately, abruptly cancelling the building contracts with the companies on Basile's list.

On the day that Gaetano Costa met with his death, Mattarella was also assassinated on his way to Mass with his wife and children. He was shot dead – by eight bullets again – on the third step outside his Palermo home. His family were too shocked to be able to help the police with any worthwhile description of the assassins. Five eyewitnesses were also interviewed. But not one of them had seen anything.

Before he was killed, Mattarella had discussed the laundering systems with Pio La Torre, Secretary of the Sicilian Communist Party and an outspoken opponent of Sicilian organised crime; he served on the anti-Mafia commission of which Terranova had been a member. La Torre initiated a bill which would give the police legal access to bank accounts they suspected to be Mafia-based and the right to tap telephones.

On 30 April 1980, on his way to Sicily's parliament building,. La Torre's car was delayed in a traffic jam. He was ambushed by three men, one riding a motorcycle. Eleven eyewitnesses were interviewed, but none of them had seen anything.

Basile died a month before the eventual raid upon the di Maggio brothers' heroin laboratories which had been located by Guiliano. And before the interrogation of the two brothers had provided firm evidence of the essential link between the Mafia and the French Connection.

The movie ends with the escape from the police of the French mastermind who smuggled ninety-seven pounds of heroin into New York in 1962. His name was Jean Jehan. In real life Jehan was closely associated with the di Maggio brothers in the early days of the Mafia's drug-trafficking activities. It was Jean Jehan – arrested by the French at the request of the Italian authorities – who introduced into the Mafia refining laboratories his ace chemist, Andreé Bousquet, always respectfully addressed as 'Doctor'.

In August 1980 Bousquet was identified by airport authorities on one of his frequent trips from France to Italy and followed to Carini, on the coast very near Palermo. In Carini he booked into the Riva Smeralda, a hotel in which Tripodi and Guiliano had sometimes eaten. The manager, Carmelo Janni, allowed detectives to book into his hotel as residents and by maintaining a twenty-four-hour watch upon the chemist they located four laboratories in the village of Trabia. When the police subsequently raided the premises, they seized a substantial proportion of the five tons of heroin manufactured every year in Sicily; they also arrested Gerlando Alberti, one of the most wanted Mafiosi in Italy. Two days later, the co-operative hotel manager was shot to death.

For once – surprisingly – a murder charge was brought: in March 1983 Alberti was jailed for twenty-four years for organising the murder.

Under interrogation Bousquet disclosed a link with a Belgian drug courier named Albert Gillet, who had been arrested at Rome Airport two months earlier with seventeen and a half pounds of heroin in his hand luggage. And interrogation of Gillet later made it possible for detectives to establish a positive link between the Mafia in Italy and the Mafia in America. The chain extended from the Inzerillo and Gambino Families in Palermo to the Gambino Family in New York.

Under the rigid control of sharp-featured Carlo Gambino, in the sixties and seventies the family rose to become the most powerful in America: Carlo was the capo di tutti capi not just of his own family, but of the Genovese, Luchese, Colombo and Bonanno Families as well. He controlled organised crime in six American states and was believed by the FBI to have been as influential – maybe even more so – than Vito Genovese had been at the Apalachin meeting in 1957. Certainly after Genovese's death Gambino became the capo di tutti capi unopposed.

Under Gambino's direction the Mafia families of New York developed their drug-trafficking business and made it more profitable than any of their other enterprises. The mastermind of the drug empire was Carmine (Lilo) Galente, who was not actually a member of the Gambino Family. While he was answerable to Joseph Bonanno, he was respected and admired by them all: indeed, when Carlo Gambino died in 1976 he was seen as a contender for the role of capo di tutti capi against the acknowledged heir, Aniello Dellacroce.

It was Galente who forged the link with Sicily, first – naturally – with the Gambino there and then with the Inzerillo. Galente's influence also extended to France, the Lebanon and Turkey.

Italian police liaised with the FBI and with the New York police over Gillet's information and American investigations confirmed the network. Which led to increased pressure from Washington for local action in Rome where the Christian Democrat Party had already been accused of being Mafia-infiltrated and therefore reluctant to move against organised crime.

Appointed to disprove that accusation was General Carlo Alberto Della Chiesa, one of Italy's best-known and feared policemen, someone who had beaten the Red Brigade terrorists and was known to be absolutely fearless and incorruptible. Della Chiesa was made Prefect of Palermo with the specific brief to curb the Mafia's activites. The sixty-two-year-old policeman arrived in Sicily with his thirty-two-year-old wife Laura and a fervent intention to succeed. He found it difficult to sustain that fervency once he realised the extent of the Mafia's power and influence, but he confirmed Basile's belief that the Mafia laundered their illegal profits through their control of the building industry and he worked hard to establish the extent of their political power, at the same time almost confirming suspicions of the Christian Democrat Party when he said, 'I am even more interested in the network that controls the Mafia, which may be in hands above suspicion and which, having placed itself in key positions, controls political power.'

He campaigned for the law proposed by Pio La Torre to be put by the Rome parliament on to the statute book and his suspicions were raised even further by the slowness with which the central government reacted.

It took Della Chiesa's death to make them implement the legislation.

On 2 September 1982 Della Chiesa and his wife were driving along Palermo's Via Carini when they were ambushed by three gunmen who raked their car with bullets, killing them both instantly. Again, none of the eyewitnesses saw anything.

There was an outburst of public protest throughout Italy at Della Chiesa's killing. His family made the direct accusation that the Christian Democrats were a subservient tool of the Mafia and from pulpits all over the country priests condemned the murder. An embarrassed parliament hurriedly passed the long-overdue La Torre law.

That legislation contributed to the eventual arrests of Rosario Spatola, Rosario and Giuseppe Gambino, Emanuele Adamati, Filippo Ragus, Tomasso Inzerillo and the other fifty-nine Mafia mobsters estimated by Judge Giovanni Falcone at their trial to have trafficked £394,000,000-worth of heroin into America, quite independently of what they had routed into Italy and Europe.

With its customary swiftness, the Mafia extracted its vengeance. Rocco Chinnici had succeeded Casare Terranova as Palermo's chief investigating magistrate and as such was heavily involved in the indictments for the trial. He was also involved in the investigations into Della

Chiesa's murder and in the continuing assault upon the Mafia drug trade.

One month after the conclusion of the Palermo trial, Chinnici was killed by a bomb, an estimated two hundred pounds of explosives, which detonated as he got into his car. None of the nine eyewitnesses had seen anything.

The Palermo trial temporarily undermined the Gambino influence in Sicily, giving the Bonnano Family supremacy.

Biggest – although still only temporary – setback to the Mafia came in July 1984, when Tomasso (Don Masino) Buscetta, who ran a £500,000,000-a-year narcotics empire that stretched from his home in Brazil, through New York pizza parlours to his Palermo birthplace, broke the oath of 'Omerta'. To save himself from being murdered in a Mafia-controlled Italian jail by Mafia enemies, Buscetta, whose two sons, a brother and a nephew died in Mafia wars, made a seven-hundred-page confession, which resulted in 366 arrest warrants being issued in Italy and New York. He detailed 120 murders, including that of General Della Chiesa. Implicated in Don Masino's confession was Vito Cianimino, a Christian Democrat ex-Mayor of Palermo.

Dramatic though the breakthrough was – an over-enthusiastic US Attorney General called it 'the single most devastating assault on the Mafia in its entire history' – a more objective view is that Don Masino was not disclosing destructive secrets about the entire Mafia, just about his personal enemies within the organisation against whom he fought and lost.

Head of that opposing, winning Corleone clan is Luciano Liggio, a paunchy, open-faced man with a receding hair-line. At the time of writing, Liggio remains free and capo di tutti capi of a multi-million-dollar narcotics empire.

Like the good businessman he is, Liggio does not, of course, restrict himself to one product. He also trades in cocaine, the cocaine of Latin America. And particularly Colombia.

15

The murder rate in Colombia's second largest city, Medellin, is six a day. To be statistically precise, it is 6.3 every twenty-four hours. Which is frequently a more accurate figure than at first seems logically possible: bodies are often dismembered or tortured. It is quite common for the nose or the ears, the tongue or the penis to be cut off before death.

This statistic makes Medellin, with its estimated 1,200,000 inhabitants, a contender for the murder capital of the world. It achieves that distinction because of its other, incontestable, claim. This Andes-cupped town with its permanent English-summer's-day climate is also the cocaine capital of the world.

Every year, forty-five tons of cocaine are channelled through Medellin into the United States, to be purchased by 5,000,000 Americans at a cost of $25,000,000,000 (£16,666,000,000). A further ten tons – usually of inferior quality, even at unadulterated source, because the customers aren't as demanding as American users – go to Europe, to the Mafia groups controlled by people like Luciano Liggio, mostly via the airports of Madrid, Lisbon and Frankfurt.

Drugs provide Colombia's biggest source of foreign income, nearly thirty-six per cent of its total Gross National Product. That income is not derived solely from cocaine: Colombia is still a major marijuana producer even though domestic production within America – there is evidence of cultivation in twenty-nine states – has made serious inroads into its market.

Between 1 October 1982 and 21 June 1983, US Customs seized 2,642,026 lb of marijuana coming *into* the country – in which there are 25,000,000 users – with an estimated street value of $750,000,000 (£493,500,000). Most of this originated from Colombia. And using the enforcement estimate of a 10 per cent seizure rate, this means that 18,300,000 lb of the drug was imported altogether.

The lawless province of Guajira is the traditional area of marijuana cultivation, but the demand is such that the plantations have spread southwards to the provinces of Cesar and Magdalena. Plantations have also been developed in the western Andes, in the provinces of Valle, Choco, Narino and Cauca. The port of Tumaco and the island of Mal Pelo, directly to the west, are the departure points for the marijuana-loaded motherships en route northwards, bound for the Caribbean and America. At the time of writing it is conservatively estimated that 125,000 acres of land are completely given over to marijuana cultivation in Colombia, although figures more than double that have been suggested to me. But even the lowest figure would produce 50,000 tons of the drug, for which Colombia has ideal, year-round growing conditions. According to the latest figures available, the Colombian authorities seized 282 tons in 1980, 3309 tons in 1981 and 3408 tons in 1982. Also in 1982 the Colombian National Police claimed to have destroyed more than 8,500,000 cannabis plants.

Colombia's involvement in drugs does not stop at cocaine or marijuana. Conscious as early as 1978 of the enormous profits to be made from all types of trafficking, Colombian narcotics barons imported vast quantities of the drug methaqualone, in bulk powder form, from the six major producing countries.

By 1980 methaqualone was being described by some – but not all – enforcement agents as the most widely abused psychotropic drug in the world, even preferred to heroin by some. Methaqualone abuse approached epidemic proportions in North America, Canada, Australia and South Africa, although it did not register as heavily in the United Kingdom.

In the autumn of 1979, a million tablets were seized in America in the space of one week. Gene Haislip, now Deputy Assistant Administrator for the Office of Diversion Control at the Drug Enforcement Administration, took a sample to the Maryland forensic laboratory where the expertise is such that scientists can 'fingerprint' pills by identifying and recognising the imperfections created during their mass production by metal punches. He asked the forensic experts to trace the source. Within hours, after microscopic examination, the scientists determined that the pills were counterfeit, not licitly manufactured, and that they came from Colombia.

Haislip travelled to the Colombian capital of Bogota to continue his detective work. The discoveries were startling: the first was that vast quantities of methaqualone powder were being produced in Hungary, East and West Germany, Austria, the People's Republic of China, Switzerland and India.

'The most startling of all,' recalled Haislip, 'was that eighty per cent of the methaqualone being produced was being channelled into illicit routes without the knowledge of the bona fide producers. And the remaining twenty per cent was medically unnecessary anyway.'

The free ports of Hamburg and Rotterdam were the initial conduits. American investigations then established that some of the powder was moving through the United Kingdom – with the rest transitting through Switzerland – en route to the Caribbean, from where it began its final journey into Colombia. From Colombia it was marketed throughout the world; Canada was the usual entry point for onward movement into the United States.

For the next two years, led by Haislip, diplomatic pressure was brought to bear upon the producing countries to cease manufacture of the powder. The first to respond – 'amazingly within three weeks of the request being made', remembered Haislip – was Hungary. The reason was an earlier diplomatic courtesy performed by Washington: in January 1978, America returned to Budapest one of its most important historical treasures, the Crown of St Stephen, together with the royal sword, coronation robes, orb and sceptre. They had been entrusted to America for safe-keeping during the war.

The only country which refused to comply with Washington's request was East Germany, although she initially assured America that she was willing to enter into a formal, written treaty. The government then insisted that the divided city of Berlin be stipulated in that treaty as the capital of Germany, which was politically unacceptable to America. East Germany therefore still manufactures methaqualone, producing between five and nine tons annually, and this supply of the drug – together with the stockpiles remaining in the former producing countries (a hundred tons or more) – prevents Haislip from achieving total eradication. He also has to contend with the problem of 'look-alike' pills which are being manufactured by the Colombians not with methaqualone but with diazepam, the non-proprietary name of Valium. The dosage in the look-alike methaqualone is far higher – five to six times greater according to analysts – and medical authorities believe this could bring about an increase in the number of overdose deaths.

The Colombians are notorious not just for the extent and the value of their drug-trafficking – which is huge – but for the violence which accompanies it. As one international narcotics expert said to me, 'The recognised Mafia will settle a dispute with an offender by murder, but only by murdering *him* because it's business. The Colombians will take out a whole family, wives, children, parents, uncles . . . everybody. And often kill the relatives first, to make the victim really suffer.' In the daily newspaper, *El Colombiano*, a whole page – and sometimes more – is devoted to detailed reports of the drug murders of the previous twenty-four hours, under the misleading heading of *La Seguridad*, meaning security.

There are more than a million Colombians living in the United States, of whom as many as ten thousand are thought by enforcement officials to be actively engaged in narcotics smuggling throughout the country. Most of those ten thousand have relatives in Colombia, regarded as hostages for their loyalty and obedience.

Orlando Galvez established a cocaine-dealing business in the New York borough of Queens, where he had a $1000-a-month apartment in the Jamaica Estates development at Astoria. His supplier in Bogota came to suspect that he was dealing with a rival source and during the last weekend in January 1982, Galvez, thirty-two, his twenty-nine-year-old wife Carmen and their two small children were slaughtered in a hail of crossfire as they were driving along Grand Central Parkway in their Mercedes. Five more Colombian immigrants later died under similar circumstances, which investigating officers came to regard as a lesson to others that loyalty to a supplier had to be respected. And on 15 April 1984 the same reprisal motivation led to the worst massacre in New York's criminal history when Virginia Lopez – five months pregnant – her four children, her cousin and her two children, and two other young members of the family were blasted to death with a shotgun. Virginia Lopez's common-law husband, Enrique Bermudez, had served four years of a five-to-fifteen-year sentence for selling cocaine and was on parole when the massacre occurred. In his Brooklyn apartment investigators recognised paraphernalia used to cut heroin. Although the victims were Puerto Rican, police thought the hit had been carried out by Colombians – 'clearly a message'.

During a visit to Medellin – a deceptively beautiful city which boasts an unrivalled orchid production – I was assured by my armed protectors that there is a regular school for assassins in the Andean foothills. There killers employed on behalf of the various drug-controlling families in the valley – and elsewhere in Colombia – are trained to murder in the manner befitting their title of 'Cocaine Cowboys'.

Like Tom Tripodi, my informant was the survivor of a

contract from the Mafia, someone whose home was watched by an armed guard around the clock and whose marriage had broken up because of the intense and frightening pressure. During the time we were together he wore one pistol in an ankle holster and another centre back, in the waistband of his trousers, fully aware that in a city of comparatively few Americans he was a known figure and that by association I would also be suspect. And a possible target.

He described the most popular form of murder to me: 'The killers are trained as a duo, to ride a motorcycle. A Honda is favourite. One steers, the other shoots. The pillion-passenger killer can put a bullet into the head of someone driving a car from a distance of twenty-five yards, while his own machine is in motion. Their accuracy is astonishing.'

So concerned was the government of President Belisario Betancur about the *asesinos de moto* that a law was introduced in Bogota and Medellin making it illegal for motorcyclists to wear close-visored, identity-concealing crash helmets, or for one to ride pillion behind the other. Those restrictions were allowed to lapse.

If they hadn't been, Justice Minister Rodrigo Lara Bonilla might have lived. In April 1984 Bonilla was hit by eleven bullets as he parked his car at his Bogota home. All were fired, with incredible accuracy, by a pillion passenger on a Honda motorcycle. Security men who failed to protect Bonilla's life because they were too far away when the ambush occurred managed to kill the rider. The pillion passenger was a youth from Medellin who told his interrogators that he had been paid $20,000 (£13,000) for the death contract by drug barons who were increasingly irritated by Bonilla's personal crusade against narcotics. After a five-month investigation into the assassination, the Colombian authorities disclosed that the murder plot was conceived at the country estate of Lara Bonilla's brother-in-law, Senor Gustavo Restrepo. An inner caucus of the country's drug traffickers attended the meeting which Restrepo hosted and agreed to contribute a total of £380,000 to arrange the killing. A warrant was issued for Restrepo's arrest.

The killing of Lara Bonilla was later recognised by the drug barons to have been a tactical mistake. Betancur, who had ignored the extradition treaty with the United States for two years, pledged at the Justice Minister's funeral that it would now be enforced. The leading traffickers fled to retrench and rethink to neighbouring Latin American countries. Three – Pablo Escabar, Jorge Ochoa and Rodriquez Gacha – arranged a meeting at the Cesar Park Marriott Hotel, in Panama, with former Colombian President, Alfonso Lopez Michelson. The former president agreed to act as an emissary with the existing government in Bogota. In response to Michelson's approach, in May Colombia's Attorney General, Carlos Jimenez Gomez, travelled to Panama to meet the three men, who claimed to represent 80 per cent of Colombia's cocaine traffickers. They put in writing their offer to the Attorney General. In return for a lifting of the government's pressure against them, they would abandon their smuggling operations, help finance the country's external debt and help rehabilitate addicts. The approach was intentionally leaked by the Betancur government and led to a public outcry. The traffickers returned to Colombia and in November 1984, bombed the bunker-like US embassy in the capital. They threatened to kill all the leading government figures, including the President, and actually offered a $350,000 contract for the kidnapping of the DEA Administrator. So concerned was Washington for the safety of its staff in the country that all dependants and children were withdrawn and some men with wives and families were reassigned to other parts of the world.

I wanted to thank my protectors in Medellin and invited them to lunch at a restaurant called Kevins where the *cazuela de mariscos* – a fish stew – is magnificent.

So is Kevins, cut into that part of the Andean mountains where the drug barons like to have their *fincas* – and where the killer school is reputed to be – with a breathtaking view of the city far below in the valley.

Kevins is owned by one of Colombia's biggest drug dealers, Jose O'Campo. It cost him more than £650,000 to build. Two days' earnings, estimated my guests.

O'Campo's mother-in-law died the victim of a motor-cycle assassination after an argument with O'Campo. So have many others. It's advisable not to offend Senor O'Campo.

Within minutes, inevitably, we were identified. In a land of pickpockets I only carried one credit card at a time – in my sock – and they didn't accept that. The pesos – in the other sock – were insufficient. No problem, assured the waiter: Senor O'Campo would be pleased to accept my American dollars. But at five pesos above the official rate. And the restaurant would be honoured if we took a compli-mentary *digestif*. We accepted, of course. It's advisable not to offend Senor O'Campo.

When we left, we found three Honda motorcycles parked four yards from our car. I suggested a photograph. We'd been a cabaret, my companions explained. They'd had their fun but they wouldn't think it funny if I photographed their killer machines. It was three miles back down the mountain and the roads twisted quite a lot. In their opinion, we'd been lucky to make it. I didn't take a photograph: it's advisable not to offend Senor O'Campo.

The US and Colombian governments have signed an extradition agreement under which Colombian traffickers convicted by an American court can be extradited to the United States. Cleverly irritating the nerve of intense nationalism that exists throughout the country by arguing that the legislation allows America to impinge upon Colombia's sovereignty, the drug barons are actively and persuasively campaigning against the agreement. The meeting at which that persuasive campaign was instigated was held at Jose O'Campo's restaurant. That night there were more than three Hondas parked outside.

As well as his money-laundering discotheque with its spectacular view of Medellin, O'Campo has a flag-bedecked, fern-cascaded shopping centre named Oviedo,

with exclusive European imports sold at the giant supermarket and the Mata Lirma nightclub and restaurant. He
also owns five *fincas*, one a lavish seafront villa on the north
coast at Nicocli, to which he takes lunch and dinner guests
in one of his fleet of helicopters. The centrepiece on every
table is a small mountain of the purest cocaine.

O'Campo is not, however, regarded in Colombia as the
premier baron, a title for which there is no formal, respectful description like capo di tutti capi. If there were such a
designation, there is no doubt it would be accorded to Pablo
Escabar.

At the time of writing, Escabar is just thirty-three years
old. Ten years ago – in 1974 – he was a jump-to-order
enforcer for another, now declining, baron named Alberto
Escabaro Prieto. Today he is estimated by enforcement officials to be one of the richest men in the world. The fifth richest,
I have been assured by one source. By another, someone who
could instantly produce well over £1,000,000,000 in *cash* if
called upon to do so, with huge additional wealth invested in
banks and property.

Escabar lives in Medellin but law enforcement officials do
not know exactly where: five homes were traced during the
time I was there and although he owned them, Escabar was
not to be found. He also has twelve office sites in the city, the
telephones of all of which are tapped either individually or
collectively. He knows it's happening because he bribes the
police, army, narcotics division and immigration authorities
in the city. From the post office – another, most important
ource – he receives early advice when someone is intending
to surrender their telephone and, more importantly, that
telephone's number. He then subscribes to that number in
the name of the original holder, thus adding another line (he
has at least fifteen officially untraceable numbers) to the
network via which he conducts his world-wide, multi-billion-
dollar cocaine and marijuana conglomerate.

Not that Escabar is a secretive, retiring person. The
opposite, in fact. A macho figure in the land of machismo,

Escabar cultivates a public personality, constantly contributing to the wellbeing of his fellow compatriots. Already he has built and given away three hundred houses to the poor in the Medellin valley. When I was in the city he was building another four thousand properties, with such miracle amenities as hot and cold running water, flushing lavatories, separate kitchens and small gardens, though the civic authorities claimed not to know the location.

All to further Escabar's public, street-level image. This is already substantial: when he and other drug barons visit Bogota or Medellin they are frequently mobbed with the frenzy accorded Hollywood film stars. Naturally this is less important to Escabar than his political influence, particularly his efforts to defeat the extradition clause in the treaty between Colombia and America. But politically he is superbly organised.

In 1981 the United States embassy in Bogota estimated that ten per cent of the politicians elected to the country's Senate and House of Representatives were the beneficiaries of financial support and electoral pressure from drug traffickers. From my own experiences it seems that thirty per cent would be a more accurate figure and an even higher number has been suggested to me.

At the last election, for instance, Escabar successfully sponsored three politicians. For one of them, Alberto Santiofimio, he is what is known as *select supplemente*, meaning that if Santiofimio is unable to sit in the parliament for any reason, without approval or recourse to those who put him into office he can ask his *select supplemente* to deputise for him. And whenever parliament is due to discuss anything remotely affecting drug legislation, Santiofimio is unaccountably occupied elsewhere and calls upon Pablo Escabar to fill his seat and vote as he considers proper. Another Escabar-supported politician, Jaime Ortega, also votes according to the wishes of his sponsor. No one, of course, is deceived by the subterfuge.

Carlos Lehder, virtual controller of the Colombian department of Armenia, is arrogantly dismissive of any cover. Perpetuating the Robin Hood myth cultivated by Escabar and others, Lehder has paved roads in a country where a track is considered a luxury, created a safari park containing every known type of animal in the world – and to which the peasants have free admission – and has publicly admitted that his 'incalculable fortune' has been gained from the monopoly of marijuana-trafficking in his region. He has further announced in print that his marijuana fortune will be used to procure him election to parliament in his own right. Which it will. His declared election platform – not surprisingly – is opposition to the extradition treaty.

It is an opposition that unites all the traffickers. Fabio Ochoa has derided the legislation. So has his son, Jorge, who now runs his father's mammoth trafficking empire while the hugely fat older man tours the word buying thoroughbred horses to breed at his *finca*, La Loma. Ochoa senior also invests his wealth in art and has bought several Picasso paintings. Outside La Loma there is a bullring – to which yet again the peasants sometimes have free entrance – where Jorge regularly demonstrates his skills as a bullfighter. Sometimes famous bullfighters are flown especially from Mexico to perform, as they are to the ring belonging to another bullfighting trafficker, Dayro Chica, at Villa Lusitania.

Bullfighting is not the only entertainment that the drug traffickers provide for the grateful population of Medellin. There are cockfights where it is as entertaining to watch the barons waging millionaire sums against one another as it is to watch the fights themselves. And bicycle racing, another popular sport in Colombia. Millionaire trafficker Pablo Correa Ramos has constructed an international-sized bicycling stadium beside his *finca*, Asis. As well as a superb track it has extensive floodlighting so that events can be staged at night. The lights are also used to guide in the helicopters Ramos uses to conduct his drug runs to the outlying despatch ports and airstrips. The helicopters deliver the European-imported delicacies and ingredients ordered by the two French chefs whom Ramos maintains on permanent, twenty-four-hour standby to prepare whatever meals he wants, whenever he wants. Such a foible is not regarded as unusual in Medellin, a city accustomed to ostentation as well as death.

The hotel favoured by the traffickers is the Intercontinental, directly before the hills which are where the mutilated and bound bodies of the daily 6.3 victims are frequently found. It is also the chosen venue for the traffickers' celebrations. When the seven-year-old daughter of Luis Carlos Milona took her first Holy Communion, he decided the event should be marked in a properly fitting fashion and told her to invite her friends to a children's party at the Intercontinental. The bill was £15,000, though it was actually quite a small affair. Milona organised a slightly more lavish occasion – the bill was over £50,000 – to thank the employees of his many investment companies. The Intercontinental was also the scene of the very first gathering of the traffickers who later formed the group 'Muerte a Sequestradores', meaning Death to Kidnappers.

There are two main terrorist organisations in Colombia: one is called FARC, the acronym for 'Fuerzas Armadas Revolucionarias Colombia', the military branch of the legal communist party, and the other is a Cuban-trained left-wing nationalist organisation known as M-19. Both recognised the potential of kidnapping relatives of Croesus-rich drug barons as a way of raising limitless money – through ransom – to support themselves and buy arms. For a while, it worked. Then Blanca Nives, the thirty-two-year-old daughter of Fabio Ochoa, was snatched. Ochoa determined that a stand should be made.

Pablo Escabar attended the meeting from which 'Muerte a Sequestradores' was later created. So did another Medellin trafficker, Manuel Antonio Garces. The meeting decided that because the civil authorities appeared powerless to protect them – a belief shared, for different reasons, by the entire 182-strong Medellin judiciary which resigned

221

en bloc in October 1980, until given army guard – then the barons should look after themselves.

The subsequent official formation meeting of 'Muerte a Sequestradores' made the 1957 Apalachin gathering of the Mafia seem inconsequential by comparison. Two hundred of the country's leading barons attended. Fabio Ochoa was naturally in the chair, supported by his sons Jorge and Fabio. Escabar and Garces were immediately alongside. Chica, Pablo Ramos and Lehder were there. Jose Alvarez-Moreno, whose children had been killed by kidnappers, flew up from Bogota, as did Benjamin Herrea Zuleta and Enriques Quintero. From the marijuana capital of Barran-quilla came Eduardo Enriques Davilla, Julio Cesar Nasser, Jorge Gomez, Lucas Gomez von Grieken – of Dutch extraction – and the husband and wife traffickers, Yvonne and Eduardo la Faurie. Both Yvonne la Faurie and Marta Ospina de Gomez, another woman trafficker, from Medellin, had lost children to kidnappers. And Veronica Rivera de Vargas and Marlene Navarro. Bernardo Londono from Bogota was there with his brother Ovido, who trafficks from Cali. Also from Cali came Miguel Rodriquez, Hernando Restrepo Ochoa and Jose Santa Cruz. Santiago O'Campo – no relation to Jose – was in the audience as well as the owner of Kevins restaurant. And Gustavo Gaviria Rivera, a cousin of Pablo Escabar who runs money-washing investment companies, Luis Milona, Alberto Prieto, Jose Jader Alvarez, Eduardo Gonzales, and Enrique Coronade and Francisco Valdeblanques, old enemies, separated by Carlos Estrada and Alvaro Crespo.

'That one day was assembled in one place the biggest and richest group of drug traffickers the world has ever known,' an enforcement official told me. 'We didn't know about it at the time, of course. Before he was killed, with his hands barbwired behind his back, the man who gave us all the details had his tongue cut out.'

The drug barons agreed that they and their families needed protection and quickly hit upon a way of providing it. The ablest gunmen from each personal bodyguard were seconded to a central, unified force, to be called upon in the event of a kidnapping. The meeting agreed, too, upon the name for their organisation – which was almost immediately shortened to the acronym MAS – and publicly announced its formation as a warning to the revolutionaries.

Blanca Nives Ochoa was released after six months, not as the result of the drug barons' vigilante group but following the payment of an undisclosed ransom by her father. But the revolutionaries *were* hit, far harder than they ever had been by any government forces: six of them were murdered in revenge for the deaths of Jose Alvarez's children. MAS also introduced punishment by humiliation, seizing people they suspected of being kidnappers and chaining them to railings in the main cities of the country, with identifying signs around their necks.

FARC and M-19 changed their strategy. Instead of working against the drug barons, they worked with them, receiving money and arms in return for service as guards and protectors on their vast marijuana estates and smaller coca plantations and at their cocaine-processing plants.

FARC guerillas receive a monthly payment of $3,380,000 (£2,331,034) from the drug barons to guard and maintain the jungle complex bordering the Yari River in Caqueta which was subject, on 10 March 1984, to helicopter assault by American-assisted Colombian police. They achieved the largest drug seizure ever in the world: 13.8 tons of cocaine with a street value of $1,200,000,000 (£827,586,000). They also seized seven aircraft – two twin-engined – a helicopter, weapons and sufficient food to sustain at least ninety people for six months.

The leader of the M-19 guerillas, Jaime Bateman Cayon, vanished in mysterious circumstances in July 1983. Some reports said he was killed in a plane crash. Others that he fled to Spain with a boyhood friend from Barranquilla, Jaime Guillot Lara, taking with him £5,000,000 gained from drug-dealing. Bateman's disappearance did nothing to affect the liaison between M-19 and the drug barons. And that alignment means there are parts of Colombia that are virtually beyond civil control. The entire peninsula of Guajira, where the marijuana plantations proliferate, is particularly lawless. From its coastal ports of Cartagena, Barranquilla, Cienaga, Santa Marta and Riohacha the marijuana boats set sail for the Yucatan Channel, the Windward Passage or the Mona Canal, or sweep wide out into the North Atlantic, to run past Florida to a state further up the American coast.

President Julio Cesar Turbay Ayala, Betancur's predecessor, tried harder than Betancur to combat drug-trafficking. He placed the Guajira peninsula under the jurisdiction of the country's armed forces and in two years six thousand tons of baled marijuana and three hundred smuggling boats and aircraft were seized. But in December 1980 that commitment was abandoned because the soldiers were needed to combat the revolutionary guerillas of FARC and M-19. Antinarcotics efforts were transferred to a US-trained national police contingent. It is ineffectual.

Although not as big a city as Cartagena or Barranquilla, Riohacha is a meeting place for the traffickers or *marimberos*. Everyone in Riohacha carries a gun and by 5 p.m. the streets are cleared for the *marimberos* to promenade, a scene reminiscent of a Wild West shoot-out. There are Americans in Barranquilla but for general US embassy personnel the rest of Guajira is off-limits unless a journey there is sanctioned by special permission and only then if the traveller is accompanied by an armed escort.

It is a sensible precaution, after Operation Tiburon. This February 1982 operation – *tiburon* means shark in Spanish – was hailed by US Attorney General French Smith as 'the most successful international marijuana interdiction to date'. Statistically it was. One fifth of the annual American consumption of the drug was seized in a campaign jointly organised by American and Colombian authorities. Almost five hundred people were arrested and ninety-five boats and planes impounded. Of the marijuana captured, 1,700,000 lb were seized in America and 4,700,000 lb confiscated in Guajira.

Kelly McCullough, thirty-nine, and his partner, Charles Martinez, thirty-four, both pilots with the Drug Enforcement Administration, both married with two children, took part in that operation.

They were asleep when the knock came at the door of their Cartagena hotel room, from men who identified themselves as police. When Martinez opened the door he faced a battery of guns. One *was* held by a policeman. The hotel staff took no notice as the two Americans were hustled out. In the car on the way out of town, towards the jungle, a nine-millimetre gun was put against Martinez's thigh and because he wasn't answering his kidnappers' questions fast enough it was fired at point-blank range. Fortunately the bullet missed the bone. In the jungle on the outskirts of town Martinez was forced to stand. The nine-millimetre pistol was pointed at his heart and fired. The bullet entered the body just above the vital organ, travelling upwards and lodging near his neck.

In the split-second distraction, as Martinez collapsed to the ground, McCullough tried to make a break. Lying wounded, Martinez saw a man, later identified as Rene Benitos, Cuban-born but a naturalised American, take aim and fire at his friend. The bullet hit McCullough in the buttocks, passed through his body and exited near his groin. McCullough kept running. The would-be assassins kept firing. Several bullets missed but then one caught McCullough in the back of the knee, bringing him down.

Martinez then saw Benitos catch up with McCullough, stand over him and fire at what appeared to be point-blank range into McCullough's face. The bullet in fact entered below McCullough's chin, missed all the vital organs in his neck and exited through his armpit, leaving a gaping hole.

Realising that they would return to finish him off in the way he believed his friend had been killed, Martinez staggered upright and managed to reach the skirt of the jungle. The assassination group saw him and started to chase, giving McCullough, who amazingly never lost consciousness, the opportunity to get up and run too, deeper into the snagging undergrowth. Bleeding, he managed to find his way back to the road and walked a mile into the nearest village to get help. The Catholic priest roused the one village police officer and, at McCullough's insistence, returned to the scene to try to find Martinez.

The killer squad were still there. Seeing the police officer, one man raised his pistol to fire again at McCullough. The police officer held up his hand and began to negotiate a bribe from the killers before he would allow the assassination to proceed!

McCullough broke away again, once more escaping into the jungle. Avoiding all intervening villages, he staggered through the night to Cartagena, helped by the fact that the blood from his wounds had clotted. It was dawn when he found a hospital and asked for treatment which was refused because there were no emergency facilities. McCullough then hailed a taxi which took him to a naval hospital: almost five hours after being shot, he finally began receiving treatment.

Martinez, meanwhile, spent the night crouched in the jungle undergrowth, several times not even breathing as the gunmen stumbled to within feet of where he lay. It was almost dawn before they gave up, deciding that he was lying dead somewhere. Martinez gave them another hour before attempting to get back to the road. He was luckier than McCullough. The first car he stopped took him for hospital treatment but first Martinez insisted on telephoning the Bogota office of the Drug Enforcement Administration to explain to station chief John Phelps what had happened and report what he believed to be the death of Kelly McCullough.

By the time Phelps helicoptered to Guajira, both men had been located and found to be alive. Phelps led the hunt for their attackers with Colombian policemen and from a description provided by the now talkative hotel staff they managed to arrest Benitos the same day. The second attacker – the Colombian police officer upon whose guarantee McCullough and Martinez had originally left the hotel – was arrested just across the border in Venezuela and returned into Colombian custody. Benitos was later convicted by the Colombian courts of attempted murder and drug-trafficking and now centres in what the American Department of Justice regard as a test case. Washington have applied for his extradition but Bogota has said that extradition will not be considered until Benitos has completed his sentence in Colombia.

There have been open moves within Colombia to legalise the vast marijuana industry and channel mammoth tax revenue to the government. During Turbay Ayala's presidency this suggestion was formally proposed by the National Association of Financial Institutions, a highly respected organisation which acts as a lobbying group and think-tank, but Turbay Ayala defeated the move by having the idea put aside by the Congressional Committee that approves bills for debate.

Then, in December 1982, President Betancur made what was in effect a direct appeal for drug money to help the government stave off the financial crisis that arose when the world price of Colombia's official best export – coffee – slumped heavily. Betancur broadcast on national radio and television and offered an amnesty to traffickers if they would deposit their money in the nation's exchequer. The amnesty, the president said openly, was to 'attract hidden capital, from wherever it comes, without looking back at its origin, without the application of any kind of sanctions, with the object that we all contribute more in the measures that correspond to us'.

The drug barons ignored him.

A month earlier Betancur had offered an amnesty to FARC and M-19, declaring, 'We cannot beat subversion with fire-power alone.' It had taken him a long time to accept this reality – that FARC, consisting of 2050 guerillas, aided by 5000 'civil defence cadres', had been confronting the 65,000-strong Colombian army for 26 years. On that occasion FARC and M-19 ignored him. Two years later, however – in April 1984 – Bentacur's government negotiated on FARC's terms and agreed to a ceasefire. During a year-long truce the agreement called upon Betancur to consider pardons to FARC fighters wanted for political crimes, bank robberies, kidnapping or acts 'committed in combat'.

Five months later – in August 1984 – Betancur's government signed a supposedly matching truce with M-19, leaving the pro-Cuban National Liberation Army the only official rebel group still operating in the country. The peace agreement with the M-19 guerillas was put in jeopardy just days before the official signing by the assassination outside his home in the provincial city of Bucaramanga, capital of Santander, of the guerilla movement's founder, Dr Carlos Toledo Plata. Dr Plata, a physician, emerged from several years underground on Betancur's assurance of personal safety. Early investigation indicated that the killing of fifty-one-year-old Dr Toledo was carried out by the 'Muerte a Sequestradores' as a warning to the guerilla groups against co-operation with the government.

Nowhere in the agreements with the guerilla movements was there any mention of their involvement with the drug barons, and an intelligence officer specifically assigned to Colombia told me, 'It's a nonsense: it gives the groups the opportunity to regroup and further entrench themselves with the drug barons. If Betancur sincerely believes this to be the breakthrough he appears to be making it, then maybe he's been at the product his country is best at producing.'

The apparent truce might also have been made to impress America. Two years earlier – in December 1982 – President Reagan specifically tailored a South American tour to include Colombia as he wanted to make a personal request to Betancur for greater action against drugs. During a public speech in Bogota, Reagan said, 'We recognise that the use and production of illegal drugs is a threat to the social fabric of both countries. I am determined to control and reduce drug consumption in my country.'

Privately Reagan made it clear to the desperate president that further financial aid to Colombia from a hostile US

Congress was dependent upon some positive response. That response came fast. On 4 January 1983 the Minister of Economic Affairs, Roberto Gerlin, made the cosmetic gesture of banning the import of ether, hydrochloride and acetone, all chemicals used to convert coca paste into cocaine. Washington was mistakenly convinced of Betancur's determination to make a more positive effort in his campaign against drugs, Bogota received its badly needed aid and the drug traffickers were affected not at all.

There are few countries in the world where the art of contraband-running is more highly developed and practised, or has a longer history. Escabar, Lehder and the other dealers can still smuggle in their chemicals with the untroubled ease with which they smuggle out their cocaine and marijuana. And retain the money they denied the president. It is not, however, that they refrain from all involvement with the Betancur family.

In Florida, in October 1982, there culminated an eighteen-month Drug Enforcement Administration investigation code-named Operation Swordfish. During that operation ring-leaders of a multi-million-dollar cocaine cartel were identified as Jose Alvarez-Moreno and thirty-four-year-old Marlene Navarro, Colombians who had attended the 'Death to Kidnappers' meeting. That both escaped was due to the crass incompetence of French Smith, who made a publicity-seeking announcement of widespread arrests *before* any action had been taken. There were, however, tape recordings of bugged telephone conversations between Alvarez-Moreno and Navarro during which the woman, who was the Miami paymaster, was instructed to open a $9500 (£6200) checking account at Miami's Intercontinental Bank.

The account was in the name of Juvenal Betancur, the journalist brother of the Colombian president. Under US forfeiture legislation the money became the 'defendant' and Betancur was required to prove in court that it was not the proceeds of drug-trafficking. After a series of legal delays his lawyer asked a Miami court – before which Betancur did not appear personally – to find that the money was legitimate. The court decided that the money was the proceeds of drug-trafficking and ordered its forfeiture.

The American government have asked Bogota to extradite both Alvarez-Moreno and Navarro for trial in the United States. The Colombian government has replied that it doesn't know where in the country the two are hiding. Both are regularly in Medellin and Bogota.

There was further indication of the cynicism or inability of the Colombian government to curb the country's trafficking activities in December 1984. On Christmas Eve Gustavo Jacome Lemus, second secretary at the Colombian embassy in Madrid, was seized on cocaine smuggling charges. Police investigations resulted in the arrest within the presidential palace of Juan Castillo and his assistant, Carlos Osorio, of the international press section. They were charged with smuggling 6 lb of cocaine into Spain in a diplomatic pouch.

There is an irony about Colombia's position as the world's leading exporter of cocaine. The country has achieved that role because of business ability and refining and distribution expertise, but in fact the coca cultivation in the provinces of Meta, Caqueta and Putumayo, although rapidly expanding to fifty thousand acres, still only accounts for less than ten per cent of the cocaine production. The remainder is imported from the other two Latin American countries where it is a major crop. One is Peru. The other is Bolivia, where the leading drug baron installed a government of his choice because he didn't like the one which had been elected democratically.

That government later fell. The baron is still in business.

16

In Santa Ana de Yacuma there has never been a fiesta to compare with the one which began that March day in 1983 when the younger Roberto Suarez finally returned from American captivity, unconvicted like his father always insisted he would be. Nor is there likely to be, ever again. Because there will probably never again be as great a cause for celebration in the Bolivian province of Beni.

There was a maracas-clicking band – one of several brought in over the succeeding, exhausting days – to greet his arriving aircraft. Fifty suckling pigs and twenty calves had already been airlifted from the provincial centre of Trinidad and were roasting in the town's garlanded square. Another charter plane brought imported whisky, beer and wine from as far away as Bolivia's capital, La Paz, for the five thousand festive townsfolk. The party went on, day into night, night into day, for a week, and whenever the food or drink appeared to be running out, fresh charter planes were despatched to collect more.

Throughout, the festivities were dominated by Roberto Suarez snr, who dominates everything in Bolivia. His own aircraft – one of his recognisable private fleet – was dutifully greeted with more frenzied enthusiasm than his son's. He started confettiing ten- and twenty-dollar bills at the aeroplane door and continued throwing them into the eagerly outstretched hands as he descended the steps and made his triumphantly royal progress through the crowds into the town. It was a gesture he could well afford, just as he could afford to pay the $50,000 (£33,000) that the week-long party cost.

After all, to secure his son's release he had earlier made it known to the American Department of State that he would settle by instalments Bolivia's $4,000,000,000 (£2,631,000,000) foreign debt. He financed and maintained in power a military government for thirteen months. He has personally built and equipped hospitals, paved roads and housed the country's poor. And created a personal bodyguard headed by a fugitive Nazi mass murderer.

Roberto Suarez snr runs the cocaine empire of Bolivia. There is nothing, therefore, that he cannot afford. And nothing that any government in the West – and certainly not in La Paz – can do to stop him.

During a lengthy Washington meeting, John Bacon and Eileen Hayes, Bolivian specialists from the Drug Enforcement Administration's intelligence division, talked to me openly about Bolivia being a 'totally hopeless situation'. Suarez, they conceded, had more resources than the then incumbent president, Hernan Siles Zuazo. Bacon said, 'I don't think we have any hope ever of any kind of eradication or control . . .'

Neither, in La Paz, do the current Bolivian government. Zuazo's inability to move against Suarez led to a weakening of his already uncertain coalition government when the leftist Revolutionary Movement gave up six cabinet posts in protest at the Minister for the Interior's open admission of impotence.

The Minister, Mario Roncal, complained to the Bolivian senate, 'They say drug-trafficking is on the increase and that is true. They say aeroplanes carrying 220 to 240 lb of cocaine leave the country and that is true. If the US, with all its resources, cannot prevent the arrival of planes loaded with drugs, less so can a poor country like ours prevent those planes from leaving.'

Zuazo also complained. While the celebration party was being held at Santa Ana de Yacuma, he told parliament, 'We are committed to arrest people like Suarez and the other godfathers. This is part of plans and operations that cannot be made public until they are carried out. The drug traffickers have a lot of money and are better armed than our National Guard.'

Zuazo and his uneasy government did not only have to deal with the traffickers. In May 1983, representatives of the eight thousand coca farmers in the department of Cochabamba, in which the growing area of Tropical Chapare is located, and the Chapare region proper, which includes the provinces of Arani, Carrasco and Tortora, concluded a three-day convention with a direct rejection of any efforts on the part of the government to curtail their annual harvest of 54,017.85 tons of coca leaf.

Of that production, only about 15,714.28 tons can properly be accounted for. The remaining 38,303.57 tons of leaf are reduced by the refining process into 191.51 tons of paste, which, once it reaches the laboratories of Colombia, converts into 76.7 tons of cocaine.

'Hopeless,' insists John Bacon.

Except for men like Roberto Suarez.

Suarez is an exception among the drug czars of Latin America: he is a sophisticated, well-educated man from an already rich and influential family. His parents were educated in Europe – predominantly Germany – and one of his relations was the first Bolivian ambassador to Britain. The son Suarez welcomed at Santa Ana de Yacuma speaks with a Texan accent acquired during an extensive American education, and the shouts of gratitude for his largesse as he dispensed bills on the triumphal passage from the airport were always prefaced with the respectful title 'Don'. The country's bankers addressed Suarez in the same respectful manner when they pleaded for dollar loans to fill an empty exchequer after US President Carter withdrew aid in protest against the drug-running government Suarez had installed in power. Suarez found no difficulty in making up the US shortfall.

Suarez was once a cattle farmer. Today he has coca plantations of vast acreages dotted throughout the Chapare, Beni and Santa Cruz regions of the country. From those estates, drug analysts in Washington estimate that Suarez is personally responsible for twenty-five of the forty-five tons of cocaine that enter America each year, giving him an annual income of around $600,000,000. He only ships a comparatively small amount of refined cocaine direct to the United States. The rest he moves as base – the yellow-coloured substance that is produced when the alkaloid is separated from the coca leaf by mixing it with kerosene, sulphuric and hydrochloric acids and bicarbonate of soda – which is refined by traffickers such as Pablo Escabar into a finished product.

Although Suarez was easily able to come to the rescue of his country when it was approaching bankruptcy – one source told me this was 'petty cash' normally used for day-to-day dealing – narcotic agents believe the majority of Suarez's enormous wealth is spread through numbered accounts in Switzerland. It was on a visit to these European holdings that his son was arrested by the Swiss authorities in December 1981, trying to enter Locarno from Madrid on a false Colombian passport. According to later investigations, Roberto Suarez jnr was carrying $250,000 in cash. He had travelled to Europe to invest on his father's behalf a further $10,000,000 that was being wired into the country.

The simple passport offence later made it possible for American authorities to extradite the younger Suarez to Miami to face charges arising from a 1980 operation for which the intended but elusive target had been the cocaine king himself. That Suarez snr avoided involvement – although unsuccessful charges were subsequently laid against him as well as his son – was due not just to the man's inherent caution but to the fact that his security adviser was an inconspicuous clerk-like man named Klaus Barbie.

The security expert had other names as well. In Bolivia, where he lived in increasing affluence from 1951 onwards, it was Klaus Altmann. In the French city where from 1942 until 1944 he was the Gestapo chief who killed and deported thousands and was personally involved in the torture-murder of wartime resistance hero Jean Moulin, he was known as the Butcher of Lyon.

Suarez bankrolled Barbie for the creation of a mercenary

protection squad called the Fiancés of Death – a song favoured by the French Foreign Legion – as his crack Praetorian Guard. The unit was in the forefront of the fighting when Suarez changed Bolivia's government. The arrest of Suarez jnr was, in fact, a serious and worrying distraction during the manipulation of that government, but his father was sufficiently confident of its success – and of the increasing fortune that was to accrue from that success – to make his four-billion-dollar ransom offer to Washington.

It was Suarez's need for ever-better outlets stimulating ever-better profits that led to his son's arraignment. In the autumn of 1979, the ground intelligence network of the US Drug Enforcement Administration picked up rumours that Suarez had fallen out with Pablo Escabar and other Colombian middlemen and had decided to reduce his reliance upon them and increase his income by dealing directly with America. His problem was establishing an American outlet. The Enforcement Agency decided to provide it.

Their opportunity came when Marcelo Ibanez, a farmer from Santa Cruz and an old and trusted friend of Suarez, travelled to Buenos Aires on a speculative selling expedition. Attached to the US embassy to Argentina was DEA agent Michael Levine: within a week he learned of Ibanez's arrival and of his purpose. From an alerted DEA headquarters on Washington's I. Street came immediate instructions: set up a sting operation.

Levine, a darkly handsome, saturnine man, typically Latino, trickled the word back to Ibanez through his underworld contacts that he was the representative of a well-established syndicate on America's East Coast, in town on a speculative buying expedition. Seller met buyer in a nightclub overlooking the old port, the Boca. The initial mutual apprehension was understandable, considering the subject of their discussion, but gradually a rapport developed between the two men. Levine assured the Colombian that his syndicate controlled clandestine airstrips and could manipulate customs and law enforcement agencies within Miami, and Ibanez assured the American that supply was no problem. When Levine asked what quantity was available, Ibanez replied calmly that he could guarantee 10.37 cwt per month – more than the administration had seized entering Miami for the entire previous year! Of greater significance for the sting operation Levine was attempting to set up, that one month's purchase would cost $20,000,000. And Levine knew the DEA could not raise that much ready cash.

Levine had an acting background which came in useful that night, sipping drinks and looking out over the Buenos Aires port. His syndicate was made up of respectable, conservative businessmen, he explained: not jewellery-laden, ostentatious Mafiosi. While he personally liked and trusted Ibanez, his colleagues would need to be convinced that the asociation under discussion would be discreet as well as worthwhile. Better, advised Levine, not to suggest over eagerness by providing too impressive an initial supply. A first delivery of half a ton would be sufficient to convince them: if each side liked the other, the shipment could then be increased to one ton in succeeding months.

Ibanez approved of the restraint, but it still left the DEA to find $9,000,000 it didn't have. However, getting the money was not the primary objective: that was getting Suarez. Levine invited Ibanez and Roberto Suarez to travel up from Bolivia to inspect his fictional set-up in Miami. Ibanez undertook to pass the invitation on to Suarez and, the following day, Levine flew to Miami to create that set-up. The Sting.

It proved to be easy to obtain finance for the supposed purchase of half a ton of cocaine, which would have netted profits of $230,000,000 once it was sold on. The agency borrowed from the Federal Reserve Bank in Florida and transferred the cash to safe deposit boxes at the Commercial Bank of Kendall, in the city's suburbs.

Enticing the Nazi-advised Suarez to America was much more difficult.

To create the ambience of an organised crime environment that Levine had described to Suarez's emissary in

236

Buenos Aires, in May 1980 the DEA rented what they considered to be a lavish beachside house in Florida's Fort Lauderdale, a luxurious three-bedroom affair with a swimming pool and a bar equipped well enough to serve any conceivable cocktail. Lincoln Continental limousines were hired, to be parked outside. A warehouse was rented and equipped as a refining laboratory for the base that Suarez was supposed to supply, and a DEA chemist – Paul Sennett – put in charge to demonstrate some technical expertise when the promised Bolivian product arrived. The most attractive female agents employed by the DEA were seconded to the house as maids and escorts for the Bolivian party. From San Francisco DEA agent Frances Johnson arrived to act as Levine's Spanish-speaking 'wife'. Richard Fiano, another Spanish speaker, was designated chauffeur but also made responsible for the Florida part of the operation that Levine had boasted spread northwards the entire length of America's East Coast. And even more impressive than the bar at the Fort Lauderdale house were the electronic eavesdropping devices that were installed to pick up conversations in every room – even the bathroom – with additional, particularly sensitive apparatus to record telephone calls. Those telephone bugs were to feature heavily in subsequent events.

From Fort Lauderdale Levine telephoned Ibanez in Santa Cruz to make arrangements for the Miami meeting. May 15 would be fine, Ibanez said: Roberto Suarez snr would definitely be coming.

But he didn't.

Only Ibanez arrived. He seemed less assured than he had been in Argentina, was distinctly unimpressed with the Fort Lauderdale house and uninterested in seeing either the carefully created laboratory or the $9,000,000 bait. And he had no time for parties. His main concern was to telephone Santa Cruz and speak to Suarez. The recordings worked perfectly.

The intended sting didn't.

Ibanez announced that Suarez – who was planning the

overthrow of the hostile government which looked likely to come to power after a democratic election – was not after all coming to America. Instead the Americans would have to fly to Bolivia to meet Suarez and take delivery of the first consignment; Suarez would then nominate emissaries to collect the money, once there was confirmation that the drug hand-over had been completed. The narcotics agents had no alternative but to agree. DEA pilots hurried to the beach house for detailed instructions about routes and landing spots. They gave Ibanez particulars of the aircraft they would be using – an ancient, creaking Convair – and they telephoned Robert Suarez jnr to talk about establishing fuel dumps at intermediary stops along the way.

They departed from Fort Lauderdale within twenty-four hours of Ibanez's original arrival, with Richard Fiano flying with him to conclude the deal. It took several days to reach Bolivia because the aircraft broke down and had to be repaired en route. During the delay, in Barbados, there were further telephone calls between Ibanez and Suarez. It wasn't easy, but the agents managed to record most of them. On 21 May the repaired Convair finally lifted off for Manaus, the Brazilian staging post where they were due to meet the thirty-year-old nephew of the cocaine king, Renato Roca Suarez. An experienced pilot, Renato produced maps and route instructions for the hand-over landing strip, a deserted dirt track carved out of the impenetrable jungle near Lake Rogagua in the Beni province.

The Americans were properly apprehensive of Suarez's informants within the Bolivian government and decided the flight had to be unofficial, without any notification – or request for assistance – from the authorities in La Paz. Renato Suarez was also anxious that the flight shouldn't be logged. The Convair's flight plan was therefore officially registered for Santa Cruz, but once en route the pilot radioed the control tower to say he was turning back into Brazil because of engine trouble. He didn't, of course. Instead he dropped to an altitude he hoped would be low enough to conceal him from any radar in Colombia's humped and ridged mountains and continued on to Lake Rogagua.

It was a rough landing – the nose wheel hydraulics were ruptured – but even before the aircraft came to a halt, Indians emerged from the surrounding jungle with the fuel that had been ordered by telephone for the flight back to America. There was no sign of Suarez. Within thirty minutes there was the sound of a small aircraft approaching. When it landed, Roberto Suarez jnr emerged and apologised for his father's absence to a disappointed Richard Fiano. He, instead, would be completing the transaction. There was not, as had been agreed, 5.67 cwt: the consignment weighed only 5.18 cwt but it was of excellent quality. As another Indian labour squad ferried black dustbin bags of the cocaine base from Suarez's aircraft to the damaged Convair, the DEA pilot took photographs of Suarez and Fiano talking together.

The overloaded, damaged aircraft only just avoided crashing into Rogagua lake on take-off. Once airborne, Fiano radioed Levine in Miami that the transaction had been completed. Ibanez remained in Bolivia and cabled a similar message to the Bolivian in Miami nominated to make the collection of the nine million dollars. The man was Alfredo Gutierrez, former President of the Santa Cruz Chamber of Commerce, owner of an air taxi fleet and a trusted friend of Suarez. But although trusted, Gutierrez still had a 'minder' – Roberto Gasser, son of Bolivian sugar millionaire and industrialist Erwin Gasser, a cocaine trafficker in his own right.

On 22 May, as the Bolivians arrived at the Commercial Bank of Kendall to collect the money, they were arrested by Drug Enforcement officers. No formal charges were made against Roberto Gasser, who returned the same day to Bolivia, but Gutierrez was indicted on charges of conspiring to smuggle cocaine into the United States and distribute it. On 3 June a Federal Grand Jury returned indictments against Suarez, his son and Ibanez, as well as Gutierrez. Bail was initially set for Gutierrez – the only accused in

239

custody – at $3,000,000. In July he sought to have it reduced before District Court Judge Alcee Hastings who, eighteen months later, was to be charged with obstructing justice and soliciting bribes for favourable treatment. Judge Hastings reduced the bail to $1,000,000. Gutierrez paid, walked out of court and caught the next available plane back to Bolivia.

Suarez's plans to install his own government were on the point of being put into operation. Those plans had been finalised with the immense care with which the cocaine barons in neighbouring Colombia had created their anti-kidnapping organisation, and for identical reasons: Suarez and the other major traffickers saw political uncertainty as a threat to their huge and lucrative operations.

For many years, the cocaine barons had not had to contend with any uncertainty. President Hugo Banzer – of German ancestry and a protector of Klaus Barbie – had been a trafficker during his seven years of office (1971–8), flying wide-bodied transporters into Colombia from the specially created airstrip on his vast estates in San Javier. Even after he had been deposed and a brief anti-narcotic campaign was being orchestrated by a police chief called Jorge Selum, a Colombian plane was observed to land and load three hundred pounds of cocaine base from Banzer's airstrip.

It was a continuation of those anti-narcotic campaigns that Suarez and the other barons feared. Even though the democratically elected Siles Zuazo had insufficient plurality to form an effective government, Suarez decided it was more prudent to install one of his own and remove any doubt. He convened a meeting of the leading barons at the Club Bavaria in Santa Cruz. As well as Erwin Gasser it was attended by a third prominent trafficker named Jorge Naller, the owner of vast plantations around Monteverde, Okinawa and Perseverancia in northern Santa Cruz. Barbie was also there, along with a contingent of his Fiancés of Death. Naller's bodyguard was a Frenchman named Jacques Leclerk, part of Jean Jehan's original

French Connection drug ring who had fled to Uruguay, and from there to Bolivia, when the organisation was destroyed in 1972.

The drug barons had been well advised about the probable reactions of the military to a well-financed coup. Their informant was Suarez's cousin, Colonel Luis Arce Gomez, who had used his position to build up a flourishing trafficking organisation of his own, establishing with Colonel Norberto Salomon a fleet of aircraft which they used to transport their cocaine into Colombia. At Gomez's suggestion, the barons made their move through General Hugo Echeverria, the army commander in Santa Cruz, and for $800,000 (£344,827) – which Suarez, Naller and Gasser provided between them – he set up a meeting with General Luis Garcia Meza, the overall army commander. Meza was offered a bribe of $1,300,000 to lead the coup, although this, the barons explained, was only a down payment against the vast future profits to be made. During that first meeting, Suarez insisted upon one important condition: his experienced relation, Arce Gomez, was to be given the most important position as Minister of the Interior.

On 17 July 1980 Meza led what was the 189th coup in the country's 157-year history as an independent state. From the first day the new regime made clear its intention of total control of the country, to be imposed by violence if necessary. Barbie's Fiancés of Death were virtually seconded to Arce Gomez's ministry, in addition to Gomez's own suppression squads, the Special Security Service. Five hundred people died in the first two weeks of the takeover and another two thousand five hundred were put into jails where torture chambers were set up. At Suarez's instructions, on that same first day Arce Gomez had every narcotics file delivered to his office. Those dossiers contained all the material upon the country's traffickers which the American Drug Enforcement Administration had assembled and provided as part of their agreement with Bolivia's authorities.

'Within forty-eight hours of the takeover there were no major traffickers unaware of any intelligence report or profile we'd ever created on them, including in some cases our knowledge of their outlets and set-up in America, which they were promptly able to change,' an American source told me two years later. 'Our anti-narcotics efforts in the country were wrecked, practically overnight.'

Throughout the country, the Fiancés of Death – operating mainly in Santa Cruz – and Arce Gomez's security squads moved against the smaller cocaine dealers nominated by Suarez, smashing their operations and seizing whatever coca base they held, to be sold through what were now officially approved channels. They also destroyed anyone they considered to be a political – or trafficking – opponent.

Marcelo Quiroga Santa Cruz, head of the country's socialist party, was killed – with other trade union leaders – at the headquarters of the Bolivian Workers Central. Juan Lechin Oquendo, a union leader, was arrested and subjected to months of torture. Nine members of the political directorate of the Popular Democratic Unity – Zuazo's party – were tortured and murdered and Zuazo fled for his life to Peru. Victims of the killer squads were Jose Reyes Carvajal, a member of the suspended congress and former National Guardsman; Artemio Camargo, the leader of the Mineworkers' Union; Ricardo Navarro Magro, a sociology professor; Pedro Mariobo, a lawyer; Ramio Valasco Arce, an economics professor; Gonzalo Barron, a university student leader; Jose Luis Suarez Guzman, a sociology professor; and congressmen Jose Valdivieso Menacho and Arcil Menacho. The nine had been meeting in La Paz to discuss the government-introduced 'austerity programme' – which cut away subsidies for food and heating oil upon which the peasant population depended – when a combined squad of Arce Gomez's security force and Barbie's Fiancés of Death broke in, tortured and then killed them. The military junta issued a statement saying that the group consisted of 'potential terrorists with criminal intent'.

Meza's government – preoccupied with their cocaine profits – abandoned the programme of stabilisation which the International Monetary Fund had created to support the country's shaky economy. He and his trafficking cabinet were unconcerned. They were no more concerned when the US government suspended foreign aid totalling nearly $127,000,000 (£54,741,000) and reduced its diplomatic representation by withdrawing Ambassador Marvin Weissman. And they were positively delighted when Carter ordered back to Washington some of the now totally ineffective drug-monitoring agents.

The next thirteen months were a halcyon period for the drug barons of Bolivia. An analyst closely involved at the time – both in La Paz and Washington – told me, 'It is impossible to calculate the money they made. Think of a preposterous figure, double it and know damned well that you've made a gross underestimate.'

Although he was Suarez's cousin, an increasingly greedy Arce Gomez closely allied himself to the other major trafficker, Jorge Naller, who was also linked to Colonel Faustino Rico Toro, head of the country's military college – he trained Arce Gomez's killer squads – and high in Bolivia's army intelligence division. Widen Razuk, the Prefect of Santa Cruz, belonged to the same faction and Jose Battista, the customs chief at Santa Cruz airport, was a conveniently placed 'enforcer' for Naller. When he was assassinated, Omer Cassib took his place as Naller's protector.

Erwin Gasser was the paymaster for another Santa Cruz prefect, Oscar Ramon Vaca, and his enforcer was the man known as Mosca Monray, 'The Fly', who was in jail when the colonels staged their cocaine coup. He was released immediately, in sufficient time to blast with a bazooka the Jesuit radio station as it broadcast news of the government overthrow.

Suarez's army friends extended beyond Meza, Arce Gomez and General Echeverria. One particular supporter was Colonel Lara, commander of the elite Rangers Regiment which – with CIA help – had killed Cuban revolutionary Che Guevara in 1967. One of Suarez's enforcers was 'Coco' Ballivian, who had actually fought with

Guevara. Another was Rudi Landivar, a former army major.

After his bail flight from Miami, Alfredo Gutierrez continued to trade. In order to do so he established close and profitable links with Colonel Airel Coca, the Minister for Education and Culture.

Halcyon though it may have been for the traffickers, it was a time of disaster for Bolivia. America was not the only country to suspend recognition. Industry was neglected. Bankers had to ingratiate themselves with Suarez to borrow money and those who didn't had to close their doors while street-corner black marketeers sold pesos from suitcases.

Belatedly realising the dangerous implications of the ostracism to which the country was being subjected, the government made the first of what was to be a series of adroit and – partially at least – successful manoeuvres to deceive Washington and other outside observers. As in everything else, Suarez was the architect.

General Meza, an acknowledged trafficker, whose accession to power had been described by the Council on Hemispheric Affairs in Washington as the 'cocaine coup', declared a cosmetic narcotics purge throughout the notorious Santa Cruz region. The declaration was made two weeks after a warning had been spread through Suarez to Naller and Gasser and some of the intermediary traffickers, giving them time to move equipment, stockpiles and aircraft away from Santa Cruz into the adjoining province of Beni. The highly publicised swoop enabled Arce Gomez's security squads to mop up the few remaining independent dealers and seize their stocks, for later re-routing and sale. And Meza could boast of the attack on Bolivia's traffickers to the Washington administration of President Reagan.

The success was marred by an internal development that Suarez hadn't anticipated: Meza, Arce Gomez and their cabinet of army traffickers overestimated their power in a confrontation with the barons. They retained the cocaine base they had seized in Santa Cruz for their own enterprises and hit the small independents so badly that the supplies upon which Suarez and the others depended began to dry up.

Gomez's biggest mistake was to indicate his over-confidence when Suarez went to him and ordered the lifting of the Santa Cruz purge to preserve the remaining supply lines. The cost, he replied, would be $50,000,000 (£23,923,000). Suarez paid the bribe because he needed the supplies. But he didn't forget the arrogance.

He was quick to exact his revenge when it became obvious that the Santa Cruz purge had had little effect on Bolivia's relationship with the US government and that foreign aid was still being withheld from his near bankrupt country. A sacrifice was needed, he convinced the government, and it had to be Arce Gomez, a man who was publicly associated with the drug trade and human rights suppression. Gomez lost the title of Minister of the Interior, although he retained his power within the group of army advisers – of which the former President Banzer was also an influential member – and, of course, the facility to continue trafficking. In addition he kept his enforcement control, not only over his own security forces but over Klaus Barbie's Fiancés of Death. These security squads were renamed Special Investigation Department, the appropriate Spanish acronym for which was DIE.

Gomez's official replacement was another soldier, General Celso Torrelio Villa, who was to figure prominently in the reorganisation of the government which Suarez orchestrated in an attempt to convince the outside world that the country was not run by gangsters, which it was.

Suarez was virtually paymaster general to Bolivia's armed forces. General Waldo Bernal was reputed to receive $150,000 (£71,000) a week for allowing air force planes to transport coca paste to Colombia and the navy's Admiral Oscar Pammo not only dealt in drugs, but was linked with Meza in the illegal export of semi-precious stones to Brazil. Pammo was more loyal, however, to Suarez, the better paymaster. So were Banzer and Torrelio Villa.

Suarez decided it was not enough to dismiss Arce Gomez:

Meza would have to go as well. His loyal military junta concurred, without dissent, and in September 1981, Meza was supposedly overthrown by a military coup and replaced by Torrelio Villa.

It was stage-managed to impress Washington and succeeded. President Reagan appointed Edwin Corr – an anti-narcotics expert – as the new ambassador and soon after his arrival in La Paz he began to send optimistic reports about the chances of government reform under Torrelio Villa. From Washington there were encouraging indications that the frozen foreign aid might be released which prompted Suarez to make one more dramatic sacrifice: he instructed Torrelio Villa to return to American custody and later trial Alfredo Gutierrez, his former friend who had jumped bail after the sting operation for which Suarez himself stood indicted.

In reality, the change of government leader meant nothing. Meza continued trading as actively as ever and Suarez remained dominant overall. In spite of the phenomenal profits made by the drug barons, peasants starved and Bolivia suffered the worst poverty throughout the Latin American continent. There were protest marches and road blockades in an effort to draw attention to the plight of the thousands who were destitute. Industry stagnated and unemployment and inflation soared. Throughout the country right-wing and left-wing factions joined forces and made increasingly angry demands for government to be wrested from the inept, corrupt military and put into the hands of a civilian administration.

In an attempt to accelerate payment of the promised American aid, Torrelio Villa deported Marcelo Ibanez to stand trial with Gutierrez; both of them were subsequently jailed, Ibanez for twelve years, Gutierrez for five. Roberto Suarez jnr was extradited to Miami for arraignment and the US authorities rejected his father's ransom offer and denied accusations of legalised kidnapping.

Suarez then replaced Torrelio Villa with General Guido Vildosa Calderon, who came to office primed to promise civilian government within a year. Again this was no more than a cosmetic gesture. Klaus Barbie was still an honoured guest at the presidential palace.

The cocaine barons traded on. Satellite photographic intelligence gathered during the year of Vildoso Calderon's puppet period in office estimated that ninety thousand tons of coca leaves were grown in the Chapare and Yungas regions *alone*. Five years earlier the same area had produced under five thousand tons. Shortly before Calderon surrendered his office to a civilian administration, army officers still loyal to Meza and Arce Gomez, and to Suarez, entered the offices of Bolivia's Narcotics Board and removed every single record, most of which had, anyway, been rendered meaningless over the preceding months. When the civilian administration came to power there was not a single document on file and the military had even taken the typewriters. Like the Nazis, Suarez didn't believe in taking any chances.

Hernan Siles Zuazo re-entered office to return the country to constitutional rule for the first time for a total of eighteen years – and two years later than he should have done – with a more popular mandate to govern than he had had at the 1980 election. He came to power supported by people at home and abroad – in Washington and throughout Latin America – all of whom hoped that he would rectify the criminal mismanagement of the patchwork military regimes and move against the drug traffickers.

From the podium of the United Nations in New York Zuazo pledged to attack his country's drug dealers.

His early achievements were impressive: Barbie was expelled to French custody to await trial for his war crimes and Meza, Arce Gomez and Torrelio Villa fled to the sanctuary of Argentina, whose military dictatorship had supported the original cocaine coup. Into exile, too, went Colonel Rico Toro and Colonel Freddie Quiroga, former head of the army special security services, which had worked closely with Arce Gomez's political extermination squads, and both Vildosa Calderon and General Albert

Natusch Busch, another former drug-condoning president, were transferred from active military duty to the reserve list. Dozens of soldiers promoted by Meza were demoted and two hundred and twenty officers were arraigned for various misdemeanours before a military honours court.

Impressive indeed. Except that Suarez remained exactly where he had been for so long, in supreme and uninterrupted control of Bolivia's drug trade, and Erwin Gasser and Jorge Naller remained there with him. General Banzer, 1971–8 president, whose party, the National Democratic Action, ruled twenty per cent of the legislature, was also committed and able to oppose Zuazo at every turn.

There are currently estimated to be a minimum of 305,000 acres of coca plantations in Bolivia, although the true figure is probably nearer 1,000,000 acres. Part of the crop is produced for the native population who traditionally chew the coca leaf – workers' contracts usually stipulate a daily allocation of leaf, as well as salary – but only 85,400 acres of cultivation are necessary to supply *all* domestic requirements.

In April 1983 US Attorney General French Smith and DEA Administrator Francis Mullen travelled to La Paz to meet Zuazo and offer a $40,000,000 crop substitution programme for those additional acres. Following the meeting a communiqué was issued, stating that the American and Bolivian governments had agreed to collaborate on the project. One month earlier a much more significant communiqué had been issued after a meeting in Chulumani attended by representatives of the 12,000 peasant families in the most important coca-growing areas, North and South Yungas and Inquisivi. It said, quite simply, that they would not allow any eradication of their crop. Their feelings were reiterated by the farmers from the Chapare region in May.

Whatever Zuazo said after meetings with visiting American statesmen, his power in the country – diminished after political defections because of his inability to move against the traffickers – was too tenuous for him to confront either the remaining military or the coca-growing peasants. Just how tenuous that power was – and how strongly the military retain their drug links – was shown in June 1984 when Siles Zuazo was seized and held for ten hours in a failed military coup. A leader of the overthrow attempt was Colonel Rolando Saravia, one of the highest-ranking officers in army intelligence who had been dismissed prior to his arraignment on narcotics charges. Another was Lieutenant Colonel German Linares, head of the US-trained anti-cocaine elite force known as The Leopards. The coup failed because the army refused to join the rebellion. Its leaders were given sanctuary in the Venezuelan embassy.

French Smith's visit to the Bolivian capital took place in the same month as his department – intent upon convincing Zuazo of their determination to break the trafficking rings – issued a formal two-count indictment against Arce Gomez, who was by then living in a luxury villa in the exclusive Palermo district of Buenos Aires. The court document identified Gomez by a trafficking pseudonym – Lucho – and charged him with conspiring, with seventeen others, to ship hundreds of pounds of cocaine into America, primarily through Florida. Also named were Colonel Jose Tito Camacho, chief of the narcotics police in Santa Cruz; Jose Luis Gutierrez, former army major and operational head of the Santa Cruz narcotics force; and Juan Carlos Camacho, an attorney for the Ministry of the Interior and the Public Prosecutor at Santa Cruz. Hinting at the degree of control that the cocaine colonels enjoyed during their months in power, the court accused Gomez of seizing the cocaine from smaller traffickers who wouldn't pay protection and actually storing it for safekeeping in the nation's empty bank vaults.

An official request for Gomez's extradition was sent from Washington to Buenos Aires and for the sake of diplomatic appearances the former Bolivian officer was placed under supposed detention. The Argentine authorities also said they were considering an extradition request from Bolivia for Garcia Meza.

Neither request was likely to be implemented while

Leopold Galtieri's military regime ruled Argentina, but democracy returned to the country in December 1983 when a civilian government was installed under President Raul Alfonsin. One of Alfonsin's first acts was to announce human rights trials against Galtieri and two other military presidents, Jorge Videla and Robert Viola, and it is certain that he will consider the extradition requests for Gomez and Meza: intelligence reports from Argentina suggest that both are considering using their huge drug wealth to bribe their way to sanctuary in another Latin American country.

In Miami, Roberto Suarez jnr's lawyer successfully argued against the admissibility of much of the carefully recorded and photographed evidence and the jury found Suarez not guilty. He returned to Bolivia immediately.

'Maybe we should have taken the four billion ransom,' said one law enforcement officer after the verdict. 'At least we would have caused Suarez some hurt. And we could have used the money to fight other sources.'

Peru is the other major source of cocaine base. It is the country where Arce Gomez and Garcia Meza apparently want to go, if they have to get out of Argentina.

17

The town's official name is Tingo Maria but it is more commonly – and appropriately – called 'Snow City' because it is the provincial centre of Peru's Huallaga River Valley, where the most potent coca in the world is grown. It is a shabby place that wears its drug-affluence like an old lady with a threadbare coat sporting a Christmas boa: serape-cloaked *campesinos* siesta under broad-brimmed sombreros outside stores that sell – for cash – television sets for which there is no transmission. Three-car showrooms supply imported Mercedes and Toyotas and the drug-dealers' favourite, the huge-wheeled Ranchero station wagons, frequently custom-decorated with flames or devil's features along the sides of the vehicle. For cash again, of course. And along the one paved street in this town of thirty-five thousand inhabitants, there are ten hotels catering for the area's most important customers, the drug growers and the drug buyers.

The cocaine king of the Huallaga Valley is Luis Lucho Porto, who has used his training as an agronomist in the creation of estates which vastly exceed his legally permitted hundred acres, although that training is almost wasted on the coca plant, which – like the opium poppy – will grow and thrive where any other crop would wither and die.

Until he was jailed in 1981 for financing a cocaine transaction, Porto's biggest rival was Guillermo Cardenas Davila, also known by the nickname 'Crazy Fly'. Like dealers in all the drug-producing countries, Davila cultivated the image of a public benefactor, binding the peasants more

251

closely to him than to any government in distant Lima. He controlled the Bellavista area, a hundred and sixty miles to the north of Tingo Maria, and when heavy rain brought flooding to the region, Davila used his drug-transporting aircraft fleet to supply – ahead of the government – food, other essential supplies and construction materials to help replace their devastated homes.

He stimulated additional interest in the area from the drug barons of neighbouring Bolivia and Colombia through relations who trade – predominantly in marijuana – from the Colombian centre of Cali. It was through the Davila family that Roberto Suarez became interested in expanding his activities beyond his own country into Peru.

President Fernando Belaunde Terry, elected in 1981 as Peru's first civilian President after twelve years of military rule, was as aware of the drug baron's power as is his successor, socialist Alan Garcia. The military made one token move into the Huallaga area and then ignored the barons like Porto and Davila and the *cocaleros*, the small coca farmers with whom Suarez has established contact.

After Belaunde's election some of the military went into exile in Argentina; it is those exiled Peruvian officers – aided by the expert Arce Gomez and Garcia Meza – whom Suarez wants to use to expand his already huge empire. This could happen.

Belaunde was uncertain of his military support and the *cocaleros* – electors as well as coca farmers – openly told him, like the growers in neighbouring Bolivia told their government, that they had no intention of switching from coca to US-sponsored substitutions such as coffee, bananas or rice, which bring in twenty times less income. Belaunde pleaded with Washington for an enormous increase in financial assistance (i.e. from $18,500,000 to $1,200,000,000) in order to launch an effective campaign against narcotics. Not only did he have to compete with the financial incentives offered by the barons, his greatest difficulty was persuading the Peruvian peasants *why* they should eradicate a crop that has been part of their culture since the Inca civilisation.

The dead were buried with coca to sustain them on their journey to the other world. Priests chewed it to put themselves into prophesying trances and at one stage it became the exclusive prerogative of the royal court to enjoy it. When the Spanish *conquistadores* first arrived they determined to eradicate its use because their priests told them it played a part in native heathen practices, but when they discovered that the local slaves worked better on coca, they initiated the practice which is still partly followed today, of paying wages in coca leaves.

The Peruvian natives call it *khoka* and regard it as a sacred plant, a gift from the gods. They mix it with lime and chew it to ward off hunger, and in addition to its nutritional value the raw leaf helps fight fatigue and improves sexual prowess. Among the Indian population, distances are measured in units of *cocada*, how far they can travel with a chew of coca until they need to create a fresh wad. It has become, therefore, a measurement of time as well – usually forty minutes.

In a country of soaring altitudes, it is legal to cultivate the coca plant above thirteen thousand feet as coca tea is supplied at tourist hotels as a remedy for altitude sickness. This is why trafficker Luis Porto is legally permitted to farm one hundred acres. Legal cultivation is controlled by the Empressa Nacional de la Coca, ENACO, which was created in 1969 to control the entire coca production in the country. Two thousand vendors are authorised to sell the crop on behalf of the legalised growers. Officially there are about 109,000 acres under government-acknowledged legal cultivation which, in 1982, produced 9747 tons of coca leaf. A conservative estimate, however, suggests that 310,000 acres is given over to illicit cultivation, and intelligence reports dating up to mid-1983 indicate that a more accurate figure is 700,000 acres. Perhaps still more, as there have since been signs that the farmers are responding to rising foreign demands.

The alkaloid content of the Peruvian coca is particularly

high and therefore much valued by chemists and users. Illegal drug-trading activities earn Peru a minimum annual income of $1,000,000,000 (£690,000,000), rivalling and some say easily surpassing the country's supposed chief export, oil.

In 1982 the intelligence unit of the American Drug Enforcement Administration carried out a theoretical survey and concluded that the clandestine coca plantations in Peru were capable of producing around 36,000 tons of coca leaf, from which 176.78 tons of drug-base paste could be refined. This, in turn, could be refined into 70.71 tons of the highest purity cocaine. As the purity level tends to be an average twenty per cent by the time the drug reaches the street, this means that every year, available for export from Peru, is sufficient paste to make 354.31 tons of cocaine.

During the Carter presidency drug-expert Ambassador Edwin Corr was appointed to Lima and persuaded Belaunde to consider eradication of the coca crop. By the time Reagan came to power in Washington, the Department of State's Agency for International Development – AID – had evolved a much criticised plan to spray the 250-mile long Huallaga River Valley with crop-destroying herbicides. The polluted river would inevitably have spread these toxic chemicals through a vast area of Latin America. At one stage the herbicide under consideration by AID was Agent Orange, the defoliant which was extensively used by the Americans in Vietnam and blamed for causing cancer and birth defects.

In fact, spraying was never introduced because Congress cut off the aid to finance its implementation, and there has been minimal manual eradication – 'just enough to impress the Americans that something is being done to justify the aid,' one source told me – by the digging up of the plants. Another expert, based in Peru, commented, 'Politically, Belaunde couldn't afford to carry out the widespread destruction that America was demanding. The peasants would have seen it as an attack upon them by central government and the military would do little to try to correct that impression. And Belaunde would have been out of office.'

Like governments in other drug-producing countries, the Peruvian government is virtually impotent in the face of the massive profits that are to be made from drug-trading: during one month in the autumn of 1982, drug agents established that £14,285,000 passed through the Tingo Maria branch of the Bank of Credit of Tocacha, another Peruvian city. Worse still, an additional problem has been introduced into the country by the Colombian drug barons.

Coca paste is created by steeping the leaves of the plant in kerosene, sulphuric acid and an alkali. The addition of hydrochloric acid provides the salt – cocaine hydrochloride – which can have a purity of ninety to a hundred per cent, depending upon the sophistication of the extracting process. After that process, however, there remains in the refining drums an impurity-packed, acid-tainted detritus which can be mixed with tobacco – sometimes marijuana – and smoked. Roberto Suarez is one of the greatest traffickers of that substance, which is known as 'bazooka'.

In Medellin, where bazooka-smoking is widespread, I was told by one drug expert, 'Nothing could be more aptly named. It literally explodes the mind. But what is peculiar about it, compared to all other drugs, is that it invariably provokes the most violent – sometimes homicidal – aggression in the user.'

Peru, like Colombia, has an extensive bazooka problem, particularly among high school children. Discussing a thirteen-day visit he paid to Latin America in 1983, French Smith said he had learned that Peru's total addict population, including the bazooka smokers, was between 140,000 and 150,000. Echoing Washington's optimism that they will eventually persuade producing countries to attempt control and eradication, he said, 'If anything gets a country's attention, it is when their own population is becoming addicted to the crops they grow!'

There is still another drug-related problem creating difficulties for the government. Peru has a group of revolutionary guerillas – the 'Sendero Luminoso' (Shining Path) – who have reached an arrangement similar to that which exists in Colombia to provide protection for some of the Peruvian coca plantations in exchange for finance and weapons. At the end of October 1983, the revolutionaries assassinated General Carlos Herrera, director of the plainclothes branch of the police training school, in retaliation for the arrest by the government of Antonio Diaz Martinez, one of the top five men in the Sendero hierarchy.

In August 1984, the 'Sendero Luminoso' drove the US-trained anti-narcotics service out of the Tingo Maria area of Monzon. The government had to use aircraft and helicopter support for a troop assault to regain limited control.

President Belaunde gave public warning that narcotics provide the principal source of finance for the terrorists within his country and that the combination of narcotics and revolutionaries poses the greatest threat to its – and his – stability. He was aware this created a climate in which the country's right-wing military might feel forced to make a coup to curb the increasing strength of the left-wing guerillas. From the remoter regions of the country – like Ayacucho, Lucanas and Huancavelica – there are reports of terror raids by the army and even massacres of peasants they suspect of supporting the revolutionaries. Under pressure, General Clemente Noel, who has authority over eleven rural zones, has agreed to conduct an enquiry into allegations of army atrocities, having originally blamed the killings upon the guerillas.

As well as the financial support provided by the narcotics trade, in their opposition to the government the guerillas have the backing and guidance of the third communist country actively engaged in the drug trade: Cuba.

18

For an impoverished country committed to spreading Left-ist revolution throughout Latin America, drugs provide the perfect answer. And Cuba provides the perfect bridge between the revolutionaries to the south and the American shoreline only ninety miles to the north.

It is conservatively estimated by US intelligence agencies that Cuba's annual income from its role as middleman in drug-trading activities is £1,379,000,000. Vice Admiral Aldo Santamaria Cuadrado, commander of the Cuban navy and one of Fidel Castro's closest advisers, has been publicly accused in Miami of conspiring to smuggle drugs. He remains free in Havana. Another Cuban indicted in Miami – but free in Cuba – is Rene Rodriquez Cruz, Director of the Cuban Institute of Friendship with the People, a front organisation for the Cuban intelligence service, the Direccion General de Inteligencia or DGI. In July 1983, a captain from the DGI – named as Perez Mendez – defected to the United States. He told his intelligence debriefers that he was in charge of a section of the Institute of Friendship known as the Overseas Community Department. As such, he claimed that at least three hundred individuals in Florida, considered by the US administration to be fervent anti-Castro exiles, were, in fact, actively trading in drugs with Havana. In secret interrogation sessions he testified further that the drug trade was under the personal supervision of Fidel Castro's brother, Raul, who benefited personally from the financial transactions.

This information matched evidence obtained earlier from

a Colombian drug runner, Jaime Guillot Lara, the contact between Cuba and the revolutionary M-19 movement. Guillot had been arrested in Mexico and said under interrogation that he was able to trade with the personal approval of Raul and other members of Castro's inner cabinet. Having supplied the information, Guillot was not brought to trial. He is now believed to be in Spain, possibly with Jaime Bateman Cayon who was his drugs-for-guns source and headed the M-19 guerilla movement until his abrupt and unexplained disappearance in July 1983.

The Reagan administration has cast aside any diplomatic ambiguity and accused Castro openly. In a statement to the Senate in April 1983, James H. Michel, Deputy Assistant Secretary of State for Inter-American Affairs, said, 'We have a report that the Communist Party Presidium, and specifically Fidel Castro, in early 1979 considered a scheme to begin dealing with narcotics smugglers, using Cuba as a bridge and support base for the networks to the United States as a means to aid Cuba economically and to contribute to the deterioration of American society.'

That scheme became known as the Mariel Boatlift, named after the Cuban port from which 130,000 Cubans fled in apparent rejection of the Castro regime in spring 1980. America was, naïvely, as sympathetic to their cause as to the Vietnamese Boat People escaping from the communist regime in Vietnam. Only later – too late – was it to emerge that the Cuban refugees included at least 3000 Cuban intelligence officers, many of whom had been trained specifically to cultivate the drug trade, and the occupants of Cuba's jails: 24,000 of them had criminal records and at least 2000 had been involved in violent crime. In the limited area controlled by the New York City Police Department, records show that between May and December 1983, there were 6288 arrests of people who had entered America under the Mariel Boatlift.

One of the agents infiltrated into America was Mario Estebes Gonzalez. That was the assumed name under which he testified to investigators. He now has an entirely new identity – including passport, social security number and bank accounts in another secret name – and a new home far from Florida where he originally settled. That protection was given in exchange for the information that Estebes provided to American investigators after being caught on a drug run. He also gave evidence before the Senate Select Committee on Crime.

Estebes, now thirty-six, was born in Havana and underwent training as a naval mechanic before being employed by the Special Bureau of Missions in the Cuban Ministry of the Interior. The Bureau is another outlet of the Direccion General de Inteligencia, which is controlled and dominated by the KGB. Russian control officers monitor activities at every level and are as involved with the Cuban secret service as they are with Bulgaria's Dajnavna Sigurnost.

The section of the US Justice Department responsible for re-allocating Cuban refugees records that Estebes left a specially created camp at Fort Chaffee, Arkansas, on 4 June 1980. His first assignment was to infiltrate a Florida-based group known as Alpha 66, an exile organisation genuinely opposed to Fidel Castro. Estebes was instructed to relay back to the Ministry of the Interior in Cuba the identities and as many details about its members as possible, and also to sabotage any vessels designated for attack or agent drops along the Cuban coast.

Two months after his release from the Arkansas refugee camp, knowing from his reports that he was now an accepted émigré into America, the Cuban Ministry of the Interior recalled Estebes to Havana. There he was given a concentrated course in drug-trafficking and a list of narcotics contacts already established in Florida, a state appropriately shaped like an accusing finger towards the Caribbean. His new assignment was to smuggle drugs through the already established networks. He was remarkably successful. When he later testified to Senate investigators – masked and then doubly protected behind a screen in a heavily guarded hearing-room – he attested under oath that in 1980 and 1981 he smuggled £3,400,000-worth of cocaine, marijuana and

Quaalude from Cuba into Florida and from there up the Eastern seaboard into New York. And there had been occasions when he personally trafficked cocaine at Studio 54, the Mecca at the time for the New York set.

Estebes identified Rene Rodriquez Cruz – also named by Perez Mendez – as the person to whom the vast drug profits were channelled. As well as being director of the Institute of Friendship with the People, Rodriquez Cruz is a high-ranking officer in the Cuban Ministry of the Interior – a member, therefore, of the intelligence service.

Estebes would have remained obedient to his Havana instructions had he not been arrested by the US Coast Guard on 29 November 1981, running 2500 lb of marijuana from an out-of-limits mothership to the Florida mainland in a smaller transport boat called *Lazy Lady*. The indictment on a charge of possessing marijuana with intent to distribute carried a maximum prison sentence of fifteen years. By co-operating with the authorities he received nine months – which, because of the time he had spent in custody, pending trial, meant his immediate release – and he was given a new identity under the Witness' Protection Programme operated by the American Department of Justice.

Estebes provided vital confirmation of earlier information supplied by Jaime Guillot, who had told his interrogators that under the protection of Vice Admiral Santamaria he had been allowed to unload his Colombian motherships at Paredon Grande in Cuba. Quite independently from Jaime Guillot, Estebes said that at a briefing meeting with Rodriquez Cruz, he was present when the Cuban naval officer issued those protection instructions. He also told his American debriefers that he was instructed on his drug-running espionage missions by Cuban intelligence officials Rodabaldo Rico and Francisco Echmendia and other instructors who used codenames such as Lt-Col. Nelson, Captain Efrain and Lt-Col. Carlos. Vice Admiral Santamaria used the alias Rene Baeza-Rodriguez.

Fidel Castro, not unnaturally, emphatically refutes any suggestion that his government is knowingly or actively involved in narcotics trafficking. In an August 1985 interview with America's *Playboy* magazine, he said, 'During the past twenty-six years Cuba's record in this regard has been *spotless* (Castro's emphasis) because the first thing the revolution did in our country, where drugs were once freely used, sold and produced, was to eradicate that problem. Strict measures were taken to destroy marijuana plantations and to strongly punish all forms of drug production and trafficking. Since the victory of the revolution, for twenty-six years, no drugs have been brought into our country, nor has any money been made from the drugs coming from anywhere else.'

Reminded that US Secretary of State George Shultz had openly said Cuba allowed overflights of aircraft it knew to be ferrying drugs, Castro said, 'Look, our country is the place drug smugglers fear the *most* (Castro's emphasis). They all try to avoid landing in Cuba or making any sort of stop on our coasts, because they have a lot of experience with the consequences and the strict measures taken in our country. . . . Small civilian aircraft penetrate our airspace rather frequently and they don't pay our interceptors the slightest attention. Having to decide whether or not to fire on an unarmed civilian aircraft is a serious, tragic question. There's no way you can be sure who's in it. An aircraft in the air isn't like an automobile on a road that can be stopped, identified and searched. The occupants may be drug smugglers but they may also be off course or trying to save fuel by taking a shorter route. They may be families, journalists, businessmen or adventurers – of whom there are many in the United States – who are afraid to land and be arrested in Cuba.

'Even though it is blockaded by the United States and doesn't have any obligation to cooperate with the United States on this or any other problem, Cuba has stood sentinel against drug trafficking in the Caribbean – as a matter of self-respect, a simple question of prestige and moral rectitude. Is it right that the treatment we receive in exchange is the infamous accusation that Cuba is involved in drug trafficking?'

261

The protestations are as empty as they read.

The government of Fidel Castro also provides sanctuary for the man who masterminded the biggest corporate robbery in United States history: in two years American financier Robert Vesco robbed hundreds of British and American piggy-bank savers in an embezzlement estimated at £146,000,000. In August 1970, at the age of thirty-four, Vesco took over the Investors Overseas Services from offshore financier Bernard Cornfeld. Over a period of two years he looted the company, selling blue-chip US securities from IOS funds and siphoning off the cash through offshore banks.

Vesco, who tried to reach a compromise with American investigators by secretly contributing to Richard Nixon's campaign fund (and later also made an approach to the Carter administration), is now a Havana-based drugs-and-gun runner and has strong links with the drug barons in Colombia and Bolivia. American investigators have found provable links between Vesco and the two Colombian billionaire barons, Carlos Lehder and Pablo Escabar. Vesco acted as middleman for Lehder and Escabar in a deal with Frederico Vaughan, an aide to Nicaraguan Interior Minister Thomas Borge, to import cocaine into the United States. Vesco was also party to a separate deal – disclosed to a US Senate enquiry by Nicaraguan diplomatic defector Antonio Farach – made between Sandinista Defence Minister Humberto Ortega, brother of the Nicaraguan leader Daniel Ortega, and Raul Castro, to import drugs into the United States using Nicaragua as a staging post. According to the United States Department of Justice, who have listed him a fugitive since 1974, Vesco has 'an arrangement of convenience' with the Castro government, with which he is actively and heavily involved shipping armaments to the revolutionary groups throughout Latin America. The headquarters of Vesco's new empire is a minuscule island called Norman's Cay, officially part of the Bahamas chain, where he has constructed an airstrip capable of handling jet aircraft, surrounded by large hangars for the storage of cocaine and marijuana en route from Latin America to Florida. Vesco pays £65,000 a month in bribes to Bahamian government officials for the right to operate unimpeded.

Although part of the Bahamian chain, Norman's Cay is, in fact, owned by Carlos Lehder, who is also president of a Bahamian-incorporated company named Air Montes. According to DEA intelligence reports, aircraft for Air Montes were purchased through an associate of the Bahamian premier. On Norman's Cay, Lehder has a Doberman pincer-guarded villa, a yacht and at one time used a fleet of nineteen motorcars. There are frequent informant sightings of Lehder and Vesco together: one of the couple's favourite sports was lizard shooting, with small bore rifles.

In October 1983 Bahamian premier Lyndon Pindling appointed a three-man commission to investigate accusations of corruption of the government by drug runners. Five ministers resigned or were sacked as a result of the probe. In August 1984 evidence of Pindling's personal finances showed he had spent £3,000,000 in seven years, more than eight times his official salary. Smuggler Edward Hayes, a former US marine pilot, said he paid $100,000 (£65,000) to Agriculture Minister George Smith for an 'umbrella of protection' over charges against him dating from 1980. Hayes testified that the money was destined for Pindling as part of a total bribe of $300,000 (£195,000). Both Pindling and Smith categorically deny any wrongdoing. Cecil Wallis-Whitfield, leader of the Free National Movement opposition party, said, 'There is perversion which exists from the top of our government right down to the bottom.'

At a meeting of the United Nations International Narcotics Control Board in Vienna in February 1984, the Bahamian delegation spoke against the suggestion of pursuing offshore financial systems established by drug traffickers.

By March 1985, the Bahamian government was sufficiently concerned by the conclusions of the Royal Commission and pressure from America to cooperate in a coordinated operation against smugglers. The operation was codenamed 'Blue Lightning' and organised from the office of US Vice President George Bush. Thirty Bahamian islands were blockaded by US Customs and Coastguards and raids carried out by Bahamian police and soldiers. Seized were 6,500 lb of cocaine, 17 tons of cannabis and several planes and boats. Value of the haul was put at £77,500,000 ($100,000,000). A Washington official described the Bahamian cooperation as 'unprecedented' but added, somewhat cynically, 'We're hoping it augurs well for the future and wasn't some cosmetic gesture on their part.'

In April 1983 President Reagan said, 'There is strong evidence that Castro officials are involved in the drug trade, peddling drugs like criminals, profiting from the misery of the addicted. Is this drug-peddling simply the act of renegade officials? Or is it officially sanctioned? The world deserves an answer.'

One month later Drug Enforcement Administrator Francis Mullen replied. Asked by Senators for his opinion, he said, 'It is difficult not to believe that the government of Cuba remains cognisant of the movement of drugs through its territory and may be facilitating this movement.'

Did that mean, Mullen was pressed, that Cuba was drug-running? Yes, he replied unequivocally.

Many other nearby islands are equally guilty.

Marijuana is a £986,000,000-a-year business for Jamaica, an export so valuable that financially pressed administrations have considered amending the law that makes it illegal to levy a tax upon it and so help to balance their exchequer. Called *ganja*, and a sacramental part of a religion of the island, marijuana was introduced in the nineteenth century by East Indians arriving to work the sugar plantations, following the emancipation of slaves in 1838. Now it is Jamaica's most important crop. Like chewed coca leaves, *ganja* makes work seem easier and the Jamaicans have evolved every conceivable way of ingesting it. It is smoked, in cigarettes known as *splif* or *sklif*. The religious Rastafarians smoke it through a *huka* or water pipe. And although the active ingredient, THC, tetrahydrocannabinol, is not soluble in water, the islanders claim to achieve highs on the *ganja* tea they brew. It is also cooked with vegetables and eaten, and brewed into a tonic by steeping the leaves in over-proof white rum for nine days, then burying the rum in the ground.

There are marijuana plantations in the parishes of St Ann, St Mary, St Thomas, St Catherine and Clarendon, St Elizabeth, Westmorland, Trelawny, Manchester, Hanover and St James. St Ann marijuana is called 'pepper' because it tickles the throat. The St Thomas crop is known as 'lambs' breath' because it is sweetly smooth.

On the former British island of two million inhabitants – where a sign near the pool of the Intercontinental Hotel says, 'smoking of *ganja* is strictly prohibited on the hotel's premises' – there are estimated to be at least thirty clandestine airstrips from which marijuana is nightly flown to the American mainland.

The religion which regards marijuana as part of its ceremonial sacrament is an offshoot of Rastafarianism called the Ethiopian Zion Coptic Church which deifies the late Ethiopian emperor, Haile Selassie. Marijuana, insist the Ethiopian Coptics, is not a drug but a herb. Drugs are liquor, wine, beer, tobacco and pork.

American enforcement officials rank Jamaica one of the largest suppliers of marijuana into the United States, but when the church was accused of attempting to import fifteen tons of the drug, the courts were persuaded to accept the sacramental argument from former US Attorney General Ramsey Clark. Intelligence organisations have been able to identify property valued at nearly £8,000,000 belonging to the Ethiopian Coptics, including a £180,000 mansion on Florida's Star Island. From the Jamaican capital, Kingston, the church runs a vast complex of trucking companies, autospares suppliers, supermarkets and furniture stores. It also has airstrips at Bryan Castle, Trelawny and Alim and it is believed to own seven thousand acres of prime agricultural

– marijuana-growing – land in Colombia. But its principal product is the highly prized and more potent sinsemilla.

The leader of the Ethiopian Coptic Church in Jamaica is Keith Gordon, also known as Edmund Gordon, formerly a marijuana trader with convictions for possession. American intelligence believes he has access to money in the Cayman Islands.

A Western intelligence source estimated that in 1982 there were a total of 19,000 acres under marijuana cultivation on the island, with an annual production of approximately 6830 tons of the drug. By the beginning of 1984 there were indications that the price of Jamaican marijuana had dropped by fifty per cent since 1982, suggesting a greatly increased production. It is even believed that considerable stockpiles exist.

'If the facilities exist to move the marijuana northwards, then it's a buyers' market,' said an enforcement official, who estimated that eighty per cent of the private aircraft arriving at Montego Bay from Nassau did so without prior clearance.

Jamaica is also emerging on to the drug scene as a major manufacturer and supplier of liquid hashish: it is thought that 220 lb are moved every month into Canada alone.

Apart from the invisible earnings generated as a minor tax haven, the principal industry of the Turks and Caicos Islands, a British protectorate since 1766, was salt exporting. When that source of income collapsed, the islands became increasingly dependent upon Britain for support aid. Against Parliamentary uproar in Britain, the government decided in 1981 to finance the construction of an airport on one of the islands, Providenciales, in conjunction with the French leisure group Club Med, who were building a complex there. The outcry was stifled when Club Med contracted a Reigate firm to carry out the construction but Chief Minister Norman Saunders still pleaded the need to Whitehall for more money.

In March 1985, London learned how Saunders intended getting some. But for himself, not for the islands.

After a three-month 'sting' operation Saunders, the 41-year-old leader of the Turks and Caicos Progressive National Party, Stafford Missick, the islands' Minister of Development and Commerce, Aulden Smith, an island MP, and Canadian drug trafficker André Fournier were arrested by Drug Enforcement agents after agreeing in a Miami hotel to allow the islands to be used as a staging post for Colombian drug traffickers.

Saunders, according to investigators, realised the vital strategic importance of the dot-sized archipelago 140 miles north of Haiti and covering an area of 200 square miles. Apart from Jamaica, there was no other grouping of islands better placed for drug-running aircraft to refuel on their way from Latin America to the United States.

The DEA film and tape recordings showed Saunders setting out his terms for allowing the Turks and Caicos to become that refuelling stop. Saunders wanted £30,000 ($63,000) for every plane carrying marijuana and £250,000 ($525,000) for every plane transporting cocaine. Saunders, a businessman who owns one of the islands upon which there is an airstrip and who also has interests in an aircraft fuel business, boasted to agents that the facilities on his islands could easily handle 1760 lb of cocaine a week. Street value of that amount in America was £500,000,000 ($1,050,000,000).

Potential profit for Saunders and the other three was £12,000,000 ($25,200,000) a year.

Saunders initially refused to resign and at first attempted to invoke diplomatic immunity, which was rejected because his trip to Miami was a private one. Found guilty in July 1985, by a Miami court, the prosecution described Saunders and Missick, 47, as men 'greedy for money'.

Every island and tiny atoll in the Caribbean is used by traffickers. The Latin Americans favour the 'double mule' method of smuggling – one carrier bringing the supply from the manufacturing or source country and then transferring his cargo to a second courier during a Caribbean staging stop. They have evolved this method to mislead

Western customs authorities who have developed a profile system similar to that employed to trace the Yakuza, checking flights or passengers beginning from source or supply countries with particular care. So the drug runners now use methods even more complicated than the 'double mule'. Instead of flying direct into the Caribbean, they might go instead to Rio de Janeiro, Buenos Aires or Caracas, sometimes extending the delivery line with the addition of a third mule at the first stop-over. From this less suspicious starting point, the couriers then route themselves to the Caribbean through Curacao, Trinidad, Barbados, Antigua or the Bahamas, for example. The islands of the Netherlands Antilles are also frequently used for refuelling stops by drug runners using their own aircraft or boats.

But America and its conveniently close Florida coastline isn't the only destination for smugglers working out of Latin America and the Caribbean. They also deliver to Canada, where there is a reliable and efficient two-wheel distribution service.

19

The initiation ceremony is obscene throughout – it involves engaging in sex with a child under age, a woman over sixty-five and necrophilia – but the culmination is the most horrifying part of all.

It is called rolling bones. Only by rolling bones does a biker completely qualify to be a Hell's Angel, a Bandidos, a Pagan or an Outlaw, and then he belongs to the hierarchy of one of the closest knit criminal fraternities in the world. And one of the biggest and best-managed drug-trafficking organisations, rivalling the Mafia in its scope and violence.

In 1983 a biker told American Congressmen what the final part of the initiation meant. In order to protect himself he wore a hood, remained behind a screen during the interview and used a pseudonym, Butch.

'When a new member joins, he has six months to roll his bones – to kill someone. If they don't roll bones, they are killed,' said Butch, whose real name was Clarence 'Addie' Crouch. A former Vice President of the Cleveland Chapter of the Hell's Angels, Crouch has been given a new identity and secretly moved far away from Cleveland by American enforcement officials as repayment for the help he provided in identifying the involvement of motorcycle gangs in international drug deals.

The motorcycle gangs in America control the pill market – particularly methamphetamine or 'speed' – and are the major chemical drug traffickers in both directions across the four-thousand-mile-long border between the United States and Canada. They have also formed close operating links with the Mafia, who frequently employ them to carry out contract killings. Crouch testified to the Senate Judiciary Committee that the Cleveland Angels murdered two people at the request of Danny Greene, the now dead leader of an Irish-dominated labour racketeering faction, in a war with a Cleveland Mafia family. One of the killings was the 1977 bombing of a man named Jack Nardi, a Mafia figure and business agent for the giant Teamsters Union.

In 1981, fulfilling another Mafia contract, the Pagan motorcycle gang bombed to death Philip 'Chicken Man' Testa in Philadelphia. Testa was manoeuvring to take over the organised crime family of Angelo Bruno who had just died. Philadelphia is the illicit pill and chemical distribution capital of America and the established Bruno Family didn't want any outside intervention. The Pagans ensured they didn't get it. The Bruno Family still control Philadelphia with Nicodemo 'Nicky' Scargo in charge.

There are a thousand drug-trafficking motorcycle gangs operating throughout every state in America and they liaise closely with similar gangs in Canada, England, the Netherlands, West Germany – although there they have been officially declared an illegal organisation – Denmark, Belgium, Austria and Australia. The total number of gangs is estimated to be 3500.

Their appearance is as uniform as their activities. A true Angel – a proper biker – only ever uses a Harley Davidson machine. Nazi helmets are *de rigueur* where the law does not decree proper crash helmets. And 'colours' – decorated waistcoats, identifying the chapter – are obligatory.

There are other obligations as well. The sexual initiation ceremonies have to be witnessed by the chapter to whom the initiate is seeking access; the under- and over-age intercourse has to be rape. A female companion – an 'old lady' – is communal chapter property, available for anybody's sexual use. Gangbangs – sexual intercourse and abuse of one woman by a group of men – are accepted practice. Hygiene – particularly sexual – is sneered upon and ignored, and intercourse during menstruation is favoured, rather than at other times during the month.

Popular names for chapters include 'Animals', 'The Dirty Few' and 'The Dirty Dozen'. They are titles in which their members glorify.

The first motorcycle gang was formed in 1948, in Oakland, California. It took its name from the 303rd Bombardment Group based at Boise, Idaho, which flew three hundred missions against Germany in the Second World War and called themselves Hell's Angels.

The current leader of the Hell's Angels, a man who has become a millionaire through his drug-dealing, is Ralph 'Sonny' Barger. He lives in Oakland, which is regarded by affiliated bikers throughout the world as the movement's shrine. His lieutenants and fellow drug traffickers are James Brandis, Kenneth J. Owen, Emanuel Rubio and Sergei Walton.

Although Hell's Angels are the founder group of the movement, the Outlaws, whose president is Harry 'Stairway Harry' Henderson, are the largest. The Pagans are led by Paul 'Ooch' Ferry, from a base at Long Island, New York State. Alvin Chester Frankes controls the Corpus Christi, Texas, headquarters of the Bandidos.

Since 1970, police have recorded thirty-six murders committed by the Angels' northern Californian chapter alone. 'The majority of the murder and violence is centred around narcotics and drugs,' a police official told me. The Angels are the largest single drug-trafficking organisation in California, producing 'speed' from twelve clandestine and until now undiscovered methamphetamine laboratories.

A confidential report produced by the US Drug Enforcement Administration says, 'Outlaw motorcycle gangs are involved in virtually every conceivable criminal activity. They are believed to control the entire methamphetamine market.'

Phillip McGuire, Assistant Director for Criminal Enforcement for the Bureau of Alcohol, Tobacco and Firearms, identified sub-divisions of the Hell's Angels and of the Outlaws, known as the Filthy Few and the SS, as being the 'Murder Incorporated' of the American bikers, the groups to which the contract killings go. 'Skirmishes over territory have turned into wars for the control of narcotics distribu tion,' he said. On occasion those wars have been fought with .50-calibre machine guns mounted on trucks – 'war wagons' as they are called.

Before rising to be Vice President of the Cleveland chapter of the Angels, Clarence Crouch belonged to the Bandidos and two smaller, subsidiary groups, the Ripe Enders and the Reapers. He personally admits to two murders and told the Senate Committee there is an 'open contract' on the Rolling Stones open to all bikers: 'There's been two attempts to kill them that I know about,' Crouch testified. 'They will someday. They swear they will do it.'

Crouch said the murder contract was issued following the killing of gun-toting spectator Meredith Hunter by Hell's Angel Alan Passaro, during a Stones' concert at Altamont, California, in 1969. The Angels were security guards for the Altamont concert – which three hundred thousand people attended – and claimed that the killing was necessary for security reasons, but afterwards the Stones 'did not back them'.

'This has been discussed many times – killing the band,' said Crouch. 'Anyone doing this would get in good grace with the California Angels.'

Two former Pagan bikers – under the pseudonyms William Costello and Edward Jackson – also gave evidence before the Senate Committee to which Crouch testified. Costello said the gang's chief source of income was from the manufacture and distribution of methamphetamine and phencyclidine, PCP, or the appropriately named Angel Dust. Jackson said in his protected evidence, 'The Pagans control the drug traffic up and down the East Coast. There is no fear of being caught. Right now the Pagans are larger than the organised crime families. Right now they are engaged in the ruthless aspect of organised crime that was common in the 1920s and 1930s.'

The blue-ribbon commission headed by Judge Irving Kaufman and established by President Reagan to investigate narcotics-related crime in the United States has undertaken to probe the involvement of motorcycle gangs. In June 1983, Associate Attorney General Lowell Jensen said that of the two hundred and sixty cases then under investigation by the task forces, twenty-six involved the major motorcycle gangs.

In May 1985, the FBI sprang against the Hell's Angels a three-year operation codenamed 'Rough Rider'. In coordinated swoops in eleven states throughout America, 1 000 law enforcement officers moved against the Angels. They arrested 100 bikers and seized $2,000,000 (£1,538,461) of methamphetamines, cocaine, hashish, PCP and LSD.

At a news conference after the arrests Attorney General Edwin Meese, who succeeded William French Smith, said the undercover operation during which agent Kevin Bonner had managed to infiltrate the organisation without having to undergo the ritual of rolling bones had averted five murders. William Webster, Director of the FBI, said the coordinated swoop had been carried out to prevent the Hell's Angels becoming an established criminal organisation.

Outside America, England has the largest number of Hell's Angels and there are extensive and close links between the two groups. The English group is known as the All England Chapter and breaks down into various subdivisions: the Exeter group, for instance, is called Satan's Slaves and a group based in Kingston-upon-Thames call themselves Road Rats.

The initiation ceremonies of English bikers do not insist upon rolling bones, although would-be members are required to bite off the head of a live chicken and drink its blood while still warm.

In Northampton there is an Angel chapter called Lucifer's Outlaws whose president, until March 1984, was thirty-two-year-old Michael Bardell. That month Bardell – whose hobby was collecting books on witchcraft, Satanism and necrophilia – was jailed for a minimum of twenty years for the murder of an Angel 'old lady', Debbie Fallon, with whom he exercised his right to sex at any time. He also murdered Debbie's fiancé, David Cox, because Cox objected to Bardell's sexual hold upon the girl.

Lucifer's Outlaw 'sergeant at arms' Stephen Parkinson was jointly charged with murdering Fallon and Cox and was also jailed for life at Northampton Crown Court. Bardell and Parkinson were further found guilty of conspiring to murder a man called Ian Turner, whose wife Susan was also Bardell's sex slave. Susan Turner wanted permanent release from the demanding Bardell, and Debbie Fallon – apart from her fiancé's objection to Bardell's sexual control – did not want to become involved in a lesbian liaison with Bardell's wife, Barbara.

The Judge, Mr Justice Jupp, found, however, that neither jealousy nor anger was a motive in the case. There was another thread.

Bardell and Parkinson had carried out the killings to impress and enhance the image of the Northampton chapter among other Hell's Angels in Britain. They took photographs of the murders, for later boastful presentation at Angel gatherings, particularly those which would be attended by the Road Rats whom Lucifer's Outlaws wanted to impress.

Peculiar to the English organisation of the Hell's Angels is a breakaway group on the outskirts of London, the Windsor chapter, who regard themselves as superior to other bikers throughout England and designate themselves by different colours – a black on white winged death's head rather than the more usual red and white.

Between the Windsor chapter and other Hell's Angels in England there is perpetual war. In 1980, while the Windsor chapter were partying in the New Forest, other bikers ambushed them and their leader, Richard Sharman, had three bullets pumped into his head. Amazingly he survived.

In September 1983, at a supposed peace gathering organised between the Windsor chapter and bikers from other groups, fighting broke out and two Hell's Angels were killed. The battle started after an argument between bikers queueing up to have sexual intercourse with an 'old lady' who was staked out naked, Indian-fashion, for their pleasure.

In 1982 police raided a terraced house in a suburb of Bristol and found it protected by steel doors and a closed circuit TV system. It was owned by a company called Hell's Angels Ltd, run by a Hell's Angel named Barry Burn, and on the premises there was £60,000-worth of cannabis and amphetamines. At a subsequent trial Judge Gabriel Hutton said, 'It is quite clear the house was used as a shop for the retail of controlled drugs.'

In Australia – the world's third largest importer of the essential Harley Davidson motorcycle – Hell's Angel chapters have been established in Melbourne and Sydney and are expanding rapidly throughout other cities in the country. Subsidiary chapters include Black Hearts, Fuhrer's Curse, Derelicts and Mad Dogs. There are strong links with the Oakland, California chapter, run by the organisation's president.

Bikers in Australia – where twenty-three-year-old Rosslyn Dillon, daughter of premier Bob Hawke, and her husband Matthew are both heroin addicts, Rosslyn with a shortened life expectation – have established a network of efficient clandestine laboratories to manufacture metham-phetamine, processing the drug from two of the accepted chemical precursors, phenylacetic acid and methylamine, which are on unrestricted sale in the country. During the first six months of 1980 – compared to the 1978 and 1979 figures taken together – sales of these two chemicals increased by over a hundred per cent. Intelligence has established that more than fifty per cent of those purchases were made by Hell's Angels or other motorcycle groups.

An international enforcement official said, 'Our biggest – and increasingly confirmed – fear is that the outlaw gangs are establishing themselves into an international traf-ficking organisation, trading and dealing from chapter to chapter from country to country. They are every bit as violent – sometimes more so – as the Colombian or Mafia gangs. They have and abide by a rigid set of rules that makes intelligence penetration extremely difficult, if not impossible. Only the top groups – the Angels, the Outlaws, the Pagans and the Bandidos – insist on rolling bones as part of the initiation but those are the controlling groups we have to infiltrate if we are to be successful in loosening and then breaking their hold on the chemical trade throughout the world. Which would mean an undercover officer, to prove his allegiance, would have to kill someone, irrespective of the other repugnant parts of their initiation ceremonies. Impossible!'

Evidence of just how violent the bikers can be came horrifyingly, in September 1984, to a family-affair rally organised in the Sydney suburb of Milperra to mark Father's Day. Without warning, a contingent of Bandidos arrived to confront an enemy chapter, the Commancheros. They fought with guns, baseball bats, spanners and bicycle chains. Eight people died in the battle. One was a fourteen-year-old child caught in the crossfire.

The fear of even closer links between chapters from different countries has already become a reality in Canada and America. The largest and best organised chapter in Canada, Satan's Choice, has forged business links with America's Outlaws – headquartered in Chicago, conveniently close – and created a combined group called the Brotherhood who wear 'colours' incorporating elements from the official designs of both chapters.

Information from street sources suggests that there are 20,000 heroin addicts in Canada and a minimum 250,000 cocaine users. The cross-border Brotherhood gives Canadian chemical drug users easy access to 150 illicit manufacturing laboratories in the United States, in addition to their own considerable methamphetamine factories, which also process the diminishing supply of methaqualone into pills. The production capacity is estimated at 30,000,000 doses a week.

There are also an estimated 1,500,000 marijuana users. Colombia is the major source of both cocaine and marijuana, and decreasing street prices indicate the abundance of supplies.

All the drugs are trafficked by motorcycle gangs, whose passage across that four-thousand-mile border is rarely impeded. The gangs work the traffic both ways but law enforcement agencies suspect that because of the task force successes in the American southern states, Canada is increasingly becoming the landing spot and distribution centre for supplies into the United States.

An official intelligence report on the narcotics involvement of bikers, prepared for circulation through the Royal Canadian Mounted Police, says, 'Their organisational structure, international affiliations and high mobility make these criminal organisations well suited to the production and trafficking of the chemical drugs such as methamphetamine, PCP and LSD. Intelligence also indicates that the activities of outlaw motorcycle gangs are not limited to chemical drug activity as these groups have more recently become involved in heroin, cocaine and cannabis markets.'

Later in that same report, predicting trends throughout the coming years, the six-man analysis team forecast pessimistically, 'Outlaw motorcycle gangs are expected to become increasingly involved in the production and distribution of chemical drugs through 1985 . . . [and] to continue to diversify their operations over the next several years by utilising a number of sophisticated money-laundering techniques such as investment in real estate and legitimate business enterprises.'

During the latter part of 1982, the predominant source of Canadian heroin switched from the Golden Triangle to the Golden Crescent. Ninety per cent was imported via commercial airlines, through Vancouver, Toronto and Montreal, but ships were also used to import the drug through Vancouver and Montreal. Mexican heroin is brought through America by motorcycle gangs.

Federal Solicitor General Robert Kaplan estimates that Canada's drug business is worth $C9,000,000,000 (£5,142,000,000) a year. It is a prize that is murderously

277

fought over, not only by Canadian gangster families but by bikers and Mafia families encroaching from across the American border.

Toronto-based Paul Volpe, a heavy, sparse-haired criminal millionaire, gained prominence as a leading mobster after being chosen – instead of the recognised American Mafia – by Haitian dictator François (Papa Doc) Duvalier, to set up gambling casinos on the Caribbean island. This naturally brought Volpe to the attention of the Mafia, particularly the Gambino Family of New York and the Bruno Family of Philadelphia who demanded the Port-au-Prince business. Volpe agreed to surrender it, in return for future co-operation and friendship, and when Atlantic City developed as America's East Coast gambling Mecca he was allowed in, along with the Gambino, the Genovese, Luchese, Buffalino and Accardo Families.

In November 1983 Volpe was found shot dead – three bullets in the neck – in the boot of his wife's BMW in the car park at Pearson's International Airport. His family had traditionally been enemies of the other prominent Toronto family, the Siderna, who were nominally headed by Dominic Racco. In 1982 Cecil Kirby, a biker hitman, disclosed an earlier contract on Volpe, put out by the Siderna. A month after Volpe's assassination, Racco, a convicted cocaine dealer, was shot down in the Toronto suburb of Milton.

Investigators believe that by stuffing Volpe's body into the boot of his wife's car, his killers were sending some kind of message to the underworld, though as yet they don't know what it is. What they *do* know is that the deaths of Volpe and Racco – and the arrest on narcotics charges of Montreal Mafia chief Frank Cotroni – have left Canada's billion-dollar drug business wide open for take-over.

The Bruno Family of Philadelphia is making the highest bid. Their chief rival is the Magaddino Family, based just across the border in Buffalo, the family which traditionally considers Canada its territory. The Magaddinos are already well established in Toronto and southern Ontario – through local, Hamilton-based families led by Giacomo Luppino and

John Papalia – and have also formed an alliance in the take-over battle with the Genovese Family in New York. The Bruno Family have the support of the New York-headquartered Luchese Family.

In opposition to the Mafia are the bikers: the Brotherhood (including Satan's Choice), the Vagabonds, Hell's Angels, the Para-Dice Riders, the Henchmen, the Coffin Wheelers, the Last Chance, the Iron Hawks, the Queensmen, the Lobos and the Pow Wow. Some of these are groups consisting of several chapters and the intelligence authorities are afraid that the groups will in turn band together to form mini armies to fight it out – literally – with the Mafia. So concerned at the prospect of all-out warfare have enforcement agencies become that a special group of police – known as Ontario's Criminal Intelligence Service – has been created specifically to fight it. And like skirmishers on the side of some medieval battle, minor fights are being fought out between Jewish and Colombian gangs trying to gain a piece of the action.

Laboratories within Canada produce not only drugs to supply the country's own illicit needs but huge exportable quantities of methamphetamines, PCP and a drug identified by the initials MDA, a synthetic amphetamine derived from nutmeg. These are the drugs the bikers take south. On their trips from America into Canada they carry LSD and the counterfeit look-alike Quaalude pills. Two-way traffic – from stolen pharmaceutical sources – includes diazepam (Valium), methaqualone when available, pentazocine, manufactured under the trade name Talwin, hydromorphone, known as Dilaudid, and oxycodone, marketed as Percodan.

Ten illegal laboratories were closed down in Canada in 1982, the last year for which figures are available. Quebec was the major manufacturing province, closely followed by British Columbia where the greatest number of Canadian addicts are concentrated.

From analysis of trends over the preceding five years, Canadian treatment specialists expect chemical drug abuse and the use of look-alikes to grow over the coming years, because of their low cost and ready availability. In Canada – as in other countries throughout the world – enforcement agencies have found that addicts now rarely remain dependent upon one drug but use a variety. It is also expected that cocaine use will increase, with Colombia retaining its significant share of the market. One intelligence report predicts an increasing number of hospital admissions and the need for treatment for cocaine injection and freebasing.

A Royal Canadian Mounted Police study for 1982 – the last year at the time of writing for which details can be obtained – says, 'The supply of cocaine remains plentiful throughout this country. Street-level purities, while averaging 49 per cent, can range from 1 per cent to 99 per cent pure. There has been little change in the price of cocaine at the retail level, a fact partially attributable to consumer acceptance. In fact retail prices have shown little long-range change during the last several years. When taken in conjunction with inflation and a rising consumer price index, the price is actually dropping each year. Cocaine is sold for between $C3000 (£1639) and $C4000 an ounce and wholesale prices are lower still and in 1982 showed a 25 per cent decrease over the previous year's price. This factor is also believed to be an indication of increased availability of the drug in 1982. Price stability at the street level demonstrates that traffickers, while making considerable profits, have also been able to meet the growing demand despite losses resulting from interdiction at the various ports of entry.'

One encouraging sign in Canada is the levelling off of marijuana abuse. The figure of 1,500,000 users in 1982 shows a considerable drop from the 4,750,000 smokers in the previous year. That trend is counterbalanced, however, by the discovery that sinsemilla marijuana, with its more potent concentration of THC, is increasingly becoming the marijuana of choice, even though it is more expensive. A proportion of the sinsemilla is cultivated within Canada but a greater concentration of tetrahydrocannabinol can alternatively be obtained by converting Jamaican, Lebanese or

Pakistani marijuana into liquid hashish. The intelligence section of the RCMP believes that laboratories have been set up specifically to process the imported marijuana in this way.

The Canadian drugs industry continues to expand unabated. But Canada isn't the only former British Commonwealth country confronting a drugs flood. Australia is another.

Australian trafficking extends far beyond the Hell's Angels organisations and their illicit chemical laboratories. Sydney is the heroin capital of the country, importing from the Golden Triangle, but cocaine – brought in from the West Coast of the United States and from British Columbia in Canada – is the new drug fashion. As in every country in the world, estimates of the addict population vary. In 1980 the figure was put at 40,000 regular users, consuming annually one ton of the drug. By 1983 the estimate had risen to 50,000 with enforcement officials calculating that Australian users spend $A3,000,000,000 (£1,400,000,000) a year on their habit. Marijuana has become the country's third largest cash crop and police rarely, if ever, enforce possession legislation.

The Mafia-type organisation heavily involved in the narcotics trade – although separate from the proper Sicilian Mafia – is called 'L'Onorata Societa', meaning Honoured Society. Another title is 'N'Dranghita', the Calabrian version of the same. The formation of the organisation can be traced to the people who emigrated to Australia from the Calabrian town of Plati.

Antonio Sergi was born in Plati. He now lives in the town of Griffith, 375 miles south-west of Sydney. Sixty-five per cent of the 12,500 inhabitants originate from Plati. Although there are cells in Leichardt and Brookvale and Fairfield, Griffith is the headquarters of the Honoured Society. Antonio Sergi is one of its leading members. Ostensibly he is a vineyard owner, wine producer and millionaire. He is, in fact, one of Australia's most important drug barons who has extended his marijuana production in and around Griffith to include heroin importation from Asia's Golden Triangle. Which is how he really made his millions. He is still free, despite being publicly named in a Royal Commission report completed in 1981 by Mr Justice Woodward, who was allowed to carry a gun throughout his investigatory hearings.

The Honoured Society is responsible for a number of unsolved murders around Griffith. Most notorious was that of Don Mackay. A solicitor and furniture store owner, Mackay also had ambitions to become a politician. During a 1974 campaign, as a Liberal candidate, Mackay learned of the extent of the marijuana cultivation around the town and considered making it an election issue. Mackay told Detective Jack Ellis, head of the town's police, of one five-acre plantation with a crop of marijuana worth about $A17,570,000 (£7,000,000), not knowing that Ellis was in the pay of the drug barons. Ellis – in 1982 to be convicted for corruption – warned his trafficking paymasters before making a token and ineffectual raid upon the plantation.

The drug barons decided Mackay was too great a threat to their operations. Robert Trimbole, also known as Australian Bob and the son of Plati immigrants, was at the time leader of the Griffith drug cartel. He paid £6 000 ($15,000) to a killer hired from Melbourne, 250 miles away, to get rid of the irritation. In July 1977, Mackay was lured to the car park of the Griffith Hotel, from which he vanished. His body has never been found.

Antonio Sergi had a foolproof alibi for the night Mackay vanished. He was eating the speciality prawns of La Scala restaurant, on Banna Avenue. His guests were Jack Ellis and two other policemen.

Mackay's opponent in his unsuccessful attempt to represent Griffith was the incumbent Labour MP, Al Grassby. He was also, until 1975, the Australian immigration minister. As such he ignored the advice of his own ministry officials and granted a short-term entry visa to Domenico Barbaro, also known as L'Australian. In 1968 Barbaro was expelled from Australia for criminal activities. On the Grassby-issued visa he returned with what investigators later learned was $A750,000 (£300,000) to finance drug deals. He came from Plati, where he remains a prominent Mafia figure.

Al Grassby is no longer a politician but is still an influential businessman in New South Wales.

Trimbole fled Australia in 1981, after being tipped off by a New South Wales policeman that his arrest was imminent. He spent three years in Italy and France, before being arrested in Dublin in late 1984.

There have been a number of Royal Commission enquiries into organised crime. The Woodward Commission found during its enquiries that the then Narcotics Bureau was hopelessly corrupt and the federal government agreed: narcotics were transferred to the jurisdiction of the Australian Federal Police, specially created to fight organised crime. The newly formed force was commanded by Sir Colin Woods, a former British Chief Inspector of Constabulary.

Evidence of organised narcotic trafficking – and doubts about the enforcement agencies' ability to combat it – led in 1980 to the creation of a further Royal Commission, this time headed by Mr Justice Stewart.

During the course of that Commission's hearings there was evidence that during a nine-month span between 1978 and 1979, a gang organised by Terrence Clark – who also used the name Alexander Sinclair, murdered six people and was, in 1983, to die Britain's richest prisoner – imported into Australia heroin with a street value of $A96,000,000 (£61,935,000).

Trimbole was Clark's partner and the man with the smuggling expertise to move huge quantities of that heroin into Britain. It was Trimbole who organised Clark's escape from Australia to avoid arrest in 1980. In 1981 Clark – under his adopted name of Sinclair – was jailed for life for the murder of another associate, Martin Johnstone, also known as Mr Asia, whose handless body was found in a quarry in the English county of Lancashire.

At Clark's inquest in October 1983, Dr Brian Cooper, the medical officer at Parkhurst, the Isle of Wight jail in which the trafficker died, said Clark had been upset at the way his outside empire of Indonesian silver mines, plantations, multinational corporations and Swiss bank accounts was being administered. To ease that anxiety he had taken tranquillisers and anti-depressant pills. He was, after all, worried about assets amounting to more than £50,000,000.

Amid reports that Clark was cooperating with the authorities about worldwide drug trafficking – and particularly the IRA role in it – in return for better administration of his fortune, Australian and New Zealand authorities requested that a second post mortem examination be conducted, to confirm the first finding of death from a heart attack. The second autopsy confirmed the first.

Yet a further enquiry into Australian crime, headed this time by lawyer Frank Costigan, created a sensation when it was published in December 1984, with claims that organised crime was rife throughout the country. Costigan demanded a further investigation specifically into what his enquiry referred to as vast heroin smuggling syndicates.

The Labour government rejected the recommendation for such an investigation.

In Griffith there has been formed a Concerned Citizens Group, to fight against the way drug traffickers blatantly operate in their town. One of its seven founding members is Mrs Barbara Mackay, widow of the murdered Don Mackay, whose body has never been found.

20

It would be inviting and conveniently sinister to imagine that Bulgaria and Cuba – dutifully obedient to Moscow as they are – trade in drugs in order to erode Western society, just as the Vietcong and North Vietnamese successfully decimated US troops in Vietnam. From a number of meetings with expert analysts in four countries, I have been persuaded that in apparent contradiction to their proclaimed, anti-capitalist ideology, Bulgaria and Cuba ply the narcotics business for exactly the same reason as every other trafficker in every other country. Money.

While there is little the Western governments can do to curb the massive profits made by these communist countries, they are not so helpless against the other traffickers. And worldwide, enforcement agencies are realising that they can win battle victories, even if the war continues largely unaffected.

America leads – as it always has done in drug preventative legislation – but in Canada and Australia legal provisions exist to seize the assets of convicted drug traffickers; the British government is committed to tightening its existing forfeiture provisions; and the International Narcotics Control Board of the United Nations is pressurising the governments of its member nations to take action against drug profits.

One country, up to now, has refused even to consider financial reprisals, even though its drug enforcement officials have convincingly argued the case.

'The problem is the memory of Nazism,' Herr Nikolaus

Haberland, of the West German Ministry of Finance in Bonn, explained to me. 'Such provisions and laws existed under Hitler and it is a period my country never wants to experience again. There were even proposals that if a trafficker were caught with a consignment of drugs and a large quantity of money in his possession then the money should be taken as chargeable duty upon the illicit drug consignment. Which was cheeky but which might have been practical. It was rejected, like every other financial suggestion. It is recognised that there is an overwhelming argument for such legislation but I am afraid it will take a long time coming here: the pendulum against Nazism has swung a long way in the other direction. I am jealous of the American laws. But then, compared to our comparatively new democracy, America has a comparatively old democracy.'

In England, Section 27 of the 1971 Misuse of Drugs Act permits the seizure of 'anything shown to the satisfaction of the court to relate to the offence' and states further that anything forfeited may be 'destroyed or dealt with in such other manner as the court may order'. Enforcement officials regard this as inadequate. It means, for example, that no seizure could be imposed upon the drug wealth of Terrence Clark.

Customs authorities can seize and enforce forfeit under Section 170 of the Customs and Excise Management Act of 1979, but the official attitude is that this – and the penalties available under the Criminal Bankruptcy Act – needs widespread reinforcement. Such a need became obvious after the successful Operation Julie case. Of the vast profits amassed by the LSD manufacturers, police traced £750,000 in Swiss numbered accounts. At the Bristol trial, the judge ordered the money forfeited, but after protracted legal argument involving the Attorney General and the Inland Revenue, the House of Lords allowed the defendants' appeal and reversed the Bristol decision on the grounds that under the 1971 Act the court had no power to order forfeiture where conspiracy was the only offence established against the trafficker.

British Home Secretary Leon Brittan crystallised the feeling of the Conservative government when he said in 1984, 'Drug traffickers make fortunes out of misery and addiction. They can net millions of pounds in a very short time and then launder the money through legitimate activity. In some cases traffickers are prepared to serve a prison sentence in the knowledge that they can enjoy the fruits of their crime upon release. Allowing this to continue would make a mockery of the penalties available. I am determined we should find more effective ways of depriving drug traffickers of the proceeds of their crime.' He added, 'I shall seek to introduce legislation during the life of this parliament to provide for the confiscation of proceeds of crime.'

The recommendation to implement such legislation came from an independent committee under the chairmanship of a judge, Sir Derek Hodgson, established by the Howard League for Penal Reform. After a three-year investigation into crime profit, the Hodgson Committee suggested that suspects' assets should be frozen at the moment of arrest and put under the control of an official 'Crime Receiver'. Upon the suspect's conviction, those assets would be seized unless a not-guilty verdict were returned, in which case the administered estate could be restored to the owner.

Pressure increased upon Leon Brittan to bring in such legislation. Against a background of international warnings that England was becoming the cocaine marketplace of the world, the Lord Chief Justice, Lord Lane, urged in a House of Lords debate in January 1985, that a new law should be introduced as a matter of urgency. He said, 'It is no longer enough even to put traffickers in hard drugs behind bars for a long time. What should be done is to make sure he is divested of every single penny of profit which he has made from his terrible trade.'

And when, after seven months, still no suggestions had been put forward, Lord Lane blasted the government for its delay in preparing what had been promised.

In America seizure provisions exist under the Tariff Act of 1930 – a statute that governs civil forfeiture under both customs and drug laws – legislation known respectively as RICO, an acronym for the Racketeer Influenced and Corrupt Organisation Law, into which Congress built sequester clauses in 1970, and the Continuing Criminal Enterprises Law. In 1978 legislation was passed applying civil forfeiture to provable proceeds from drug trafficking. Being a civil action, it is not necessary for those proceeds to be part of a criminal conviction or an indictment. In 1983 the House of Representatives proposed a law called the Comprehensive Drug Penalty Act – officially entitled HR 3299 – which was supported by the White House, who had already proposed its own comprehensive legislation to the House, HR 2151.

Supporting the Drug Penalty Act, but urging inclusion of some of the President's proposals, James Knapp, the Deputy Assistant Attorney General of the Criminal Division of the Department of Justice, told the House Subcommittee, 'The goals of this legislation, strengthening the use of forfeiture as a weapon in attacking drug-trafficking and increasing the fines available for serious drug offences, are ones which this administration regards as of the highest priority, for they are essential to our efforts in combatting one of the gravest crime problems facing our country: the importation and distribution of dangerous drugs.'

There were already examples of the effectiveness of existing seizure laws. In January 1982 a federal prosecution successfully proved that profits from the marijuana enterprise run by Texas millionaire Rex Cauble had been channelled into his legitimate businesses and got a forfeiture ruling on a third of the millionaire's holding company, Cauble Enterprises. That meant that the government became a partner in three Texas banks, six Texas ranches, a high-priced chain of Western menswear shops called Cutter Bills, the Miley Horse Trailer Co. and a steel mill making parts for caravans. Also seized was a third of Cauble's $20,000,000 investment in Exxon shares. Normally the US Marshals are responsible for administering seized assets, but in the Cauble case Washington chose instead to pay

Cauble – who was free on bail – an annual income of $10,000 to manage the frozen holding company.

The Cauble case was brought under federal law and provided an example for American state legislatures who are gradually recognising the advantages of forfeiture. Florida was the first to take action and, in 1980, amended a state law giving the police the right to keep cash and equipment seized from traffickers. Orange County Sheriff Lawson Lamar now drives a 1981 Cadillac Eldorado that came from a drug arrest and Sumter County law officers all use seized vehicles. In addition, a captured van has been turned over to the school board, the dog catcher has been given a four-wheeled truck that once hauled marijuana, eight brand new cars are now being utilised for undercover work and a seized caravan has been used to provide extra office space. Missouri, Utah, Maryland and Illinois have passed similar legislation. New York State has plans to do so and California has improved its forfeiture laws.

The Drug Enforcement Administration has authored a model Drug Profits Act that has been adopted by ten additional states, enabling them to realise the benefits of seizure not enjoyed by federal authorities. Property seized by the federal authorities reverts to the general treasury, with no benefit to such agencies as DEA, FBI or Customs. State-seized property can be held by that state and channelled directly to its law enforcement bodies, boosting their budgets. Florida is practically self-financing.

During his appearance before Congressional legislators, Knapp said that under the RICO statute the government were unable to seize assets until after a criminal conviction, which gave guilty traffickers time to conceal or transfer profits in advance of any trial and so retain the proceeds of their crime. The President sought an amendment enabling assets to be seized and held pending an indictment, and also the provision of a substitution clause. As the law stood, a prosecution, in order to seize assets, had to prove in a criminal trial that specified property had been used or obtained in such a way as to render it subject to forfeiture. The substitution clause would enable the Department of Justice, if it found that the specified assets had been disposed of, concealed or removed, to apply to the courts for other assets of the defendant to be sequestered.

The White House further proposed to extend Section 102 – which allows the civil forfeiture of property used to store drugs or manufacturing equipment – to include land upon which marijuana is cultivated.

Marijuana, particularly sinsemilla, is America's second largest cash crop, second only to corn and slightly ahead of soybeans. California produces most, followed by Arkansas, which cultivates a local product known as 'razorbud' in the trade, but it is clear to the government that domestic cultivation of marijuana for commercial distribution is increasing, and not only on the private farms: clandestine growers have established plantations in all of America's 155 national parks in 43 states. The annual income of $20,000,000 (£13,245,000) from marijuana cultivation in the Ozark and Ouachitas national forests is more than the revenue from timber, in a state where forestry accounts for a third of its income.

The vast drug profits are laundered, and always through tax haven countries.

Switzerland is universally recognised for its discreet banking laws but has recently become less attractive to traffickers wanting to conceal drug profits because it has negotiated with America a treaty under which the traditional privacy is abrogated if the United States can satisfactorily prove that money has been earned through drug transactions.

In addition, the laws regarding companies set up in Switzerland are disadvantageous: the government withholds thirty-five per cent of corporation interest and dividend payments, substantial minimum capital must be invested and the majority of directors of a Swiss corporation must be Swiss citizens.

When the primary business is the administration of

holdings in other firms, companies are designated holding companies and are assessed for tax on capital, plus a low federal income and net asset tax. Participation companies are partly holding companies, partly operating companies, the distinction being that administration of a holding firm must not be the primary business. Service and domiciliary companies are those based in Switzerland but primarily serving foreign interests. Federal income and capital taxes are levied on the income of both types of companies.

The most attractive aspect of Swiss banking is therefore its ability to set up a trust in another country.

Under the Mutual Assistance Treaty in Criminal Matters, signed between Switzerland and the USA in 1977, if America can prove that money deposited in Swiss banks has been generated from drug-trafficking, the Bern government will provide all bank and transaction details and, at Washington's request, freeze the identified accounts. Further, if the money is proved under Swiss law to be profits from narcotics-dealing, the accounts can be forfeited – but to Switzerland, not to America.

The traffickers are therefore looking for alternative sanctuaries and finding a number of no-tax or low-tax countries who are less concerned about the source of the funds which wash through their financial institutions. A surprising number of those countries – estimated by the Permanent Subcommittee on Investigations of the United States Senate's Committee on Governmental Affairs to wash at least £30,000,000,000 a year – have affiliations with Britain.

No tax at all is exacted by the Bahamas, the Cayman Islands, the Turks and Caicos Islands of the Caribbean or the islands of Vanuatu and Nauru in the Pacific. Low tax countries include Bermuda, the Netherlands Antilles, the Channel Islands, the British Virgin Islands, Monserrat, Panama, Liechtenstein, Monaco, Bahrain and Hong Kong.

The laundering methods are varied and provide huge profits for the commission-earning, soap-holding middlemen.

The bulk of cash is a significant problem for a drug trafficker: £1,000,000, for example – a moderate profit for a moderate narcotics deal – *weighs* heavily and is difficult to carry. If it is to be removed physically from the country where it has been earned – the riskiest way – then before it is laundered, it has to be 'refined', changed upwards into high-denomination notes, simply to reduce the weight. This is a tedious process – involving visits to numerous banks so that the amount will not arouse suspicion – and is therefore avoided by traffickers if at all possible.

Money exchanges, accustomed to handling large amounts of currency, are frequently used, particularly among the barons of Latin America. Throughout the tax-haven countries there are thousands of corporations and businesses which exist only as paper companies. Using his carefully established, non-existent corporation, the baron notifies a foreign lawyer representing his interests that he wants to make a large cash transfer to his corporation's foreign account through a particular money exchange, be it in New York, London or Hong Kong. The notification, therefore, is communicated to the exchange not locally but from abroad. The courier then arrives and the money he carries is legitimately transferred to the foreign account of the corporation, in accordance with every banking provision.

Using this method, the barons have evolved a way of tripling their profits. Having established substantial, multimillion assets in his haven country, the trafficker will then 'borrow' back already untaxed money to invest, usually in real estate. Alternatively, he might bring the money back as a corporate investment and benefit again either from the income tax allowance against the interest he is repaying on a loan to himself, or from the favourable provisions that the US government allows on foreign investment. In the case of property purchase, it means the trafficker is paying little or no tax on the money held in his foreign account, is simultaneously claiming tax relief from the government on his 'loan', and furthermore owns real estate or investments which are increasing in value year by year.

Brokerage houses are also utilised by traffickers taking advantage of the benefits of foreign holdings, another system which operates through paper companies. In this case the trafficker's lawyer advises an established foreign bank that the company wishes to buy gilt-edged securities. The order for those securities is then placed by the bank, with the advice that on the settlement date a courier will hand-deliver to the brokerage house cash in payment for the ordered stocks. The brokerage house obtains the stocks and on the appointed day the courier deposits his drug money in exchange for the securities, which can be re-exchanged whenever he wishes for clean, laundered money.

The haven countries also operate schemes whereby banks offer fiduciary accounts separating the name of the holder from the account itself, and some have 'omnibus' accounts which are operated by foreign banks with American brokerage houses. A trafficker can operate such an account from abroad, in the name of the omnibus account, with no listed details of the trafficker's involvement.

Traffickers also use the havens to create trusts, as well as corporations. The Bahamas, which is not a signatory to any tax treaties, and does not impose income tax, capital gains tax, estate, inheritance or gift tax, is a favoured location for this type of laundering, particularly as the details of bank accounts are confidential. It is possible to set up resident or non-resident companies and to establish trusts, even retaining the assets in another country. If it is a non-resident trust, assets can be invested in any currency. It is because the Bahamas is a recognised financial outlet for drug runners that its government officially opposes any international laws facilitating pursuit.

Bermuda has become a recognised haven for drug barons wanting to incorporate what are known as captive foreign insurance companies, holding institutions for which tax treaty benefits are unimportant, and trust establishments.

Captive insurance companies are incorporated and owned by large American multinational corporations, the parent companies. The captive company insures the foreign risks of its multinational parent, which could otherwise be covered only at a rate the parent would regard as prohibitive. Captive companies can provide equivalent coverage at a lower cost, are not restricted to outside insurance laws and can make speculative investments that would – in America, for instance – be illegal. Premiums paid to Bermuda-established captive insurance companies by their parent companies are considered tax-deductible expenses.

The Cayman Islands are another popular tax haven for traffickers, specialising in the establishment of trusts, companies and banks. The Caymans allow the establishment of 'exempted' trusts which carry a government guarantee that no taxes will be imposed for fifty years from the date of the trust's establishment, provided that no beneficiary becomes a Cayman resident. These trusts can be administered by a foreign bank – from Switzerland or Hong Kong, for instance – with the trust assets held in another haven country. Exempted trusts are used by criminals who wish to have the tax advantages of the Caymans but who do their main business outside the islands; such companies cannot trade in the Caymans except to further the business carried on outside the island. They are not required to reveal the identity of shareholders and anonymous bearer shares – voting as well as non-voting, dividend as well as non-dividend and preferred, redeemable stock – can be issued for cash, property or services. In 1984, however, the US reached an agreement with the British government similar to that which exists between America and Switzerland, allowing investigators access to bank accounts believed to be the result of drug-trafficking. The access is strictly limited to narcotics investigations.

The Channel Islands of Jersey and Guernsey also operate rules and regulations regarding trust funds in the common-law manner of the Bahamas and the Caymans. A document known as a Declaration of Trust can be executed by a trust officer and the holder's name need never appear on the trust documents. Non-resident companies are called corporation tax companies and to qualify, either the place of formation or the place of control of the corporation – that control being determined from where directors' meetings are held – must be outside the islands. Although these companies are required to maintain a list of shareholders, they can be nominees. Notes of annual meetings have to be maintained and the issue of bearer shares is not permitted.

Enforcement agents rightly regard Hong Kong as the most important tax haven in Asia, despite the investigation law which was passed in 1983. The island's principal advantage is that no taxes are imposed on any income from foreign sources for companies incorporated there. The local source tax is seventeen per cent and free exchange rates exist for nearly all currencies.

Liberia, the only tax-haven country in Africa, has advantages beyond its well-known flags of convenience for merchant shipping. Non-resident companies which are more than fifty per cent foreign owned are not taxed on their foreign-sourced income and there are no exchange controls. Liberian corporations can be formed within forty-eight hours, annual meetings can be held anywhere, there are no government reporting requirements and bearer shares can be issued.

Liechtenstein's laws do not require registration of the names of the real owners of a company, only the name of the company or trust and of the lawyer who manages it. This means that only the lawyer knows the name of the owner and can open a Swiss bank account on his behalf in the name of the paper company, although some traffickers prefer to have a Swiss banker arrange for the incorporation of their Liechtenstein company. In this case, the Swiss national would be listed by the lawyer as the owner of the Liechtenstein company and the real ownership could only be proven if a copy of the secret trust agreement between the criminal and the Swiss banker came to light. For additional safety, that agreement can be held in a safe-deposit box in a bank in any of the other tax-haven countries. Enforcement officials believe this system has been operated successfully by Roberto Suarez snr.

Other methods of concealing illegal drug profits in Liechtenstein are provided by foundation corporations (known as a *Stiftung*), trust corporations (*Anstalt*) and ordinary corporations (*Aktiengesellschaft*). A *Stiftung* is more or less synonymous with a charitable foundation, except that the beneficiaries are private, non-charitable individuals. However, responsibility for control of the funds is vested not with the founder of the *Stiftung* but with the board which can amend the articles, add or delete beneficiaries or even dissolve the foundation. A *Stiftung* cannot be used to engage in business.

More favoured by traffickers is the *Anstalt*, a corporation which does not issue shares either for the benefit of the founder or of others. Instead the founder – or current holder of the founder's certificate, which is a bearer instrument showing all the ownership rights – has the power to amend the articles of incorporation, appoint or remove directors and also to name beneficiaries. An *Anstalt* need not be profit-making, nor does it have to operate a business. It can hold financial interest in foreign firms (controlling or otherwise) as a holding or investment company.

There are two different forms of *Aktiengesellschaft* in Liechtenstein. Those which hold investments in other companies, patents, or intangible property rights are designated holding companies. Alternatively, if an *Aktiengesellschaft* is headquartered or domiciled in the country but carries on no commercial activities there other than operating an office, it is regarded as a domiciliary company. Neither pays any regular income tax, only 0.1 per cent annual tax on capital and reserves – as do the *Anstalt* and *Stiftung* – and a 4 per cent tax on dividends and interest. Bearer shares controlling either the total capital or some part of it are permitted.

In Monaco, companies doing more than three-quarters of their business there pay no tax and companies with administrative officers in the country but doing no business there pay tax of just under three per cent of their local office expenditure.

In the Netherlands Antilles there is a 'free zone' where

the tax on companies operating from the islands is two per cent of net. A tax treaty which has been negotiated between the Antilles and the United States enables investments or holding companies in the islands to make their payment in either country.

Vanuatu permits exempted companies and, as in the Bahamas, the government guarantees confidentiality for the required annual financial reports. Trusts can be established under British common law, but there is no trust law.

The attractions of Panama are that there is no tax on foreign-source income of either companies or individuals and the cost of establishing a company is probably lower than in any other haven. In addition, it is flexible both about the location of the company and its meetings, there is no tax on bank interest and details of bank accounts are confidential. Further, owners of a Panamanian company are not required to disclose their identities but can operate through a local lawyer.

Financial treaties similar to the Swiss-American Mutual Assistance Treaty have been agreed between the USA and Italy, Germany and Holland, and an agreement with Colombia is currently awaiting ratification from Bogota. Efforts are also being made by Washington to reach a formal agreement with the Netherlands Antilles, but there is little evidence of interest in such an arrangement from Panama or the Bahamas, who allegedly derive twenty to thirty per cent of their income from illicit banking activities.

The obstacles that litter the financial trail left by drug traffickers are raised at home as well as abroad – as has been recognised ever since the 1931 conviction of Al Capone when US law enforcement agencies acknowledged the benefit of close liaison with the country's Internal Revenue Service. In 1957 Mafia figure Frank Costello was jailed for tax evasion and Joseph (Doc) Stacher, a successor to Bugsy Siegal in the Meyer Lansky organisation, was convicted on the same charge in April 1964. That close liaison was misguidedly limited, however, in the mid-1970s, when Donald Alexander was appointed head of the IRS. Setting out his new policy, Alexander said, 'Selective enforcement of tax laws designed to come down hard on drug dealers and syndicated crime, for example, may be applauded in many quarters but it promotes the view that the tax system is a tool to be wielded for policy purposes and not an impartial component of the democratic mechanism which applies equally to all.'

This view was not the only difficulty placed in the way of enforcement agencies pursuing drug money. The second resulted directly from the Watergate disgrace that forced Richard Nixon – an ever-strident narcotics opponent – from the presidency.

During the investigation into the Democratic HQ burglary, there was abundant evidence that the American president had sought from the Internal Revenue information about the financial affairs of people he considered enemies or opponents. Congress consequently introduced the Tax Reform Act of 1976, which was signed into law by Nixon's successor, President Gerald Ford, and imposed severe restrictions on the information federal law enforcement agencies could request from the IRS. Further, it tightened and actually made cumbersome the procedures agencies had to follow in order to obtain information.

Already working to the non-cooperation policy dictated by Commissioner Alexander, the IRS interpreted the law to – and in some cases beyond – the letter. The situation actually reached the point of absurdity, with some agents genuinely believing that the 1976 Act prevented them from reporting outside their own service information they might come across indicating that a major non-tax crime was being planned. For example, US Senators later discovered that in the early days of the legislation, a DEA agent had given an IRS investigator a list of people whose activities might be of interest in future tax cases. He then mislaid his own list and asked the IRS official for a copy. The IRS investigator refused, saying the list had become a tax matter and the Reform Act made it illegal for him to share it with anybody, including the agency which had provided it in the first place.

The Senate Government Operations Committee, later

renamed the Government Affairs Committee, were already justifiably concerned that the Drug Enforcement Administration and the US Customs Service were feuding internally over petty infringements of each other's jealously guarded territory. That concern intensified when the Department of Justice, the FBI, the DEA and even some officials within the Department of the Treasury itself complained that the straitjacket into which the IRS appeared willingly to have strapped itself was rendering even more ineffective the efforts to trap narcotics smugglers.

An investigation was set up under a permanent subcommittee chaired by Senator Sam Nunn. Opening the enquiry he said, 'Obviously the IRS must be aggressive in collecting the nation's taxes from all sources, but I can understand the scepticism of a small-town waitress who is caught for underreporting her tips when organised crime millionaires escape without even filing a tax return. If the average taxpayer knows that the IRS can successfully collect taxes from the mob, he is a lot more likely to ante up his fair share, if for no other reason than the fear of being caught. More likely, the average taxpayer will have confidence in our voluntary tax collection system and feel that his taxes are being well spent, at least on federal law enforcement activities.'

Setting out what has increasingly become an established policy among enforcement agents worldwide, Senator Charles Percy, the Ranking Minority member of the investigating committee said, 'Drug dealers come in all shapes and sizes. They range from the pre-teen peddler to the transcontinental trafficker. But arresting the street corner pusher, although necessary, will not end the problem. The big money is going to people who never touch the contraband. No matter how effective our drug interdiction programme or trafficking laws are, this upper echelon of crime operates with no fear of arrest. Yet these people who are orchestrating these illegal operations and gleaning enormous profits are the very ones we need to put out of business. The key to prosecuting and convicting them rests in the profits they make. They are vulnerable only to the most

299

complex and detailed financial investigations.'

During the Senate investigations, members of the sub-committee produced evidence of 'unbelievable' cash flows generated by narcotics trafficking. Irvin Nathan, Deputy Assistant Attorney General of the criminal division of the US Department of Justice, cited the situation that had arisen in 1978 when the Federal Reserve banks of Florida reported a currency cash *surplus* of $3,200,000,000 (£1,675,000,000) from drug dealings. And there were frequent examples of people walking into banks to open accounts carrying up to $1,000,000 in cash in paper bags, boxes and suitcases.

Even after Donald Alexander resigned from his position as Commissioner in 1977, his attitude of opposition to law enforcement activities was upheld within the service, so much so that high-ranking officers flagrantly misled the investigating Senators. On six separate occasions, IRS witnesses – trying to convince the politicians that they had not reduced their anti-narcotics activities – testified that they had obtained convictions against twenty-two high-ranking drug dealers in 1979 even though the Department of Justice had no record of having supplied prosecutors. The IRS witnesses, including Jerome Kurtz – Alexander's successor as Commissioner – said on 14 December 1979 that they didn't have the details at hand but would provide them later. When no details had arrived by 24 January 1980, the investigating Senators wrote asking where they were. Kurtz didn't reply. The Senators pointed out they had to close their hearing by 7 March. On that date Kurtz replied to say they would not provide details of the twenty-two cases because they 'may not be a matter of public record and therefore not properly disclosable'. In that same letter Kurtz qualified his earlier testimony. Having originally talked of the convictions being of 'high-level drug financiers and traffickers', he now said that 'in several instances the classification of the cases as a high-level narcotics trafficker was questionable'.

The investigating committee determined to examine the

IRS claims further. On 28 March 1980 Thomas J. Clancy, the Director of the IRS Criminal Investigation Division, wrote to Chairman Nunn saying that the disclosure provisions of the Tax Reform Act which had caused the enquiry in the first place prohibited them from identifying any individual convicted of a tax crime as a drug dealer. And in an act of either arrogance or contempt he attached an eight-foot-long computer print-out listing every person convicted of a tax crime during 1979. There had been a total of 1622 convictions and the investigating Senators' support staff estimated that to work through each one in the attempt to isolate the supposed twenty-two would take a squad of men, working full-time, more than a year. Once again the Senators demanded the names, aware from the letter which had accompanied the monstrous list of the IRS's belated embarrassment. Clancy had conceded, 'Three of the twenty-two cases should not have been included in the project because the field investigation failed to develop information establishing narcotics involvement. On the other hand that review [of the applicable IRS files to locate the twenty-two cases] convinced me that ten to twelve of those convictions involved high-level drug leader cases, while the remainder involved persons whose narcotics activity had been established but not necessarily at very high levels . . . we believe our field people were justified in including them in the project.'

The investigators' view was that the IRS certainly hadn't been justified in including these names in a statement specifying 'high-level drug financiers and traffickers'. The list of twenty-two names was never produced.

In 1982 amendments were introduced to lift some of the restrictions imposed on disclosures in the 1976 legislation and more are pending. But it had become evident during the committee's enquiry into the liaison difficulties with the IRS that their interpretation of the 1976 Act was not the only difficulty other federal agencies were experiencing with those responsible for financial investigation.

In the 1970 Bank Secrecy Act – formally entitled Currency

and Foreign Transactions Reporting Act of 1971 – there are two sections relating to the financial pursuit of traffickers. Form 4789 requires banks to return to the Internal Revenue Service details of any financial transaction in excess of $10,000 (£6896). The Act also requires anyone transporting, mailing or shipping $5000 in to or out of the United States to file Form 4790 with the US Customs Service.

Although the Secrecy Act became law in 1970, it was not until 1979 that the Department of the Treasury started to make full use of Forms 4789 and 4790, and even then it was largely as the result of pressure from one man who correctly realised its potential.

Initially businesses which were daily involved in substantial currency transactions had been allowed exemptions, including banks and financial institutions. Others simply disregarded their legal responsibilities and those that did comply had their returns ignored by the Internal Revenue Service, which allowed them to pile up unread at service centres throughout the country.

David MacDonald, a former Assistant Secretary of the Treasury, told probing Congressmen, 'IRS would not cooperate in our effort to make this information available as Congress had intended. This caused years of delays in dissemination of vital information which could have been used to track down narcotics traffickers and organised crime figures.'

The investigating Senators reached their conclusions by June 1980: 'There is great demand for illicit drugs in this country,' they said. 'Until demand subsides the problem will still exist. However, it is also apparent that the availability of illicit drugs has reached epidemic proportions. Law enforcement cannot reduce demand. But it can do a better job of controlling the supply of drugs being sold. To that extent, it should be a deep embarrassment to the United States government that this nation is literally awash in illicit drugs. Heroin, cocaine, marijuana and all varieties of synthetic drugs are available to anyone who wishes to buy. The richest nation in history is also the most dependent on drugs – and the least capable of controlling their importation, distribution and use.'

As a result of the Congressional investigation, a number of amendments were introduced, one of the most important of which was the creation of the Treasury Financial Law Enforcement Centre – known as FLEC – at Customs headquarters. Maintained by the Customs and the IRS, it is a computer system designed to receive and process the information on Forms 4789 and 4790. It is programmed to respond automatically if the name on the form is that of a known drug trafficker and it also reacts to any Colombian, Bolivian, Peruvian or Mexican passport as well as to any transaction over $50,000 involving an individual with an address in a source country. It also provides a referral system for any enforcement agency with a query on a named, suspected individual.

Loopholes still exist, however. Form 4789 requires notification of money in excess of $10,000 being 'transported, mailed or shipped' in or out of the country, meaning that any wired financial transaction – an extremely common form of currency transfer between financial institutions – is not covered by that legislation. Another extremely successful way of moving money is to get a line of credit transferred within a casino chain, with branches both in America and on one of the offshore islands. The trafficker can establish his credit by depositing drug funds, go to the casino, withdraw the money in chips, cash them at another casino without playing and thus successfully launder his dirty money. The IRS, which has now reversed its former obstructive policy, is encouraging legislators to include casinos under the provisions of the Bank Secrecy Act.

The other enforcement agencies have evolved various ways of chasing the finances of drug traffickers. Operation Swordfish, a sting operation orchestrated by the Drug Enforcement Administration, might have been extremely successful if the US Attorney General hadn't mistimed his announcement about it and enabled the major ringleaders to escape.

In 1981 the DEA established in Miami Lakes a

303

multinational financial organisation called Dean International Investment Inc. President Frank Dean was, in fact, DEA agent Frank Chellino and is still an active operative in Miami. The title of the corporation was evolved by his wife Sally: it stood for her husband's employer – DEA – with the final 'N' for 'Nah, nah nee, nah, nah' in anticipation of their triumphant capture.

The creation of the company was planned in minute detail. Well aware that traffickers, with enormous wealth and frequently corruptible officials at their disposal, carry out the most rigorous checks on the credentials of their laundering organisations, verifiable antecedents had to be created for everyone involved. The story they prepared was that Frank Dean was an Italian-Jewish businessman out to make money, and had come with Sally to Miami from Chicago. Fictitious details about both of them were entered into credit computers in Illinois and Florida, and a house in which they never lived was rented in their new names in an exclusive residential area of Miami, with all the requisite documentation. The telephone recorded under the name of Frank Dean at the false address had a switch device that routed any incoming calls to Chellino's home. He had a social security number in the name of Frank Dean and it was the name in which he rented the impressive Cadillac, the name to which he became used to responding automatically whenever he was addressed by it. And the name in which he borrowed $2,000,000 to spread through various bank accounts to prove his investment company was a reputable one, with more than adequate funds to use in its business of money-laundering.

For eighteen months Chellino went nowhere near the DEA or any other law enforcement headquarters. He underwent a crash course in economics at the University of Miami law school and every night, returning home, he drove by a circuitous route, constantly checking to see if he were being followed. Once, when he washed and then passed on some drug money which turned out to contain some counterfeit bills, he became the subject of a police investigation himself and had to get his superiors to alert the police to the situation.

Essential to the success of the operation was spreading the word of Dean Investment's existence. The men who helped build its reputation were Roberto Darias and Fillipe Calderon, both well known within Miami financial circles. Calderon is a Colombian banker, Darias an anti-Castro Cuban lawyer who had previously been parachuted nine times into Cuba to work for American intelligence. Both men gave evidence at the subsequent trials of the seventy-seven people who were indicted at the end of Operation Swordfish and a murder contract now exists upon each of them.

Calderon and Darias never carried guns, unlike Chellino whose attention to protective detail extended even to the sort of weapon it was: instead of the regulation – and therefore recognisable – ·38 six-shot Smith & Wesson revolver, he carried a ·38 *five*-shot. The protection was necessary because Dean Investment acted predominantly for Colombians who, according to Chellino, carried machine guns in preparation for every eventuality.

Chellino was never offered drugs for his personal use but had it happened he had prepared his reaction. 'I would have refused. I was a businessman, interested only in making money, not sampling the product. It was an attitude they would have understood, like carrying a gun.'

He was never involved in any shoot-outs, either, but midway through the operation there was a telegram – paid for in cash and therefore untraceable – that said, 'We know who you are. Close up your business or else.'

Chellino said, 'We decided to do nothing. We just went with it. To this day we don't know what it indicated or who did it. Later, as we got towards the end, there were a couple of telephone calls to the office. "We know who you are." What do you do? You close up the whole operation because of that? Or do you just sit it out? Fortunately nobody was hurt.' Dean International Investment Inc. became both well known and highly respected among drug dealers, many

305

of whom would enter the glass-fronted office carrying triple-suit cases crammed with twenty-dollar bills. Some of the bankers they dealt with became so impressed with the expertise of their operation that they sought to become partners. During the company's eighteen-month existence a total of $20,000,000 was washed while Chellino and his agents built up their subsequent indictments through video and tape recordings of every transaction. During that period they made $125,000 commission and when they swooped they seized $5,000,000 in assets. Even so, this and other similar operations – an FBI sting called Bancoshares, for instance – have been criticised because traffickers still profit from them financially.

Law enforcement cannot be assessed on the basis of cost effectiveness. Swordfish led to the indictment of seventy-seven people, including Manuel Sanchez, Vice President of the Intercontinental Bank and one-time employee of the Bank of Miami, Lionel Paytuvi, former Vice President of the Greater American Bank of Dade County, and Eloy Cepero, who was associated with the Metropolitan and Loan Association of Hialeah. Miami lawyers S. David Jaffe and Lester Rogers were charged with conspiracy to import cocaine and launder drug money and the same charge was made against a third lawyer, Arthur Karlick, the honorary Austrian consul in Miami who had served as Assistant City Attorney and City Prosecutor for Miami Springs in the early 1970s. And Dr Jorge Suarez-Menendez, a thirty-seven-year-old Miami Beach plastic surgeon, was charged with conspiracy to distribute profits from a Colombian drug operation.

The purpose of Swordfish and other such operations is to hit just such people and deter other bankers, financial experts and professional people who might similarly be tempted to enter the drug business.

Swordfish was also an instructive exercise, further educating the DEA in the ramifications of cleaning drug profits. Sanchez and Paytuvi, for instance, were found to have moved their money to two banks in Panama, the First

Inter Americas Bank and the Banco Nacional de Paris. Chellino travelled to the Cayman Islands to set up cash outlets and in doing so he learned about the island's then conveniently easy banking systems and the people who operated there. But his enquiries extended beyond the Caymans. Operations were established in Switzerland, the Dominican Republic, Japan and Spain, as well as Panama.

'After Swordfish, banks got a lot tighter on accepting customers with bags full of money,' said Chellino. 'We frightened a lot of people and a lot of people have stayed frightened.'

They did not, however, succeed in ensnaring the ringleaders they sought, Colombian Jose Alvarez Moreno and his Miami-based financial expert Marlene Navarro, who headed a syndicate that smuggled just under twelve hundredweight of cocaine from Colombia into the United States over a two-year period. Through Dean Investment Navarro laundered almost $6,000,000, frequently using the money-wiring technique to return the profits either to Colombia or to Panama.

Marlene Navarro lived in a lavish, $300,000 townhouse in Estepona Avenue, near Miami's Doral golf course. She had a special white telephone by her bed – tapped by DEA agents – which she used most nights to speak to Alvarez Moreno. In the study was the framed certificate of her Bachelor of Arts degree from the University of Miami. The bookshelf contained volumes on economics in both Spanish and English and DEA agents later found on her desk the International Monetary Fund's publication, *The Role of Exchange Rates in the Adjustment of International Payments*. She had a substantial financial interest in the Valleys of Kendall, a forty-two-unit condominium.

Navarro escaped capture because of the Attorney General's premature announcement of the conclusion of the operation, before any arrests had been made. A lot of other traffickers heard the radio or television reports as well and some actually telephoned the offices of Dean Investment to check if it was still safe to trade. Each caller was guaranteed there were no problems and as they arrived they were seized.

'The pressures at the very end were monumental,' Chellino recalled. 'I don't think any of us slept more than a few hours during those last two weeks. We were trying to time drug deals and co-ordinate with the US Attorney's office and with banks all over the world.'

It was during Operation Swordfish that the DEA taped the conversations involving the $10,000 and the Colombian president's brother, Juvenal Betancur.

Operation Swordfish was not the only sting operation to target drug finances, nor the most elaborate. The claim for that accolade comes from Operation Greenback, an investigation of narcotics money by the customs authorities which is still being pursued, under a different name – Operation Eldorado – by Customs, Internal Revenue inspectors and DEA agents. Greenback brought a successful prosecution against the Great American Bank of Dade County for laundering – over a two-year period – drug money amounting to $36,608,978. Lionel Paytuvi was convicted again.

The architect of Operation Greenback was a bespectacled, affable financial detective named William Rosenblatt, whose official designation is Area Special Agent in Charge of the US Customs Service in Florida's South-east Region. It was Rosenblatt who first recognised the potential of Forms 4789 and 4790, persuaded the Customs Commissioners to finance his research programme and almost single-handedly brought FLEC into being. Its data base now contains four million entries. 'We're targeted on the criminal hierarchy, the Mr Bigs of the narcotics industry,' says Rosenblatt. He regards the drug organisations *as* industries, corporations run by presidents or chairmen who create an infrastructure staffed by lawyers and financial experts just like any multi-billion-dollar multinational.

'People thought I was crazy when I proposed pursuing narcotics traffickers through an audit trail,' he reflected. 'Nobody thinks I'm crazy any more. It's a very arduous, long-range type of investigation, but the pay-off is big. We have now got a computer system that can tell us a lot of things about people who are moving money and why they are moving money and who they are moving money for.'

Rosenblatt was one of the first to suggest that the way to attack drug barons was through their mega-figure financial incomes. And he was the man who ran through his computer the returns from the country's 14,630 banks in order to monitor their compliance with the Bank Secrecy regulations requiring notification of deposits of over $10,000. He made several discoveries from that check: one was that a large number of banks weren't bothering to make the return at all, but the most important revelation was the huge pool of money that existed in the State of Florida, at that time the major entry point from Latin America.

'The authorities went crazy with excitement when they realised it was possible to follow a money trail,' Rosenblatt told me. He was allocated a special division for his financial detective work. Initially there were teething troubles and inter-agency rivalries but despite these difficulties there were impressive results. Rosenblatt's expertise made it possible to bring charges against the banks who were failing to comply with the regulations and the publicity those early prosecutions generated led to a greatly improved response from financial institutions throughout the country.

By early 1984 Customs had returned forty separate indictments involving 152 people, of whom 111 had been arrested. The remaining 41 had fled the country. Nearly $25,000,000 had been seized in currency, in addition to property worth $2,000,000 (£1,315,789), including aeroplanes, vehicles and boats. The government had also collected $1,650,000 in bail bond forfeiture and instituted Jeopardy Tax Assessments involving nearly $113,000,000, and under its own entitlement law Customs made civil seizures of assets and property amounting to $33,069,492. One of those seizures involved $9,400,000 (£6,184,210) in cash from one particular narcotics ring which, according to account books uncovered by customs investigators, in a single year had channelled $500,000,000 through Miami financial institutions.

The Customs seizure entitlement, which was instituted in the latter half of 1981, is officially called Customs Asset Attachment Programme. Said Rosenblatt, 'With that programme we're taking the motive away from these people who deal in drugs. If we catch them, through our financial investigations, they don't just lose their liberty. They lose their houses and their cars and their jewellery: everything, in fact, that we can prove has been acquired from drug-running.'

From its first attempt at drug preventative legislation in 1906 – the Opium Exclusion Act – the US has had to persevere for the better part of a century before achieving its first notable victories in the drugs war.

A long struggle lies ahead of the Eastern bloc which has still to acknowledge officially it's at war at all. But while the regimes of some Communist countries have benefited financially from drug-running, other Communist regimes have become the victims.

21

Officially drug abuse is a rarity – if it exists at all – in Eastern-bloc countries. I have been assured by drug experts from the Soviet Union, East Germany and Bulgaria that their difficulties are minimal and that any problems they encounter arise because of foreign nationals trafficking on their territory.

The reality is far different.

My information about the degree of addiction spreading throughout the Soviet Union as a result of the Russian presence in Afghanistan comes not just from one but three independent and authoritative sources. They say that the Russian soldiers returning from Afghanistan mostly smoke their heroin – the traditional method of ingestion in Afghanistan, Iran and Pakistan – but that there are increasing reports of injection. One expert told me, 'Russia's greatest difficulty is that they occupy a major source country, where heroin is available not at the 3 per cent to 3.5 per cent purity of New York, or even at the 30 per cent high of London, but at 60 per cent at its lowest and more often than not in the region of 90 per cent. At strengths like that, it's easier to become addicted than it is to catch a cold.'

A revealing insight into the extent of drug use within communist countries came in 1980, with a surprisingly frank admission from Zeigniew Thielle, head of the Polish drug treatment programme and a psychiatrist at Warsaw University's medical school.

At a conference in Amsterdam advocating the legal use of cannabis, Dr Thielle disclosed that in 1972 a Polish research unit had determined that between 48,000 and 71,000 youngsters used 'opiate-type' drugs, and that in a follow-up survey in 1976, that figure had risen to between 174,000 and 294,000.

Contrary to the official view that drugs are always imported, Dr Thielle said the Polish addicts do not use foreign heroin but have created their own supply, injecting diluted dehydrated juice from unripened poppy heads. They have also evolved a way of producing what in street slang is known as 'soup', a concentrated version of the drug manufactured from poppy straw, the unlanced poppy from which it is much more difficult to obtain a morphine base. The customary glass of 'soup' contains up to 3.08 to 4.62 grains of morphine and there is a growing tendency to try to inject the potion.

By the beginning of 1985, the estimate of users had risen to 200,000 and an alarmed Polish government introduced a law in an attempt to curb the growing of poppy and hemp. As well as attempting to restrict cultivation, the law also gives police powers to move against the street sellers common on the avenues of Warsaw and to enforce the registration of addicts.

In Vienna, resident DEA agent Thomas O'Grady – who maintains the liaison with Warsaw – told me, 'The relationship between our two countries is both excellent and sensible. There aren't borders or ideologies with drugs: just trafficking. And profit.'

Hungary is co-operating fully with the West in its anti-narcotics efforts. Government officials, who have admitted discovering marijuana cultivation within the capital of Budapest itself, encourage visits from American anti-narcotics experts to lecture at week-long educational courses, and Hungarian customs officers are regularly sent to the USA to study American interception methods. Particular training is given in profile recognition, because intelligence reports indicate that Hungary is a popular transit route.

Heroin as well as marijuana is a growing problem within Hungary. It is the same in Yugoslavia whose addict population, using psychotropics as well as heroin and marijuana, numbers twenty thousand. A thirty-bed sanatorium for the treatment and detoxification of addicts is scheduled to open in Belgrade in April 1985. The country's particular problem is the long border it shares with free-trading Bulgaria, although Sofia is not the only source of drugs: customs officials at Koper recently seized six tons of marijuana from Karachi, intended for Europe via Trieste.

'Unquestionably the police control in the Eastern bloc has enabled the communists to retain a better handle on the situation than has been possible in the West,' an enforcement agent said in Vienna. 'But there is increasing evidence that despite that control the situation is changing and that their abuse problems are getting out of hand.'

The same is true of the undeveloped countries of Africa.

The majority of African countries have inadequate or corruptible customs controls and in its most recent review of the world situation the United Nations International Narcotics Control Board warned, 'Traffickers are endeavouring to establish Africa as a major source of cannabis supplied to Western Europe as well as a major illicit market for psychotropic substances and a transit point for the traffic in such substances.'

Heroin has not yet become a major problem in Africa but there is increasing evidence of a cocaine trade, particularly among the wealthy, and in Nigeria where intelligence reports have already established trafficking links between Lagos, Kano, New York and Chicago. That trafficking is in both cocaine and marijuana.

Enforcement problems in Nigeria extend beyond official corruption, which is high. It is a vast country and has virtually open borders with the surrounding nations of Dahomey, Niger, Cameroon and Chad, making it impossible to police.

An additional difficulty is that for many years there was little official deterrence from trafficking. During the secessionist war between Biafra and Nigeria the Nigerian government supplied marijuana to its soldiers before battle and the trafficking penalty was cut from its previous ten years to six months. Succeeding governments did not repeal the legislation. In July 1984, the government of Major General Muhammad Buhari announced a clampdown on the country's soaring crime rate and said that under a new law drug traffickers could now face a firing squad.

There is widespread and unchecked marijuana cultivation throughout East and West African countries, all of which are developing severe internal problems. On the streets of Lagos it is not uncommon to see children as young as ten smoking a marijuana cigarette.

'If we were to eradicate completely opium poppy and marijuana cultivation in Latin America and South and East Asia – which we will never be able to do – then Africa could step right in and fill the market,' a narcotics official told me in Vienna. 'What's more, we're damned sure they would do. A lot of people in a lot of African countries have already seen the potential and are getting into the business. And as little, if anything, can be done about Latin America and Asia, it just means that more drugs are going to be available. If more are available, it follows that the prices will be cheaper. And more people will be able to get hooked. You know the problem with narcotics? You can't win: that's the problem. It's a bastard, but it's true. Just can't win.'

One African leader making positive efforts to stop his country being affected by narcotics is Zambian President Kenneth Kaunda, who declares a horror of all addictive drugs. When the Third Secretary at the Zambian High Commission in London, Godfrey Lubinga, invoked diplomatic immunity when British Customs wanted to question him about a £500,000 heroin shipment in March 1985, the President personally intervened and lifted that immunity.

Afterwards President Kaunda said, 'I did not hesitate for an instant. It was, I am told, an almost unprecedented reaction to a very uncommon request. But in the fight we all must wage against this terrifying menace I am convinced I was right.'

Upon orders from the President, Zambian police and customs authorities cooperate fully with other world agencies in attempting to trace drug routes, some of which pass through Zambia. The President further believes that other countries should be prepared, as he was, to lift diplomatic immunity when a member of their diplomatic staff comes under investigation. He said, 'I am certain that a way could be found of enabling diplomats to do their job in foreign countries without at the same time providing a blanket shield for murder, terrorism and the plague of drugs. It must be found.'

Conclusion

At no time in world history has drug addiction been greater. Or growing faster. At no time in world history have traffickers been so rich. Or getting richer.

Enforcement has failed utterly to halt the explosion of drug-trafficking. And maintenance – and every other form of treatment – has failed utterly to halt the explosion of drug-taking.

Those conclusions are unpalatable but undeniable.

Equally undeniable is the fact that an answer has to be found. As British Home Secretary Leon Brittan said in December 1983, 'The price of ultimate failure is unthinkable.'

There is no overnight solution to be found, either by politicians or by bewildered, disillusioned parents.

Enforcement is a part: a vital part. So is treatment. And maintenance. But only parts, small parts of an as yet undiscovered whole.

For thousands of years people have taken substances to improve or heighten their feelings. And they always will, despite attempts to prevent, dissuade or penalise them.

This is the reality to which I referred at the beginning of this book, a reality that governments refuse to accept. But after sixty years of patchwork, piecemeal, disorganised and conflicting policies, affected – and afflicted – countries and governments must recognise that they have to start again. Completely. And achieve a greater degree of success than they have done so far.

They have to refashion their attitudes, which means

recognising the truth of history: that some people will always take drugs; that some actually *need* drugs.

From conversations with sociologists, doctors, psychiatrists and treatment specialists in several countries – but particularly in the United States and Britain – I believe that small amounts of marijuana for personal use should be decriminalised internationally. I do not expect blinkered critics to countenance such an argument because they would consider decriminalisation to be synonymous with legalisation. But this isn't the case, any more than the *de facto* attitude among some British constabularies, the customs authorities, the government's Advisory Council on the Misuse of Drugs, or the governing bodies in the eleven American states and the European countries that have already passed personal possession legislation indicates a junkies' charter.

Surveys throughout the Netherlands in 1976 showed that fifteen per cent of the population between the ages of thirteen and twenty-five were using marijuana. By the end of 1983 – after cannabis was made available from controlled distribution centres – the figures for the same age group had dropped to between one and two per cent.

If cannabis were legalised, much of its appeal would be lost. What's more, I have encountered no statistical evidence to back the claim that use of marijuana inevitably leads to hard drugs. While *some* marijuana smokers progress to cocaine or heroin, as many others remain on marijuana. Marijuana is an integral part of West Indian culture: progression to other, harder drugs because of marijuana use is an exception rather than the rule among West Indians.

The dangerous, progressive link from soft to hard drugs is encouraged only by the black market and the Dutch scheme making cannabis available to youngsters was designed to lure them away from the sometimes irresistible pressures on the streets. It is a policy which I think other countries might beneficially adopt.

Certainly outright prohibition, backed by legal penalties, will continue to be a lamentable failure. Just as those legal penalties are often archaic and even counterproductive.

Prisons create, not cure, drug awareness.

At the annual conference of the British Prison Officers' Association in 1981, chairman Colin Steel said, 'I do not think that if the public knew how much of a problem drug abuse in prisons was, they would be as quiet as they are.' Two years later that same conference was told of cannabis parties being held in some British jails, in the majority of which drugs have replaced tobacco as the traditional currency. And at the conference in May 1984, warning was given that soon murders would be committed in British prisons 'as a direct result of drug-taking and abuse'. Mr Roy Richards, a delegate from Albany Prison on the Isle of Wight, accused the Home Office of failing to recognise the growth of the problem in British jails and said, 'Within the last two years we have experienced not only a full-scale riot but serious stabbings and slashings, all of which can be attributed to the control and misuse of drugs.' He added, 'We are forever fearful that one of those murdered is going to be one of us.'

In America many prisons are run by drug gangs. In California the narcotics business *within* correctional institutions is valued at more than $1,000,000 a year and run by the Nuestra Familia (Our Family), the Mexican Mafia, the Aryan Brotherhood and the Black Guerilla Family. Robert (Big Bob) Vasquez, an inmate of Folsom Prison in Represa, California, is currently disputing leadership of the Nuestra Familia and control of its drug business with Robert Rio Sosa, who is serving life in California's Vacaville jail. In Washington State the Wells Spring Commune and the George Jackson Brigade supply marijuana, heroin, LSD and pills to prisoners – 'anything that's wanted, they've got' according to an enforcement official.

It is true to say of every marketplace that demand dictates supply. If the supply and demand for marijuana were controlled officially, I believe that the black-market trade would dwindle to an infinitesimal proportion of what it is today, in every country in the world.

It is also true that traders rarely restrict themselves to one kind of merchandise, but adjust to changing requirements. If the demand for marijuana diminished, it would be logical to expect the billionaire barons and their middlemen to concentrate on cocaine, heroin or psychotropics, in which many of them already deal anyway.

Here again I consider there is a way to exercise better control than exists already, providing greater medical benefits for the addicted and – most importantly – weakening the hold on the market currently enjoyed by the traffickers.

The recommendations of the second Brain report in Britain were unquestionably better than those of the ill-considered first, but with the benefit of hindsight the treatment centres have not been as successful as they were expected to be. The main problem – which is why the Advisory Council to the British government is considering alternatives – is that addicts simply do *not* attend.

Conditions differ significantly from the time when it was first proposed – addicts then were usually medically hooked, from earlier treatment – but why not attempt a variation of the enlightened system proposed by the earlier Rolleston report? Rolleston thought addicts should be treated like anyone else with an illness, by their own general practitioners. In Britain the Association of Independent Doctors in Addiction still believe and argue that. And the original intention of the Harrison Act in America was to put addicts into doctors' care, not at the mercy of revenue men armed with guns and grenades.

I have not overlooked the fact that the second Brain Committee was created specifically to examine over-prescribing by doctors. And found gross examples of it. Nor am I naïve enough to believe in a foolproof system for supervising GPs. But as governments all over the world have learned to their cost, there can be no final solution, only at best a compromise.

One of the flaws in my proposal is that not all doctors would be prepared to treat addicts. But those willing could be licensed and their prescriptions subjected to independent check which, together with an extension of the Misuse of Drugs Act to cover *any* opioid, would strengthen overall control. These changes, if adopted, with the existing Home Office index, would in time expose any over-prescribing so that the offenders could be brought before a disciplinary body and, if necessary, struck off. Such systems could – without too much bureaucracy – be established in every other country in the world. Governments with larger areas to monitor could set up controls at state, provincial, cantonal, leander or district levels, channelling up to a national oversight agency or regulatory medical body.

And for every one maverick doctor there would be hundreds treating their addict-patients not with drugs cut and diluted and in some cases actually poisoned by additives but of a guaranteed strength and purity. And administered in sterile conditions, not with a communal needle carried in some dirty pocket or handbag, guarded jealously and used indiscriminately until it breaks. And only then after a cure had been attempted; the usual attitude of doctors, very properly, is that freely to give an addict the drug of choice without any remedial effort is not treatment but a confirmation and continuation of his addiction.

And I do not consider – in the case of heroin addiction – that the treatment should be that of methadone. Having discussed it in great detail with a number of treatment specialists – particularly the now-critical Dr Patrick Mullin in Glasgow – I am convinced of the findings of that other critic, Dr David Ausubel of New York who, in a paper published after exhaustive study, declared that the substitute drug 'has inadvertently created incomparably more primary methadone addicts than it has cured heroin addicts'. No treatment that afflicts in greater proportion than it remedies can logically, let alone medically, be considered a satisfactory alternative.

Why not heroin itself?

The sepsis and the hepatitis and the ulcers suffered by heroin users are caused by dirty needles. Or by mixing their street-bought fix with vinegar or lemon juice or lavatory-bowl water. Or by diluting that fix with talcum powder or quinine or glucose or baby food or wall scrapings or chalk or strychnine. Heroin produced under controlled conditions, of a known strength and administered to addicts with a known tolerance, would cause far less organic damage than either the freely available, heavily advertised, and lucrative – to the government as well – alcohol or tobacco.

Addicts assured of a supply of medically pure heroin of a guaranteed strength would, I believe, go to a doctor to get it. Certainly more readily than they currently go to treatment centres. And contact with a doctor would surely be an initial step towards some sort of remedial treatment which is more than the sixty-six thousand unnotified users are currently receiving in Britain. Such a supply would, too, be a further attack upon the obscene monopoly and manipulation of addicts' lives at present exercised by traffickers, but not – by any stretch of the imagination – another junkies' charter. For if treatment of all opioid addiction reverts in Britain to properly licensed and properly controlled general practitioners prepared to take on the responsibility, then the decision whether or not to prescribe will remain, as it always has, at the discretion of the doctor. It is certainly a system that has worked for Dr Kanagaratnum Sathananthan, the only doctor in England to be licensed by the Home Office to prescribe heroin privately. Dr Sathananthan works south of London with the positive support of the Home Office, some officials of which consider his approach better than the uncertain policies adopted by various National Health clinics. Dr Sathananthan urges patients who seek maintenance to stabilise their dosage and then dispenses heroin of a known purity. Any addict seeking a cure is helped towards it. Dr Sathananthan says his cure success rate is fifteen per cent.

In July 1985, the Controlled Drugs (Penalties) Bill was enacted to come into force in September of that year, increasing the maximum penalty for trafficking in Class A drugs – heroin, cocaine and marijuana – from the previous fourteen years to life. Also promised at the Conservative

321

Party Conference in Brighton in October 1984, and repeated at the 1985 Conference, was legislation to seize traffickers' assets. Life imprisonment and forfeiture provisions are necessary and overdue for big-time dealers. But getting them on to the statute book will be an insufficient deterrent unless courts and judges are publicly seen to impose them to their maximum.

In most countries of the world teenagers – and children – can freely buy cigarettes, a drug responsible for more disease, death and addiction than heroin, cocaine, marijuana and psychotropics combined. Mr Everett Koop, US Surgeon General, reported that cigarettes were responsible for 90 per cent of the 60,000 deaths associated with obstructive heart disease in America in 1983, 170,000 deaths from other heart disease and 130,000 cancer deaths.

Since the introduction of health warnings on packets, restraints on advertising and counter-propaganda in schools, cigarette consumption has dropped dramatically.

I accept, of course, that cannabis abuse would explode if it were made available as I suggest. But I believe that the same sort of sensible, intelligent campaign that has so effectively reduced cigarette-smoking would correct the balance and in time – I say again, there is no overnight cure – diminish that abuse.

The main thrust of the campaign would have to be educational, with the dangers set out in as explicit detail as possible for the benefit of teachers and pupils alike. As they should be with solvent abuse. There are few schools in Britain in which children do not know about glue-sniffing – even if they don't practise it – so films portraying catatonic youngsters with ulcerated, suppurating faces would have a far greater deterrent effect upon an impressionable young teenager than a dozen 'teacher says it again' lectures.

I am aware of the doubts among experts concerning such an approach. The Advisory Council, for instance, feel shock or scare tactics could be positively harmful and, further, that unless any educational approach is carefully considered and designed there is a risk of creating in children an interest they might otherwise not have. Some enforcement officials favour such a programme.

Sir Patrick Hammill, Chief Constable of Strathclyde, called publicly in March 1984 for an advertising and educational campaign to combat drugs. He quoted the successful anti-cigarette series of health-warnings on television and urged that a plan be evolved for educationalists and pupils throughout the country.

It is tempting to try to diminish the importance and dangers of drug abuse by dwelling on the comparatively small numbers involved.

The effect of the social fallout of drug addiction is not only to be seen in the squalor of London's Piccadilly or New York's Lower East Side or Washington's 14th Street or Amsterdam's Veedik. The damage is far greater. To sustain a heroin habit in Britain, an addict needs on average £350 a week, for a 7.7 grains, £50, daily buy. Even those on the Home Office index, receiving what methadone maintenance continues to be offered, regularly cheat as they need money for their black-market purchases. This, for the 66,000 heroin addicts alone – not counting the estimated additional 150,000 who buy cocaine or marijuana or psychotropics – amounts to £1,201,200,000 a year. And nearly all of this is obtained through larceny, robbery, violence and prostitution.

An illicit psychotropic habit in Britain – which excludes the thousands being prescribed by National Health doctors – costs a minimum of £175 a week to sustain. Using the lowest figure suggested to me – 40,000 – that represents a yearly expenditure of £364,000,000, nearly all of which is obtained through larceny, robbery, violence and prostitution.

The lowest figure suggested to me for cocaine abusers is 10,000. It costs a minimum of £193 a week to sustain a cocaine habit – £100,360,000 over a year, nearly all of which is obtained through larceny, robbery, violence and prostitution.

The lowest figure put forward for the number of people in England using marijuana is 100,000. A minimum marijuana habit costs £13.80 a week to support. That means a yearly

323

expenditure of £71,840,000, nearly all of which is obtained through larceny, robbery, violence and prostitution.

In America – where a Justice Department study in 1984 proved 42 per cent of the country's bank robbers were drug users – Blue Cross and Blue Shield, health insurance organisations, put the economic, social, health and crime-related losses caused by drug abuse each year at between $10,000,000,000 (£6,578,947,000) and $20,000,000,000 (£13,157,894,000).

Apart from the ever increasing use and trafficking and the personal degradation of the addicted, can England afford a total of £1,737,400,000 a year in drug-related crime? And America $20,000,000,000?

The cost is too big and too extensive to ignore or to attempt to diminish with an argument about priorities.

To invoke the familiar cliché of the subject, many battles have been mounted against drugs. Few – far too few – have been won. In a war, when battles aren't won, fresh strategies are devised and introduced.

Glossary

Drug terms among the street people rise and fall with the speed of a bad fix. Early on during the year I spent with more than a hundred different enforcement officers from at least fifteen countries, I realised few narcotics agents use slang: heroin was usually called heroin, and cocaine, cocaine. 'Slang gives it a glamour it hasn't got,' explained an agent in New York. The following lexicon includes some words and terms still in use, some of which have dropped out of favour and others – as with most fashions – are waiting for the style to return.

AB	An abcess
ABC	A bad – adverse – behaviour report
ACE	A twelve-month sentence
ACAPULCO GOLD	Marijuana, gold in colour, grown in the Acapulco area of Mexico
ACID	LSD
ACID HEAD	An LSD user
ACTION	Drug dealing
AFRICAN BLACK	A type of marijuana, black in colour
A-HEAD	Heavy user of amphetamines
AEROPLANE	Butt of a marijuana cigarette
ALLEY JUICE	Methyl alcohol
AMPS	Amphetamines
ANGEL DUST	PCP or phencyclidine. Ingestion method is to sprinkle on to mint, parsley or sometimes a marijuana cigarette and smoke
ANTI-FREEZE	Heroin
ARMY DISEASE	Addiction to opiates. It dates from the period when cocaine and morphine were the standard pain relievers given to soldiers

ARSENAL	Drug supply
ARTILLERY	Injection equipment
BABY	A beginner in drug use. Also sometimes, but not often, used to indicate a small habit
BABYSITTER	Someone caring for another on a drug trip, usually LSD
BACKTRACK	To pull blood into a syringe during the act of injection
BAG	A packet of drugs. Also, someone's preferred activity or job
BAGMAN	A supplier of drugs. Also, BIG MAN; BINGLE
BALE	A pound of marijuana
BALL	The use of cocaine through the genitals
BALLOONS	Drugs sold in contraceptives
BAMBOO	Paper in which a marijuana cigarette is rolled
BANG	The act of injecting drugs and the excitement that injection causes
BAR	Marijuana in the form of a chocolate bar, the weed bound together by honey
BARF	To be sick, to vomit
BASH	Marijuana
BATTED OUT	Arrested
BEANS	Amphetamines. Also, BLACKBIRDS; BOMBITAS
BEAT	To cheat
BE AWAY	Imprisoned
BELLY	To take drugs orally
BELONG	To be on the habit
BELT	Euphoria
BENDER	An orgy
BENNIES	Benzedrine
BENT	Depressed. Influenced by drugs
BERNICE	Cocaine. Also, BERNIE'S FLAKE; BIG C; BOUNCING POWER
BHANG	Ground marijuana. A paste either eaten as a pill or used to make marijuana tea
BIG CHIEF	Peyote
BIG D	LSD, Also, BLACK TABS; BLUE ACID
BIG JOHN	Policeman
BIG O	Opium. Also, BLACK STUFF
BINDLE	A street-purchased, ready-for-use packet
BING	To inject

326

BIRD'S EYE	Small quantity of a narcotic
BISCUIT	Methadone
BIT	A jail sentence
BLACK BEAUTY	Amphetamine sulphate. Also, BLACK BOMBER
BLACK MOLLY	Diet pills in a black capsule
BLACK MOTE	Marijuana in honey
BLACK RUSSIAN	Black opium
BLANK	Phoney or low-grade drugs
BLAST	To smoke marijuana; the effect it has on the smoker. Also, BLOW A STICK – usually a Thai stick.
BLAST PARTY	Several people smoking marijuana
BLIND MUNCHIES	Food craving frequently brought on by marijuana
BLOCKED	High on drugs
BLOW	To inhale the drug
BLOW A VEIN	To fail to enter the vein for an injection
BLOW CHARLIE	To snort cocaine
BLOW HORSE	To sniff, rather than inject, heroin
BLUE ANGEL	The barbiturate amytal
BLUE BIRDS	Barbiturates. Also, BLUE BULLETS; BLUE DEVILS; BLUE DOLLS; BLUE TIPS; BLUES
BLUE CHEER	LSD and Methedrine, mixed together
BLUE HEAVEN	Sodium amytal
BLUE VELVET	A mixture of antihistamine and opium – containing paregoric. It is injected
BOMBAY BLACK	Potent Indian hashish
BONG	A hashish or marijuana pipe
BONITA	The milk sugar used to cut pure heroin
BOOT	Drug euphoria
BOY	Heroin
BREAD	Money
BREAK THE NEEDLE	To break a habit
BRIDGE	A device to hold a marijuana cigarette to enable it to be smoked to the very end
BRING DOWN	The feeling when drugs have worn off
BRODY	Feigning illness to get drugs from an unsuspecting doctor
BROKER	A dealer
BROWN	Mexican heroin

BROWN SHOES	Someone who does not use drugs
BUMMER	A bad drug trip
BUNDLE	A supply of drugs. Usually ten or fifteen packets
BUSINESS	Injection equipment
BUST	Arrest
C	Cocaine. Also, CANDY; CARRIE; CECIL; CHALK; CHARLIE; CHOLLY; COKE
CALIFORNIA SUNSHINE	LSD
CANADIAN QUAIL	Methaqualone
CANDYMAN	A dealer
CANNON	A hypodermic syringe
CATNIP	A fake drug
CHASING THE DRAGON	Preferred Asian – particularly Chinese – way of taking heroin. The heroin is heated over tinfoil and the fumes inhaled through a straw
CHINA WHITE	Methyl analog of fentanyl, once wrongly believed to be a super grade of heroin
CHIP	To use heroin only occasionally. Hence, CHIPPER, CHIPPING
CHULLUM	A hashish pipe
CLEAN	Someone cured of addiction
COATING	High
COCKED	Euphoric on cocaine
COLD TURKEY	To attempt withdrawal, usually from heroin, without any medical assistance. Addicts believe it causes physical agony but prevalent medical feeling is that the symptoms are no worse than bad flu
CONNECTION	Source of supply
COOK	To heat opium for smoking
COOK-UP	Heat heroin, with water, vinegar or lemon juice, ready for injection
CRASH	To sleep under the influence of drugs, usually heroin, which is a soporific
CRASH PAD	Somewhere to sleep
CROAKER	A crooked doctor who will sell illegal prescriptions
CRYSTAL	Methedrine
CUBES	LSD on a sugar cube
CUT	The adulterating of drugs before street sales

DAGGA	Marijuana. Also, DINKY DOWS: a name that originated in Vietnam
DEALER	One who sells drugs
DECK	A small quantity of narcotics
DEUCE	Two-year jail sentence
DIANE	Meperidine
DIBBLE AND DABBLE	Occasionally to use drugs
DIME	A ten-dollar packet of drugs
DOWNERS	Depressants and sedatives
DOWN HABIT	Chronic addiction
DRY OUT	The process of detoxification
DUSTER	A heroin or PCP cigarette
EIGHT	An eighth of an ounce of heroin. A street quantity
ELEPHANT DUST	PCP
EVERY MOTHER'S BLOOD	A cocktail of hallucinogens
FACTORY	Equipment for taking drugs, generally used to mean hypodermics. Also, FIT
FAMINE	Absence of drugs on the streets
FIX	To inject
FLAKE	Cocaine
FLASHING	Solvent – or glue-sniffing
FLUSHING	Drawing blood into the syringe before an injection, to ensure that the vein has been properly penetrated
FREEBASE	To ingest a purer form of cocaine by holding an extraction pipe over a flame to burn away the hydrochloride salt
FRENCH BLUES	A combination of barbiturates and amphetamines
GAGE	Marijuana. Also, GANJA; GHANA; GOLD; and GRASS, which also means to inform
GEAR	Equipment for taking narcotics. Also, the drugs themselves
GIRL	Cocaine
GOUCHING	Nodding off after taking narcotics, usually heroin
GONG	Opium pipe

H	Heroin, Also, HORSE; HELEN; HENRY
H & C	Drug dependence. A user's daily need.
HAWAIIAN SUNSHINE	LSD. Also, HAWK
HEAD	A person addicted to drugs, particularly narcotics
HEAD SHOP	A drug paraphernalia shop. Extremely common throughout America but gradually being eradicated by state legislation
HIGH	Drug-induced feeling of euphoria
HIT	To purchase drugs. Also, to be arrested
HITTING	Adulterating drugs
HOG	PCP or benactyzine
HOOKAH	Hashish pipe
HORN	To snort cocaine or heroin
HUSTLING	The means by which a habit is supported
ICE-CREAM MAN	Opium seller
INDIAN HAY	Marijuana
J	Marijuana cigarette. Also, JOINT
JACK UP	To inject
JACKING OFF	Slowly depressing the hypodermic plunger, to prolong an injection
JEE GEE	Heroin. Also, JOJEE; JONES; JOY POWDER
JUNK	Narcotics
JUNKIE	An addict
KEE	Measure of quantity: a kilogram or 2.2 lb
KENTUCKY BLUE	Marijuana grown in Kentucky
KICK	Drug euphoria. Also, to stop using
KIEF	Hashish
KIF	Marijuana
KIT	Equipment for taking drugs
LAND	Come down from a trip
LIEUTENANT	Intermediary between the dealer and street people
LITTLE D	Dilaudid
LSD	Lysergic acid diethylamide
LUDING	To take methaqualone
LUDES	Quaalude. The drug methaqualone

330

MACHINERY	Equipment for taking drugs
MACK	A hustler
MAGIC MIST	PCP
MAGIC MUSHROOMS	Psilocybin
MAINLINE	To inject directly into a main vein
MAINTENANCE	Treating addiction by supplying an addict with the minimum quantity of a drug necessary to support his habit. In the case of heroin addiction, the substitute drug is usually methadone. It is, however, equally addictive
MANICURE	The preparation of a drug – usually marijuana – for use
MARK	A victim
MEET	The transaction appointment between addict and dealer
MELTING	Undergoing cold turkey
MERCHANDISE	Drugs
MEXICAN BROWN	Marijuana. Also, MEXICAN GREEN
MEXICAN RED	Sodium capsules
MICKEY MOUSE	To use heroin occasionally only
MISS	Failing to enter a vein cleanly on injecting
MONKEY	Drug habit
MONKEY ON THE BACK	Early withdrawal symptoms
MONSTER	Methedrine
MOOTER	A marijuana cigarette
MORPHIE	Morphine
MOTHER	A dealer
MOUSE	A stoolpigeon. A grass
MRS WHITE	Heroin
MUD	Crude opium. There is a brand known as MEXICAN MUD
MULE	A drug courier, transporting from production point to marketplace. Mules from Latin America are traditionally poor peasants or workers who swallow a number of pellets of cocaine wrapped either in condoms or the sealed fingers of surgical gloves. The pellets are excreted and recovered when the mule has successfully passed airport or port checks

NAIL	A hypodermic needle
NARCO	A narcotics detective. Also, NARCO-BECKS: money gained by trafficking
NEEDLER	Someone who gets satisfaction from using the needle while injecting drugs. Also, a recreational, weekend user
NICKEL BAG	A five-dollar purchase of heroin
NOD	To sleep after injecting heroin
OD	To overdose
ORANGE SUNSHINE	LSD
OUTFIT	Equipment for taking drugs
OUT OF IT	Strung out on a drug trip
PACK	Marijuana cigarettes
PANAMA RED	Marijuana from Panama. Also, PANAMA REED
PAPER	A container of narcotics
PAPERS	The paper in which marijuana is rolled to create a cigarette
PAT DOWN	A body search by a narcotics officer
PEACHES	Benzedrine
PEAK	The apogee of a drug trip
PEANUT BUTTER	Heroin
PEPS	Amphetamines
PICKED	To break a habit. Also, to be arrested
PIN	A well-made marijuana cigarette
PINK CHICKS	Barbiturates. Also, PURPLE HEARTS
PIN-SHOT	A way of taking drugs when a hypodermic isn't available. A hole is made in the skin or vein by jabbing with a needle and the drug fed into the hole with a medicine dropper or fountain pen filler
PIPE	An artery or large vein
PITCH	To sell
PLAY THE POINT	One of a steerer's many functions: to act as lookout for a police raid
POINT	A hypodermic needle
POISON	Any opiate, particularly cocaine. Also, a grass
POKE	To smoke marijuana
POP	To inject drugs under the skin, rather than in the vein. Addicts frequently begin this way,

frightened of actually entering a vein. And end that way as well, when their veins have collapsed and can no longer be made to stand out to receive the needle. Also, to ingest a pill

POT	Marijuana
POTHEAD	Someone heavily dependent upon marijuana
PRICKLY	The sensation of air entering a vein during a clumsy attempt at injecting
PSYCHED	High on a trip or excited
PUFF	To smoke opium. 'Puff the Magic Dragon' was an in phrase as well as a children's song during the Beatles' era
PUSH	To sell narcotics. Hence, PUSHER – a dealer
QUAALUDE	The trade name for methaqualone. Also, LUDES
QUARTER	A measure: a quarter ounce of a drug
RAP	To talk, during a trip. Also, a prison sentence
RARE	To ingest heroin or cocaine by inhaling it through the mouth. Smoking
READER	A narcotics prescription
RED BIRD	Seconal
RED CHICKEN	Chinese heroin
REDS AND BLUES	Barbiturates
REEFER	Perhaps the most common word to describe a marijuana cigarette
REGISTER	Drawing blood into the hypodermic to ensure the vein has been penetrated
RIFF	To talk
RIG	Equipment for taking drugs
RIP	To steal. But to be ripped is to be high on drugs
ROACH	Something – usually a long pin or hatpin – that can be inserted into a marijuana cigarette so that it can be smoked to its full extent. Also, ROACH CLIP
ROCK	Crystals of cocaine, usually after distillation by the free-base process. Also, crystals of heroin
ROOT	Marijuana
ROPES	Large veins. Arteries
RUNNER	Someone selling on a dealer's behalf. A go-between
RUSH	The initial euphoria of a hit

SACK	A quantity of heroin
SACRAMENTS	LSD. Also, STRAWBERRY FIELDS. The Beatles' song 'Strawberry Fields Forever' had a particular meaning for addicts
SCAG	Heroin. Also, SKAG; SMACK
SCOFF	To take narcotics orally
SCORE	To buy drugs. To find a dealer
SCRIPT	A prescription for drugs. Hence, SCRIPT MILL
SCRIPTERS	Someone with a prescription who sells on some of his drugs
SET	Drug-taking equipment and paraphernalia
SHAKE	To break a habit
SHARPS	Needles
SHIT	Generic term for all drugs. Also, for any purchase of drugs which turns out to be of bad or inferior quality
SHERM	A PCP-impregnated cigarette
SHOOT	To inject
SHOOTING GALLERY	A place where an addict can inject himself, having scored
SHOT	An injection
SKIN POP	To inject under the skin instead of into a vein
SLEEPERS	Barbiturates. Also, SOFTBALLS
SMACKER	A heroin addict
SMOKE	Marijuana. Also, SNOP
SNOW	Cocaine. Also, STARDUST
SNOWBIRD	Someone addicted to cocaine
SPEED	Methedrine or methamphetamine
SPEEDBALL	A mixture of cocaine and heroin
SPLASH	Amphetamines
SPLINTS	Marijuana cigarettes
SPOON	A measure of heroin. A quarter spoon is the usual dosage
SPORT OF THE GODS	To snort cocaine
STEERER	The man who guides buyer to seller
STONED	Completely under the influence of drugs
STRETCH	To cut
STRUNG OUT	Extended either by the strength of the drug or by constant use, thus exhausting the addict
SUNDAY HABIT	Infrequent, recreational drug abuse
SWALLOWER	A mule who ingests drugs for smuggling

SWEET LUCY	Hashish
SWINGMAN	A supplier of drugs
TABS	Drugs in pill form
TABBING	Placing LSD on tablets or paper
TAKE OFF	To shoot up. Also to steal
TEAMAN	A marijuana user
TEXAS TEA	Marijuana
THAI STICK	A cigarette-sized package of marijuana. Also, a marijuana cigarette
TICKET	An LSD-impregnated piece of paper, which is ingested
TIE	Rubber tubing or any binding wrapped tightly around the arm or leg to make veins protrude for injecting
TOAT	To smoke marijuana. Also, TOKE
TOOL	Cocaine
TOOLS	Equipment for taking drugs
TRACKS	Needle scars
TRIGGER	To take LSD and then immediately to smoke marijuana
TRIP	To experience psychedelic drugs, usually LSD
TURKEY	A look-alike placebo
TURKEY TROTS	Tracks
TURNED ON	Into drugs. Experiencing the sensation of drugs
UP	High
UPPERS	Amphetamines. Also, cocaine, psychedelic drugs, stimulants
UPTOWN	Cocaine
VALLEY	The inside elbow. Normally the first place where a heroin addict mainlines
VIPER'S WEED	Marijuana
VIRGIN	Someone using drugs but not yet addicted
WAFERS	Methadone
WAKE-UPS	Amphetamines
WASTED	Someone at the extreme end of drug usage. Very much under the influence. Also, WIPED OUT; WRECKED
WEED	Marijuana

WEEKEND WARRIOR	A recreational user
WHITE BOY	Heroin. Also, WHITE GIRL
WHITE LIGHTNING	LSD
WINGS	The very first shot of heroin
WORKS	Equipment for taking drugs
YELLOWS	Phenobarbital sodium
YOKE	A job. A way of raising drug money
ZEN	LSD
ZONKED	Knocked out by drugs
ZUNKED	Someone addicted to hard drugs

Bibliography

Brown, Peter and Gaines, Stevens, *The Love You Make: An Insider's Story of The Beatles,* Macmillan, London, 1983

Fallon, Ivan and Srodes, James, *DeLorean: The Rise and Fall of a Dream Maker,* Hamish Hamilton, London, 1983

Hersh, Seymour, *The Price of Power: Kissinger in the Nixon White House*, Summit Books, New York, 1983

Judson, Horace Freeland, *Heroin Addiction in Britain,* Harcourt Brace Jovanovich, New York, 1973

Trebach, Arnold S., *The Heroin Solution,* Yale University Press, New Haven, 1982

Sources

'Australian Royal Commission of Inquiry into Drug-Trafficking', February 1983

Ausubel, David P., 'Methadone Maintenance Treatment: the Other Side of the Coin,' *The International Journal of Addiction*, 1983

Burr, Dr Angela, 'The Piccadilly Drug Scene', *British Journal of Addiction*, 1983

Connell, Dr Philip, 'Drug Dependence in Great Britain: a Challenge to the Practice of Medicine', 1967

Connell, Dr Phillip, 'The Impact of the New Approach to the Problem of Drug Dependence in Britain', 1970

'Co-operation: the Backbone of Effective Law Enforcement', 5th edition, US Department of Justice

'Drug Misuse in Ireland, 1982–3', The Medico-Social Research Board

'Drugs: a Study in Dublin Post-Primary Schools', *Irish Medical Journal,* July 1982

'FBI Laboratory', US Department of Justice, 1982

'Handbook of Forensic Science', US Department of Justice, 1981

Paxton, Roger, Mullin, Patrick and Beattie, Jack, 'The Effects of Methadone Maintenance with Opioid Takers', *British Journal of Psychiatry,* 1978

Spear, H.B., 'Drug Abuser Deaths,' *British Journal of Addiction,* 1983

Spear, H.B., 'The Growth of Heroin Addiction in the United Kingdom', *British Journal of Addiction,* 1969

'The Supply of Drugs to the US Illicit Market from Foreign and Domestic Sources in 1980 (with Projections through 1984)', The National Narcotics Intelligence Consumers' Committee

Drug Enforcement Administration
'The Carter Administration Weighing the Objectives', August 1977

'Medical Practice Under the Law', December 1977
'The Investigation of Nicky Barnes', July 1978
'Federal Interagency Co-operation', September 1978
'Asian Narcotics: the Impact on Europe', February 1979
'Drugs of Abuse', July 1979
'National Drug Law Enforcement', October 1979
'The Early Years', December 1980
'The Current Challenge: Southwest-Asian Heroin', Summer 1981
'Dealers, Dollars and Drugs', Summer 1982
'Counterattacks on Cocaine', Fall 1982

United States Congress
'Hearing Before the Committe on Expenditures in the Executive
   Departments', 27 June 1947
'Southeast-Asian Narcotics', House Select Committee on Narcot-
   ics Abuse and Control, 12 and 13 July 1977
'Oversight Hearings on Federal Drug Strategy', House Select
   Committee on Narcotics Abuse and Control, 23 September, 6
   and 12 October, 15 and 16 November 1977
'Yacht Hijacking and Drug Smuggling', House Subcommittee of
   the Committee on Merchant Marine and Fisheries, 22 and 23
   November 1977
'Drug Abuse in the Military', House Select Committee on Narcot-
   ics Abuse and Control, 27 April, 24 May, 2 and 16 June, 27 July
   1978
'Cocaine and Marijuana Trafficking in Southeastern United
   States', House Select Committee on Narcotics Abuse and Con-
   trol, 9 and 10 June 1978
'Drug Abuse and Trafficking in the State of Hawaii and the Trust
   Territory of Guam', House Select Committee on Narcotics
   Abuse and Control, 4 and 5 July 1978
'Study Mission on Narcotics Trafficking and Production in
   Thailand, Hong Kong, and Macau', House Select Committee
   on Narcotics Abuse and Control, 6–16 July 1978
'Problems of Law Enforcement and Its Effort to Reduce the Level of
   Drug Trafficking in South Florida', House Select Committee on
   Narcotics Abuse and Control, August 1978
'Stopping "Mother Ships": a Loophole in Drug Enforcement',
   Senate Sub-committee of the Judiciary, 22 August 1978
'Drug Abuse in New York City Schools', House Select Committee
   on Narcotics Abuse and Control, 30 and 31 August, 1 September
   1978

'Use of International Cargo for Narcotics Smuggling', House Select Committee on Narcotics Abuse and Control, 24 October 1978

'Scope of Drug Abuse in Puerto Rico: Supply and Demand Reduction', House Select Committee on Narcotics Abuse and Control, 19, 20 and 21 April 1979

'Federal Drug Enforcement and Supply Control Efforts, Fiscal Year 1980', Senate Committee on Appropriations, 25 October, 16 November 1979, 14 April 1980

'Patterns of Currency Transactions and Their Relationship to Narcotics Traffic', House Subcommitee on General Oversight and Renegotiation of the Committee of Banking, Finance and Urban Affairs, 29 November 1979

'Drug Use and Abuse in the Memphis–Shelby County School System', House Select Committee on Narcotics Abuse and Control, 17 and 18 January 1980

'Interdiction of Drug Trafficking in Georgia', House Select Committee on Narcotics Abuse and Control, 29 February, 1–3 March 1980

'Increased Heroin Supply and Decreased Federal Funds: Impact on Enforcement, Prevention and Treatment', House Select Committee on Narcotics Abuse and Control, 2 May 1980

'Illegal Narcotics Profit', Senate Permanent Subcommittee on Investigations, 4 August 1980

'Recommendations for Continued House Oversight of Drug Abuse Problems', House Select Committee on Narcotics Abuse and Control, 24 September 1980

'Community Action to Combat Drug Abuse', House Select Committee on Narcotics Abuse and Control, 22 and 23 April 1981

'Annual Report of the House Select Committee on Narcotics Abuse and Control', 1982

'Drug Abuse in the American School System, 1982', Senate Subcommittee on Investigations and General Oversight of the Committee on Labour and Human Resources, 27 January 1982

'Narcotics Law Enforcement', House Select Committee on Narcotics Abuse and Control, 30 April 1982

'Further Investigations of Look-Alike Drugs', House Select Committee on Narcotics Abuse and Control, 12 August 1982

'Organised Crime Drug Enforcement, Fiscal Year 1983', Senate Committee on Appropriations, 9 December 1982

Appendix I

Bodies in Britain from which information can be obtained on factual and educational material concerning drug abuse:

The Institute for the Study of Drug Dependence and also *The Standing Conference on Drug Abuse*, both at 1–4 Hatton Place, Hatton Garden, London EC1N 8ND

Release, 1 Elgin Avenue, Maida Vale, London W9 3DR

The Health Education Council. 78 New Oxford Street, London WC1A 1AH

The Teachers' Advisory Council on Alcohol and Drug Education, 2 Mount Street, Manchester M2 SN9

Lifeline Project, Joddrell Street, Manchester M3 3HE

The Schools Council Health Education Project 12–19, Health Education Unit, Education Department, Southampton University, Southampton

National Youth Bureau, Albion Street, Leicester

Narcotics Anonymous, PO 246, London SW10. Telephone 01–871–0505

Families Anonymous, telephone 01–278–8805

Appendix II

American efforts to implement the extradition treaty between Washington and Bogota and smash the stranglehold of Colombia's cocaine barons was wrecked in November, 1985, when M–19 guerillas staged a suicide raid upon the Palace of Justice in the capital. First action of the guerillas was to seize twelve members of the Colombian Supreme court who were processing America's extradition requests and kill them. They also seized all the documentation connected with the extradition proceedings and burned them. Any papers missed were subsequently destroyed when the building was gutted by fire in the efforts of President Betancur's army to recover the building. After the suicide raid – more than a 100 people died in the battle, including all the guerillas – Justice Minister Enrique Parejo Gonzalez openly accused the cocaine traffickers of involvement. He said the killing of the Supreme court examining justice and the destruction of the extradition documentation was 'clear evidence that behind the siege was a defensive action on behalf of the dark interests of the drug racketeers.'

Colombia was one of the 30 countries invited to London in March, 1986, to attend a World conference on drugs convened and hosted by Margaret Thatcher. At the time of writing the drug producing countries of Bolivia, Peru, Pakistan and Thailand were also on the invitation list.

The London conference preceded by two months that planned in Japan by leaders of the seven industrialised nations of the World. The Big Seven gathering was conceived a year earlier in Bonn. That intervening year was spent by health experts and enforcement officials of each of the countries formulating concrete proposals to combat drug production, trading and drug-related crime.

Mrs Thatcher prepared for both conscious that despite all government efforts drug-trafficking and abuse in Britain showed a constant upward climb. And that in the country there was widespread criticism of those efforts. Some of that criticism came from an all-party Parliamentary Social Services Committee which examined Britain's drug problem. In June, 1985, that Committee concluded that treatment services were 'woefully inadequate' underfunded and often inaccessible. Any rehabilitation offered, accused the report, usually came from voluntary organisations unable to plan ahead because of uncertaintly of secure funding. The committee found little sense of direction in the Government's preventive efforts. Insisted the report: 'The government must put forward a clear, long-term strategy for the coordinated development and maintenance of services for drug users' and in another section it said: 'Drug misusers can be helped to come off and stay off drugs. There are a number of examples of services which work. Drug misuse can be tackled, but only if expressions of concern are matched by action.'

Critical of apparent lack of compassion, the report said 'Drug dependency is no more self-inflicted than a vast range of diseases which absorb most hospital medicine. We do not refuse treatment to lung cancer sufferers where it is caused by smoking cigarettes, nor to heart patients suffering as a result of over-indulgence. It is intolerable that those few specialist facilities that are available (for drug addicts) should have to battle even to maintain their service.'

One of the report's recommendations was that every school in the country should appoint a trained teacher to educate pupils of the dangers of drug misuse.

Index

351

354

Stacher, Joseph, 297
Standing Conference on Drug Abuse, 46
Steel, Colin, 318
Stephenson, Michael, 51–2
Stevenson, Robert Louis, 81
Stewart, Mr Justice, 283
Storey, Francis, 75
Studio 54, 260
Stuurman, Jan, 62
Suarez, Renato Roca, 238
Suarez, Roberto jnr, 231, 233, 234, 238, 239, 246, 250
Suarez, Roberto snr, 231–50, 255, 295
Suarez-Menendez, Jorge, 306
Sullivan, Manly, 86
Sumiyoshi-Rengo, 170
Swan, Christopher Michael, 17, 18, 31, 34

Takenaka, Masahisa, 170
Taoka, Fumiko, 170
Tasita Imports Ltd, 166
Taylor, Elizabeth, 129
Teen Titans, 133
Terranova, Casare, 203, 208
Testa, Philip 'Chicken Man', 270
Thames Valley Police, 42–3
Thielle, Zeigniew, 311–12
Thompson, Frank, 105
Tiegs, Cheryl, 132
Tocco Family, 97
Toledo Plata, Carlos, 228
Toro, Faustino Rico, 243, 247
Torrelio Villa, Celso, 245–6, 247
Trafficante, Santos, 116
Trafficante Family, 97
Travolta, John, 132
Treasury Department (US), 83, 85, 86, 91, 94, 104, 299
Treasury Financial Law Enforcement Centre (FLEC), 303, 308
Trimbole, Robert, 282–3
Tripodi, Tom, 198, 199–201, 203, 214

Tripp, Margaret, 35
Trotter, Neville, 61
Trupiano Family, 97
Trynant Pharmaceutical Ltd, 45
Tsui Fong, 38
Turbay Ayala, Julio Cesar, 224, 227
Turkes, Alpaslan, 193
Turkish Federation, 193
Turner, Carlton, 10, 103, 106–7, 109, 111, 112–13, 125, 133
Turner, David, 46
Turner, Ian, 274
Turner, Susan, 274

United Nations, 88, 93, 162, 180, 195
United Nations Fund for Drug Abuse Control, 13, 93, 158
United Nations International Narcotics Control Board, 10, 16, 162–3, 179, 189, 285, 313

Vaca, Oscar Roman, 243
Valachi, Joseph, 89–90
Valdeblanques, Francisco, 222
Van de Kamp, Joseph K., 138
Vanderberghe, Francis, 197
van der Reijden, Joop, 192
Vang Pao, 164, 165
Vasquez, Robert, 318
Vaughan, Frederico, 262
Veitch, John, 62
Verne, Jules, 81
Vesco, Robert, 262–3
Victoria, Queen, 81
Videla, Jorge, 250
Vientiane, 163, 165, 166
Vildosa'Calderon, Guido, 246, 247
Viola, Robert, 250
Vitosha, '82, 184, 185
Volpe, Paul, 278
von Grieken, Lucas Gomez, 222

Wald, Jeff, 129
Walker, John, 148

AND I DON'T WANT LIVE THIS LIFE
by Deborah Spungen

'Harrowing, brutally honest and beautifully written' *Woman*

They called her 'Nauseating Nancy' – the outrageous girlfriend of Sex Pistol Sid Vicious. She died as she had lived – shockingly, in a sleazy New York hotel. Sid would be charged with her murder before his own untimely death. But what the lurid headlines didn't reveal was the family heartbreak behind the horror: 19 years of struggling to understand a daughter who, even as a toddler, rebelled against everything her parents stood for. Now, at last, her mother has broken the silence . . .

And I Don't Want To Live This Life is a powerful and moving insight into the structure of a modern family. It is a twentieth century tragedy, whose final message shining through the darkness is one of hope.

'One of the most heart-rending books a mother has ever written about a daughter' *Daily Mirror*

'A most remarkable book . . . a harrowingly honest, hypnotically readable account of a modern tragedy' *Dublin Evening Herald*

'Engrossing where you expect it to be superficial, harrowing where you expect it to be harmless and a testament of the will which battled against the obvious conclusion to Nancy's life, which was fraught with unpredictable violence and could only be expected to end within those confines' *Time Out*

0 552 12589 X   £2.50

'H'

Autobiography of a Child Prostitute and Heroin Addict
by Christiane F.

The most shocking account of young people caught up in the dark world of drug abuse since *Go Ask Alice*.

'Afterwards, you might feel like chaining your teenage offspring to the kitchen table'
Sun

'Clear, unsentimental, strongly reminiscent in tone of the shrewd, sharp ginswilling London children interviewed by Mayhew more than a hundred years ago'
Observer

'If you fail to buy it as a parent you are neglecting your duty. It is as simple as that'
Bedfordshire Times

'Riveting'
Sunday Times

Filmed as CHRISTIANE F.

0 553 11772 2   £1.95

GO ASK ALICE
by ANONYMOUS

Alice is fifteen, white, middle-class. She diets. She dates. She gets decent grades. She thinks someday she'd like to get married and raise a family.

On July 9, Alice is turned on to acid. She digs it. Acid makes the world a better place. So do all the other ups. They open up the world of sex. They make Alice feel free. Sometimes Alice worries about taking drugs. She thinks maybe she shouldn't. But, she figures life is more bearable with drugs than without.

Alice's parents don't know what's happening. They notice changes. They have no idea she's on drugs. They cannot help her.

The difference between Alice and a lot of other kids on drugs is that Alice kept a diary.

0 552 09332 7   £1.95

LIFE WITHOUT TRANQUILLISERS
How to survive stress and anxiety without drugs
by Dr Vernon Coleman

'A godsend'
Daily Telegraph

Back:
LIFE WITHOUT TRANQUILLISERS

Valium, Librium, Mogadon: these are just some of the brand names of drugs in the benzodiazepine group which today pose a horrifying addiction problem for many ordinary people.

Although they are widely prescribed by doctors, these drugs are not only highly addictive but they can cause brain damage, mental confusion and anxiety itself – which is the very symptom for which the drugs are most commonly prescribed.

LIFE WITHOUT TRANQUILLISERS gives you the harsh facts about the dangers of these 'happy pills' and being hooked on them. There are wise guidelines on how to relax and how to overcome the stresses of modern life without turning to pills for help.

Most important of all, Dr Coleman clearly explains exactly what action you should take so you can safely cut down on and then stop you drug intake.

0 552 12718 3   £2.95

DRUGWATCH
Just Say No
by Shaun Woodward and Sarah Caplin
Foreword by Esther Rantzen
Based on the BBC TV Survey

The BBC Drugwatch survey is the largest study ever undertaken in Britain on drug abuse. Approximately 50% of the questionnaires were filled in by drug addicts themselves and the rest by relatives or close friends of drug users who, in many cases, had died as a result of their addiction.

Just Say No is far more than a compilation of the startling conclusions of this survey because it is a vital and compelling series of case-histories in which the addicts and those nearest to them have written of their own tragic experiences.

The survey shows:
★ 15½ is the average age that a teenager begins taking Heroin and Cocaine.

★ Cannabis was the first drug ever taken by virtually all addicts. It is the getaway to later drug abuse.

★ Once addicted, it is inevitable that you pay for your habit by dealing or turning to prostitution or crime.

★ Dealing is a huge underground network which no amount of policing can combat.

★ Hot to get treatment.

★ How to help an addict.

★ How to stay off the drug.

★ Drug use is not restricted to the big cities. It is now endemic throughout Britain.

★ The drugs included in the survey were Heroin, Methadone, Diconal, Morphine, Palfium, Tuinal, Valium, Mandrax, Cocaine, Speed, Glues – 'Solvent-Abuse' – LSD, Hash, Grass.

0 552 12820 1   £1.95

INDECENT EXPOSURE
by David McLintick

A True Story of Hollywood and Wall Street

It began with a $10,000 cheque – a cheque with a forged signature. It became the biggest scandal and the most vicious power struggle in the history of Hollywood and Wall Street.

'Compulsively readable – you can't put it down' *Guardian*

'A bombshell! Mario Puzo could not have invented a more colourful cast of cutthroats' *Newsweek*

'Explosive. An absolute must. Enthralling, suspenseful, and heroic. Makes Nixon and his bunch of cover-up artists look like a bunch of clods' *Los Angeles Times*

'Investigative journalism at its best, crisp, uncluttered, full of drama' *The Observer*

'Engrossing . . . fear, loathing and embezzlement among the six-figure executives of Hollywood . . . McLintick's skill in this blow-by-blow chronicle is breathtaking' *The Standard*

0 552 12389 7   £2.50

THE CONCISE MEDICAL DICTIONARY

The CONCISE MEDICAL DICTIONARY will be an indispensable aid for nurses, physiotherapists, social workers, medical secretaries, hospital adminstrators, radiographers, technicians and other paramedical workers.

Compiled by practising physicians, surgeons and experienced medical writers, it will also be invaluable for doctors, medical students and members of the general public.

0 552 11934 2   £4.95

A SELECTED LIST OF
AUTOBIOGRAPHIES AND BIOGRAPHIES
AVAILABLE FROM CORGI BOOKS

☐	09332 7	GO ASK ALICE	*Anonymous*	£1.95
☐	99065 5	THE PAST IS MYSELF	*Christabel Bielenberg*	£2.95
☐	12708 6	KNOCK WOOD	*Candice Bergen*	£2.50
☐	12548 2	KLAUS BARBIE: BUTCHER OF LYON	*Tom Bower*	£2.50
☐	12718 3	LIFE WITHOUT TRANQUILLISERS	*Vernon Coleman*	£2.95
☐	12553 9	SWINGS AND ROUNDABOUTS	*Angela Douglas*	£2.50
☐	11772 2	'H' THE AUTOBIOGRAPHY OF A CHILD PROSTITUTE AND HEROIN ADICT	*Christiane F.*	£1.95
☐	12501 6	BEYOND THE HIGHLAND LINE	*Richard Frere*	£1.95
☐	12675 6	MAFIA PRINCESS	*Antoinette Giancana & Thomas C. Renner*	£2.50
☐	99066 3	NAMESAKE	*Michel Goldberg*	£1.95
☐	99098 1	AUTUMN OF FURY	*Mohamed Heikal*	£3.95
☐	12389 7	INDECENT EXPOSURE	*David McClintick*	£2.50
☐	12655 1	BUNNY: THE REAL STORY OF PLAYBOY	*Russell Miller*	£2.95
☐	12378 1	CORONER TO THE STARS	*Thomas Noguchi*	£1.95
☐	08433 6	EVERY NIGHT, JOSEPHINE	*Jacqueline Susann*	£1.50
☐	12589 X	AND I DON'T WANT TO LIVE THIS LIFE	*Deborah Spungen*	£2.50
☐	12820 1	DRUGWATCH	*Shaun Woodward & Sarah Caplin*	£1.95
☐	11934 2	THE CONCISE MEDICAL DICTIONARY		£4.95